The Welfare State

THE WELFARE STATE
Its Aims, Benefits and Costs

J. F. Sleeman

London · George Allen & Unwin Ltd
Ruskin House   Museum Street

First published in 1973
Second impression 1974

ISBN 0 04 360028 X hardback
     0 04 360029 8 paperback

Made and printed in Great Britain
in 10 point Times New Roman
by William Clowes & Sons, Limited
London, Beccles and Colchester

Contents

1 What is the Welfare State?   *page* 1
2 The Origins of the Modern Welfare State   9
3 Development of the Social Services, 1900–1948   23
4 The 'Beveridge Revolution'   39
5 General Description of the Post-1945 Welfare State   49
6 The Limitations of the British Welfare State   87
7 The Economics of the Welfare State   105
8 International Comparisons   136
9 The Future of the Welfare State   161
   Bibliography   192
   Index   194

Tables

1 The growth of social service expenditure in Britain   *page* 3
2 The main forms of social service spending in the inter-war period   37
3 Public expenditure on the social services in the post-war period   80
4 The main branches of public expenditure as percentages of national product   106
5 Government expenditure and gross national product at current and at constant 1900 prices   107
6 Consolidated social service expenditure, 1970–71   117
7 Average source of local authority revenues—current account 1970   118
8 Public expenditure on social services as a percentage of gross national product, in selected countries   136
9 Average ratios of certain types of social security benefit to average earnings, 1960   138
10 Family allowances as a percentage of national income per head of the occupied population, 1960   139
11 Distribution of social security cash benefits between the main forms, 1960   140
12 Social security contributions as a percentage of gross national product, 1967   157

Abbreviations

Cmd and Cmnd	Command Paper
GNP	Gross national product
IEA	Institute of Economic Affairs
NAB	National Assistance Board
NHS	National Health Service
NI	National Insurance

Chapter One

WHAT IS THE WELFARE STATE?

The phrase 'the Welfare State' has passed into our common language, often without much thought about what it really means. According to one recent authority,[1] it was probably first used in print by Archbishop William Temple, in his pamphlet 'Citizen and Churchman', published in 1941, in which he says, 'In place of the concept of the Power State we are led to that of the Welfare State.' Whatever its origins, it came into general use in the years after 1945 to describe a phenomenon which everyone recognized, when the Government's responsibility for the provision of social services was extended. With the development of National Insurance, National Assistance and Family Allowances, with the setting up of the National Health Service and the extension of public educational provision, with the growth of welfare services for old people, children and families in trouble, and with the spread of the public provision of subsidized housing, it was generally felt that we had a new kind of State, a Welfare State. No longer was the State merely the policeman who kept law and order, or the arbiter who settled disputes and upheld the sanctity of contracts. No longer was its concern only to relieve the most acute cases of need or inequality. Its business was now positively to promote the welfare of all its citizens.

Unfortunately, the concept has also become embroiled in political controversy. For some it is the very symbol of the role which the State should play in modern society, in which participation in the social services should be one of the rights and duties of citizenship; the services provided by the Government to promote the common welfare of all the citizens should also be constantly improved and extended. Hence it is to be defended against all attacks by reactionaries. For others, it is the symbol of 'feather-bedding', of a tendency to provide help to people irrespective of whether they need it or not, an excessive care for the needs of all which is in danger of sapping self-reliance and initiative. Hence as incomes rise it should be expected to wither away, and people should become more able to provide for themselves.

Most people probably fall somewhere between these two extremes, accepting the benefits which the services provide for them, thankful that we are now able to meet the needs of the less fortunate so much better than we could in the past, uneasily aware of the many gaps which still exist in our services, and yet perhaps a bit apprehensive whether perhaps we have gone too far in the direction of feather-bedding. To examine the historical developments which lie behind the present forms which our welfare services take will be part of the business of this book; in so doing, it will look at the ideals which underlie them and the effects which their working is liable to have on the economy. Thus we shall attempt to throw some light on this controversy, and draw some conclusions about how the services may be expected to develop in the future. But first we must see how spending on the social services has grown over the years.

THE RISE IN PUBLIC EXPENDITURE, ESPECIALLY ON THE SOCIAL SERVICES

Comparisons of the real national product of a country at widely separated periods are difficult, because there are so many changes in the types and qualities of the goods and services produced. We have motor cars, television sets and washing machines today, unknown or virtually unknown at the turn of the century. We eat different kinds of food and we have them increasingly pre-packaged and prepared. We tend to buy them at the supermarket instead of at the family grocer's, and we do our washing at the launderette instead of employing a washerwoman. Electricity, a luxury in 1900, is now an everyday necessity. On the other hand, we no longer use candles or horse buses, and domestic service has become a rare luxury. Nevertheless we can say in rough terms that the average Briton is perhaps twice as well off in the 1970s as he was in the early 1900s, in the sense that real national product per head is about double today what it was in 1900.

Of course the product is not shared out equally. Kuznets quotes the following figures for Britain, based on income tax returns.[2]

	1913	1938	1949	1957
Percentage of income before tax received by:				
Top 5 per cent of income units	43	29	23·5	18
Top 20 per cent of income units	59	50	47·5	41·5
Percentage of income after tax received by:				
Top 5 per cent of income units	not	24	17	14
Top 20 per cent of income units	avail- able	46	42	38

These figures would imply a considerable reduction of inequality, especially after deduction of income and surtax. In fact, their significance is problematical; those people with the highest incomes have a number of ways of reducing their taxable incomes relative to their actual spending power, through settlements, trusts, gifts, insurance, capital gains and so on; large numbers of the lowest incomes are not subject to assessment and so escape accurate record. What is clear, however, is that there has been a growing redistribution of income between the working population and the non-working population, through taxation and spending on social security benefits to the old and the sick, and through education and health services.[3] Also, improved educational opportunities and health facilities make it easier for more people to enter the better-paid white collar and professional occupations, in which the demand for labour has been growing anyhow.

In any case, the rise in the real national income has been accompanied by a massive growth in the share of it passing through the hands of the public authorities. In the early 1900s they spent only some 10 to 12 per cent of the national product; of that, more than a quarter went on defence and almost a tenth on the service of the National Debt, which was largely the cost of past wars. Between a quarter and a third went on social services, and that was spent almost entirely by the local authorities.

By the early seventies, in contrast, the public authorities together were spending 40–50 per cent of the national product, about half in services in kind, such as defence, education or medical services, and about half in transfers of cash, for example social security benefits and interest on Government securities. Defence now takes only some 11 per cent of this total, or 6 per cent of the gross national product. Interest on the National Debt accounted for 10 per cent of total public spending, transferring some 5 per cent of the national product

TABLE 1 *The growth of social service expenditure in Britain*

					Public spending as percentage of total public spending		
	Total	Defence	National debt service	Social services	Defence	National debt service	Social services
1910	12·7	3·5	0·9	4·2	27·6	7·3	33·0
1938	30·0	8·9	4·0	11·3	29·7	13·3	37·7
1970	50·4	5·7	4·9	23·7	11·4	9·8	47·1

Public spending as percentage of gross national product

Source: Peacock and Wiseman, *The Growth of Public Expenditure in the United Kingdom* (Allen and Unwin, 1967) and *National Income and Expenditure* (HMSO, 1971).

3

from taxpayers to holders of Government and local authority securities. The social services, including housing, accounted in 1970 for 47 per cent of total public spending, or 23½ per cent of the gross national product, including current services in kind, like education and medical treatment, capital expenditure on houses, schools and hospitals, and transfers such as social security benefits or housing subsidies. Table 1 summarizes the position; further details are given in the first section of Chapter 7.

The exact relationship between the growth of the national product and the growth of public spending, particularly on social services, is a matter of some controversy, which we must consider in more detail later. Undoubtedly it is a two-way relationship. As the country becomes better off, the evils of poverty and lack of opportunity stand out more clearly, and the community takes a political decision to spend more on providing for the needs of the less well off. An urbanized, industrial community also has a greater need to spend on public services than a rural, agrarian one, since town life demands public health and welfare services for civilized living, and an industrial society needs a higher level of formal education. On the other hand, expenditure on education and health services and, in varying degrees, many of the other social services are also a form of investment in human capital. This in turn bears fruit in greater productivity and a more rapid growth of the national product. Attempts to measure the rate of return on educational expenditure in the United States, for instance, using expected additional life-time earnings achieved by those attaining higher levels of education, suggest that it is comparable to the return on investment in physical capital.[4]

A CHANGE IN THE CONCEPT OF THE STATE AND ITS FUNCTIONS

Whatever may be the causal relationships, there is no doubt that we have seen a change in the concept of the role of the Government in the community which is one of kind rather than merely of degree. The term 'Welfare State' reflects an attitude towards the State, which sees it as a positive agent for the promotion of social welfare. In this it can be contrasted with the *laissez-faire* ideal of the State rather as a policeman or arbiter. The believers in *laissez-faire* saw the functions of the Government as being primarily those of protecting the community against external attack, maintaining internal law and order and guaranteeing contracts; thus it provided a framework within which private enterprise and the free market could work. Beyond this, they only recognized a very narrow range of public services as being justified on the grounds that private enterprise could not provide them. These included a minimum provision for the relief of the destitute, or the undertaking of public works such as harbours, canals or lighthouses. In general, they believed that public enterprise was likely to be inefficient and wasteful and that taxation was a necessary evil, draining away money which would be better left to fructify in the pockets of the people.

In contrast to this *laissez-faire* attitude, we now accept that social welfare demands a much wider and more pervasive range of Government activity. Not only should the Government provide social services, such as social security, medical treatment, education, welfare facilities and subsidized housing, but these should go beyond the provision of a bare minimum towards ensuring that all have equal opportunity, so far as the country's resources allow. There is difference of opinion as to how this can be most effectively done and what degree of public provision it should involve, relative to private, but the principle that this is a proper public concern is generally accepted. It is also generally accepted that the Government has an obligation to steer the working of the market economy in the directions considered to be socially desirable. Fiscal policy and monetary policy should be used to combat unemployment and inflation and promote steady growth. Encouragement should be given to types of investment thought to be desirable, by means of investment allowances and grants. Help should be given in developing new industries in those areas of the country which are unduly dependent on declining industries and hence lagging in growth and incomes. The Government should intervene in some cases to prevent the restriction of competition by monopolies and trade agreements, where greater competition is thought necessary for economic efficiency; in other cases, it should promote mergers of firms into larger units, where this is necessary for effective competition in world markets. In a crowded country like Britain, moreover, control of the physical environment becomes ever more necessary, if people are to be decently housed, industry is to be located where it can grow with best advantage, and the effects of the motor car are to be coped with.

The concept of the Welfare State thus involves much more than the social services. It is concerned with the Budget and tax policy, with the Bank of England and the control of the money and credit supply, with industrial location and the development areas, with the Monopolies Commission, the Restrictive Practices Court and the Industrial Re-organization Commission, with Town and Country Planning and the New Towns, to mention only the main examples. But the social services are nevertheless its most characteristic element,

5

since they are concerned with the positive provision of services to individuals, of a type and on a scale that they would not obtain through the free market. The aim of the modern social services goes beyond providing the basic minimum of poor relief, elementary education or protection against epidemic disease, which is essential for civilized urban society. The Welfare State ideal conceives that an increase of social welfare is brought about if people can get a secure minimum income when they cannot earn, medical treatment suited to their needs when they are ill, educational opportunities according to their age, aptitude and ability, a chance of decent housing at rents they can afford, welfare services for the old and the children, and so on. It sees these as more likely to be provided adequately by Government action than through the market.

In other words, the type of services most characteristic of the Welfare State is those which meet what Musgrave calls 'merit wants'.[5] They are not concerned with pure public wants of a kind which cannot be satisfied through the market, because the benefit from them is almost entirely social and there is little or no private benefit. Services such as defence, law and order, general administration, town and country planning, street cleansing or the provision of lighthouses are of this type, in that if they are provided at all, the whole community must by and large benefit from them and no one can be excluded from them. Hence it would not be worth anyone's while to pay a price for them since, if they are provided, he can get their benefit for nothing; therefore they cannot be sold through the market and must be provided by the State and paid for out of taxation.

Education, medical treatment and social security, for instance, are not of this type. They provide distinct benefits to individuals; they can be, and are, provided through the market and sold for a price. We have private fee-paying schools, doctors in private practice and private nursing homes, private insurance against sickness, widowhood and old age. But an element of social benefit, from an educated and healthy community, or from ensuring that all members of the community are guaranteed a minimum income in the event of inability to earn, is held to arise over and above the private benefits to individuals. If the provision of these services was left to the market, in response to the demand of those willing to pay the full market price for them, they would not be supplied in the socially optimum quantity. Hence the community takes a political decision to provide them communally and make them available either free or at heavily subsidized prices, paying for the necessary resources of labour and capital out of taxation. In the case of education up to the statutory school-leaving age, we even make its consumption compulsory, to ensure that children are not deprived of education because of the negligence of their parents.

Recognition that the social services are of this kind, namely services the provision of which involves a high ratio of social benefits to private benefits, leaves unsolved all sorts of questions about the extent to which they should be provided and the methods by which they should be supplied. Public opinion about what constitutes social benefits changes and develops. At one time their scope was narrowly conceived, as involving only a bare minimum of, say, elementary education, relief of the destitute, or the prevention of epidemic diseases. As time has gone on, we have come to see benefits more in terms of securing equality of opportunity for all as far as possible, and as a form of investment in improving the quality of the country's human capital, as well as enriching the lives of those otherwise impoverished. With the rise in national income there is difference of opinion as to what this should imply for the further development of the services. Are these social ideals better secured by extending the range of public services available to all, or by encouraging the better off to meet their needs through the market and concentrating State benefits on those least well off? In so far as the public interest is held to justify public spending on a service, is this best met by the Government itself providing the services, as against subsidizing their provision by private agencies?

It is with the development of thinking and policy on matters such as this that we shall be largely concerned in this book. To begin, we must look back into history and trace the origins of the concepts underlying the modern Welfare State. That is done in Chapter Two. Chapter Three traces the development of the social services in the first half of the present century and shows how they grew up, largely piecemeal, to meet particular needs. Chapter Four deals with principles of the Beveridge Report, which underlay the re-organization of the services after 1945. Chapter Five outlines the main features of the Welfare State as it took shape after the Second World War, while Chapter Six points out some of the limitations in this system as shown up by twenty years of changing economic and social conditions. Chapter Seven attempts to deal more systematically with the economic implications of the Welfare State and the interactions between the social services and the working of the economy. Chapter Eight makes some comparisons between the development of the social services in Britain and in certain other countries, such as those of Western Europe and North America. Finally, in Chapter Nine there is a discussion of the conflicting views about the future development of the social services and an attempt to assess likely future trends.

NOTES

1 P. Gregg, *The Welfare State* (Harrap, London, 1967), pp. 3–4.
2 S. Kuznets, *Modern Economic Growth* (Yale University Press, 1966), Tables 4–5, p. 208.
3 See Chapter Seven, pp. 119–22; The extent of redistribution of income.
4 Compare, for instance, T. W. Schultz, 'Investment in Human Capital', *American Economic Review*, Vol. 51 (1961), pp. 1–17. Reprinted in M. Blaug (ed.), *Economics of Education* (Penguin, 1968), pp. 13–31.
5 R. A. Musgrave, *The Theory of Public Finance* (McGraw-Hill, New York, 1959), pp. 13–14.

Chapter Two

THE ORIGINS OF THE MODERN WELFARE STATE

THE ROOTS GO BACK FAR INTO THE PAST

The roots of the concept of the Welfare State go back far into the past. The members of local communities have always tended to feel a sense of collective responsibility for their less fortunate brethren. Thus the trade and craft guilds of medieval and early modern times frequently made provision to maintain those of their members who had fallen on poverty or ill-health; sometimes these were through cash payments and sometimes through providing accommodation in hospices and almshouses. Similarly they sometimes established schools for the education of their members' children. Some of the best known of the latter-day public schools have their origins in foundations of this type, such as Merchant Taylors, or Oundle, which was founded by the Grocers' Company. Wealthy philanthropists also often endowed local charities to relieve the poor and the sick and to provide education, and in some cases the municipal authorities made themselves responsible for such foundations.

Up to the end of the nineteenth century it was generally accepted that the responsibility for such welfare services as were provided should be a local rather than a national one. Indeed, the central Government had neither the resources nor the administrative machinery to intervene effectively itself. Nevertheless, it had come to be accepted that the Government had the responsibility for ensuring that certain basic needs were met, and of seeing that the local authorities had the power and the financial means to carry them out. Thus in England public responsibility for the relief of the poor and the prevention of destitution was accepted with the passing of the Elizabethan Poor Law Act of 1598. This called for the appointment of overseers of the poor in every parish to set the able-bodied on work and relieve those who could not work, and for the levying by each parish of a local rate to provide the means. This provision was strengthened by the Act of Settlement of 1662, under which everyone had a parish of settlement which was legally obliged to relieve him if he fell into need and under which there began the system of removal of those in need to their parish of settlement.

Throughout the chequered history of the Poor Law in the seventeenth and eighteenth centuries, Parliament was constantly driven to intervene to try to make these provisions more effective, in face of the weaknesses of the local government machinery of the times and the lack of any adequate central administration to enforce standards. Thus the Acts of 1723, 1756 and 1782 encouraged the coming together of parishes to form larger Unions capable of building and maintaining workhouses for the non-able-bodied. Meanwhile the practice was growing of giving the able-bodied outdoor relief in cash, instead of work, which could not usually be provided. From the 1790s this became the general practice in southern England under the so-called Speenhamland System,[1] whereby the rise in bread prices during the Revolutionary and Napoleonic wars was met by the supplementation of wages by poor relief.

In Scotland, public responsibility for poor relief was recognized, for instance in an Act of the Scottish Parliament of 1579; however, in practice, this responsibility remained with the church authorities, it being the duty of the Kirk Session of each parish to provide outdoor relief for the non-able-bodied, mainly from church collections. Powers existed to levy a rate, but even as late as the early 1840s only about a quarter of Scottish parishes had recourse to this. Poorhouses were rare exceptions in Scotland, and payment of relief to the able-bodied was expressly excluded, at least in legal theory.

On the other hand Scotland, unlike England, had accepted in principle the need for the provision of a general system of public education. This had been an ideal of Knox and the Reformers, but it fell down on the unwillingness of the local land-owners to provide the means. An Act of 1696 called for the provision of a school-house and a teacher's salary in every parish; although compliance was far from universal, the general level of education in eighteenth-century Scotland was certainly in advance of that in England. In the larger towns the burgh schools also provided some measure of secondary education for the 'lad o' pairts'. With the rise of the urban population in the industrial areas in the early nineteenth century, however, the public education system in the towns tended to break down.

THE PERIOD OF *LAISSEZ-FAIRE*

During the early nineteenth century the general prevalence of *laissez-faire* beliefs was unfavourable to the development of welfare services. This was the culmination of a trend of opinion beginning as early as the late seventeenth century, and it gradually gained strength. Attempts by the State to regulate the working of the economy came under growing disfavour; this was due to experience of their ineffectiveness at a time of rapid economic change and weak Government institutions, and to a growing belief in the virtues of free enterprise under the stimulus of the profit motive, regulated by the invisible hand of competition. These ideas received their most effective formulation in Adam Smith's *Wealth of Nations* (1776). Hence the provisions of the Statute of Apprentices calling for the fixing of fair rates of wages by the justices of the peace fell into growing disuse in the eighteenth century, though not formally repealed until 1812 and 1814. The same applied to statutory provisions for the regulation of prices and qualities of goods.

During the period of rapid industrialization in Britain the climate of public opinion was unfavourable to generosity towards the poor. There was a great belief in the virtues of hard work, frugality and enterprise, for industrial development seemed manifestly to depend on the efforts of those who worked hard and ploughed back their savings. It was generally believed that the poor would not work if their conditions were made too comfortable. Current opinion was reinforced by the teachings of the classical economists. Ricardo taught that a rise in the wage bill could only take place at the expense of profits, on which business enterprise and hence employment depended. Malthus taught that a rise in earnings would be followed by such a rise in the birth rate as would swallow up any gains. Hence the so-called 'Iron Law of Wages', which implied that the level of wages could not rise much above subsistence level.

There was a general hostility to intervention by the Government in the working of the economy. This was partly because of ideological belief in the virtues of free enterprise and the invisible hand of competition, and partly because of experience of the usually ineffective working of the public administration in the days before Civil Service reform. This belief went to reinforce the vested interests of those who were opposed to any Government interference with the conduct of business, or any attempts by the central Government to correct the ineptitudes of the unreformed local authorities.

The rapid rise of population and the growing urbanization probably also had the effect of leading to a harsher and less understanding attitude towards those in poverty and need. In the smaller communities of the past, the better-off had the poor always close at hand and were forced into at least a paternalistic concern for their welfare. As the nineteenth century wore on, the poor were more and more segregated into the working-class slums of the large towns, or into separate mining and mill villages, whereas the comfortably-off moved into the 'better class' residential areas in town and country. Thus there arose the 'two nations' attitude deplored by Disraeli, with the better-off knowing little of how their less fortunate fellows lived. This was enhanced by the endemic social unrest and disorders in the industrial areas in the first four decades of the century, themselves the product of the hardships and insecurity caused by rapid technical and industrial change. The middle and upper classes tended to retreat into a kind of siege mentality before the possible dangers of riot and revolution on the part of the masses.

THE NEW POOR LAW

In the social service field these trends found expression in the Report of the Royal Commission on the Poor Law of 1834 and in the Poor Law Amendment Act which followed it. The Commission reacted sharply to the evils of the Speenhamland System of supplementing inadequate wages with outdoor relief, with its pauperization of the labourers, its burden of rising rates and its encouragement to farmers to keep down wages at the expense of the ratepayers. Hence the New Poor Law, as established under the 1834 Act, embodied the principle that the condition of paupers should be made less eligible (i.e. less attractive) than that of the lowest-paid independent workers. In general, able-bodied workers were not to be given outdoor relief, but to be offered entry into the workhouse as a test of genuineness of need. Parishes were compulsorily grouped into Unions to enable larger workhouses to be built, in which it was hoped that more appropriate treatment could be given to different classes of the non-able-bodied who needed institutional care. For the first time, a central Government authority, the Poor Law Commission, was set up to supervise the Boards of Guardians of the Unions. This was succeeded in 1847 by the Poor Law Board which became the Local Government Board in 1871.

As the century went on, it proved impossible to administer the Poor Law according to the strict principles of 1834. Trade depression, for instance, caused large-scale unemployment among the able-bodied on a scale which could not be met by applying the workhouse test, and outdoor relief had to be given, especially in the industrial areas. On the other hand, the hopes of 1834, of applying more appropriate forms of treatment for the sick, the children, the feeble-minded and the old, were largely frustrated by the generally parsimonious spirit of the Poor Law administration and by the small size and limited resources of many of the Unions. The general mixed workhouse still prevailed even at the time of the Royal Commission on the Poor Law of 1905–9, except that a good deal had been done to set up separate children's homes and separate hospitals for the more seriously sick. The payment of outdoor relief to the non-able-bodied in their own homes also remained largely a matter of giving inadequate pittances with little investigation of the circumstances leading to poverty. In fact, in the words of the Minority Report of the Royal Commission, the Poor Law remained deterrent in principle and indiscriminate in practice. It was dominated by the fear of encouraging pauperism by too generous treatment, yet was unable adequately to discover and remedy the causes of poverty.

In Scotland relief through the Kirk Sessions of parishes, financed by voluntary collections, remained the general rule up to 1845, but it proved to be increasingly inadequate to deal with the problem of poverty in the growing industrial areas. The effectiveness of the church authorities as agencies of relief was further weakened by the spread of sectarianism, culminating in the Disruption of 1843, which tore the National Church in half. Under the Poor Law Act of 1845, Parochial Boards were established in each parish, succeeded in 1894 by Parish Councils; the levying of poor rates soon became general. A central Board of Supervision was set up, which in turn became the Local Government Board for Scotland in 1894. In principle the Poor Law in Scotland was just as deterrent as in England and Wales, and in some ways even more parsimonious. By law, no relief at all could be given to the able-bodied, though this had to be winked at in times of severe trade depression. For the non-able-bodied, outdoor relief continued to be the rule and there was less use of the poorhouse than in England.

The spirit which underlay the Poor Law, namely the fear of encouraging idleness and improvidence, inspired other developments in the mid-Victorian period. For instance, the Charity Organisation Society was founded in London in 1869 in an effort to curb the abuses of indiscriminate private charity; this arose from the existence of numerous funds which doled out small sums of cash or benefits in kind such as coals, clothes or grocery tickets. The aim was to encourage the channelling of all such giving through the Society, which would carry out an investigation of circumstances to ensure that help was given only to the deserving. The Society was not popular either with those in need or with other charities, which disliked being coordinated; its attitude tended to be unduly harsh and restrictive. Through its insistence on thorough investigation and adequate help to those genuinely in need, however, it pioneered the tradition of family case-work, which continues under its present name of the Family Welfare Association (adopted in 1944). Similar societies were founded in a number of provincial towns, and they have developed on the same lines.

FACTORS LEADING TO A CHANGE OF ATTITUDE

Nevertheless, as the century wore on, a number of factors began to lead towards a more positive attitude towards State action for social welfare. They included intellectual trends, such as utilitarianism; experience of the pressing dangers to public health arising out of conditions in the growing towns; the needs of an industrial society for some degree of education; the pressures of political democracy as the franchise was extended; experience of the inadequacies of the market to provide for urgent social needs, and realization of the continued wide extent of poverty among the unskilled masses at a time of generally rising prosperity.

THE INFLUENCE OF UTILITARIANISM

The spirit of utilitarianism, which sought to justify political actions on the basis of the contributions towards increasing human satisfaction and decreasing dissatisfaction, had its positive as well as its negative results. While it led to the sweeping away of many inefficient forms of State intervention by querying their usefulness, it also encouraged purposive intervention by the State where greater happiness could be held to be promoted by it. Hence there was support for Sadler and Shaftesbury in their campaigns for factory legislation to protect children and young people in industry. This began effectively with the Factory Act of 1833, under which the first inspectors were appointed; it continued with the Mines Act of 1842, forbidding underground work for women, girls and boys under ten; the Act of 1844, further limiting working hours for women and children in textile mills, and that of 1847, establishing a ten-hour day for these same groups. No attempt was made to regulate the working hours of adult men, this being regarded as too severe an interference with freedom of contract, but in time the limitation of hours for women and children also brought about shorter hours for men, though this was delayed for many years after 1847 by the device of employing children in relays; this was eventually prohibited in 1874.

THE NECESSITIES OF PUBLIC HEALTH

It was in the public health field that intervention was to be most decisive, forced on by the experience of the evils of life in the growing industrial towns. Here tens of thousands of men and women were packed into overcrowded and poorly-built housing, completely lacking adequate sanitary provision or pure water supply. Conditions which had been tolerable in the country villages and market towns of the past were found increasingly hazardous to health as towns grew in size. The cholera epidemics of 1831–32, 1848–49, 1853–54 and 1866, with their sudden and disastrous impact and heavy mortality, did much to force home lessons not sufficiently learned from the endemic presence of less dramatic diseases such as typhus, typhoid, measles, scarlet fever, diphtheria and tuberculosis. The dependence of infection on bacteria and viruses was not yet known, nor had it been proved that cholera and typhoid frequently are water-borne, and typhus carried by lice. Nevertheless such visitations made clear the connection between disease and filth and, by the general alarm which they caused, went far to break down the inertia of the vested interests of property-owners.

The leading figure in bringing about this awakening was Edwin Chadwick, the first Secretary to the Poor Law Commissioners. His Report on the Sanitary Conditions of the Labouring Population, published in 1842, was the first large-scale presentation of the full horrors of the situation. Chadwick was able to make it the more telling to the public opinion of the time by stressing the burden to the rates caused by the additional poverty resulting from the ill-health due to such conditions. This report and similar ones did much to dispel the comfortable ignorance of the living conditions of their less fortunate compatriots behind which the well-to-do middle classes had tended to shelter. It was followed by the report of the Commission on the Health of Towns in 1844–45, which led in 1848 to the first Public Health Act. Under this Act, Local Boards of Health could be set up with powers over services such as water, cleansing, draining and paving of streets, where these powers did not already exist under private Acts. A central General Board of Health was also established. Many of the powers were, however, permissive, and action followed only slowly. For instance, although Liverpool appointed the first Medical Officer of Health in 1847 and the City of London followed the next year, it was not until 1872 that their appointment became obligatory. Local opposition to the supervisory functions of the General Board of Health was so great that its powers were not renewed when they lapsed in 1854.

Experience in the next twenty years showed that, in those towns where effective sanitary measures were enforced, mortality was reduced, particularly during the cholera epidemic of 1866. It was not until the early 'seventies, however, following a Royal Commission in 1869, that a uniform system of sanitary authorities with adequate powers covering the whole country was established. It was consolidated in the Public Health Acts of 1872 and 1875, and the Local Government Board was made responsible for public health as well as for the Poor Law. Medical Officers of Health and sanitary inspectors were now installed throughout the country and there were mandatory powers to provide proper water supply and sanitation and to deal with nuisances. New buildings were subject to bye-laws laying down minimum quality standards, and infectious diseases gradually became compulsorily notifiable. In Scotland events took a similar course under the Public Health (Scotland) Act of 1867 and subsequent Acts. In both countries the reforms of local government and the introduction of County Councils, followed in England by that of Urban and Rural District Councils, hastened the process by providing popularly elected authorities in areas outside the corporate towns, where previously they had not existed.

THE NEED FOR PUBLIC EDUCATION

Pressure of events also led to the Government eventually taking greater responsibility in the field of education.

In England and Wales the development of a nation-wide school system was delayed by rivalries between religious denominations as well as by prevailing *laissez-faire* attitudes. Elementary schools were provided by the National Society (Church of England) and by the British and Foreign School Society (Non-conformist), both of which went back to the early years of the century. Government grants were given to the two societies from 1833, and were extended in 1838 when a Committee of the Privy Council was set up to supervise them. However the voluntary system proved incapable of meeting the needs of the growing population and in the 'sixties less than half the children were receiving instruction. In Scotland public education was stronger, but the parish school system was also failing to provide for the growing towns.

Growing industrialization was increasing the need for workers who could at least read and write, and the achievements of mass popular education in the United States and in Prussia were felt to lie behind their growing commercial achievements as well as the military successes of the North in the American Civil War and of the Prussians against France in 1870. The extension of the franchise to the mass of urban workers in 1867 made it more urgent to 'educate our masters'. Hence the Education Act of 1870 and the corresponding Scottish Act of 1872 set up elected School Boards to provide schools in areas not covered by denominational schools; in Scotland, they took over the existing parish schools. Education in England and Wales became compulsory in 1880, and the minimum school leaving age was gradually raised, reaching 12 in 1899, with power to make it 14 by local bye-law. It was not until 1918 that 14 became the universal minimum age. In Scotland attendance was compulsory up to 13 from 1872. Up to 1891 small fees were charged, but from that year (1892 in Scotland) elementary education was free.

Provision of secondary education was left mainly to the market for considerably longer. The Victorian era saw a big development of fee-

16

paying schools for the middle classes. Some of them were ancient endowed foundations intended to give free schooling to bright, poor boys, which were transformed into the so-called Public Schools, giving a boarding education to the wealthier upper middle classes, under the influence of such leaders as Arnold of Rugby, Thring of Uppingham and Butler of Shrewsbury. Others were new foundations intended to give an education at a moderate price to the sons, and increasingly also to the daughters, of the trading and professional classes. By the 1880s and 1890s, however, there was beginning to be concern that the provision both of secondary and technical education in Britain was falling behind that in other countries. In particular, the Germans were beginning to invade our export markets, especially with the products of the science-based industries, and this was felt to be due at least in part to their much better educational system. In Scotland the burgh schools made a wider provision available, while in Wales there developed a system of intermediate schools. In England there was no publicly provided system of secondary schools before the passing of the Education Act of 1902. Some School Boards had begun to provide 'higher grade' schools, but the Cockerton Judgment of 1899 ruled that this was outside their powers.

Meanwhile the newly established county councils had been authorized since 1889 to provide technical, evening and other advanced classes, and it was to them that the further development of education in England and Wales was to be entrusted.[2] Under the Education Act of 1902 the county and county borough councils replaced the school boards and were empowered to create secondary schools, charging small fees; they also provided some free places by scholarships from the elementary schools. The new secondary schools were for long to be used mainly by the middle classes, but they opened the road towards a more comprehensive national system of education, which was later to be slowly widened, notably by the Education Acts of 1918 and 1944.

THE INADEQUACIES OF THE MARKET

Education was one of the first fields in which it came to be realized that the free market could not be relied upon to provide services to the extent adequate for social needs. There were other spheres also in which the authorities tried to intervene in a limited way, to deal with obvious abuses, only to find that the market could not be relied upon to fill the gaps in social provision revealed by this action. Examples are to be found, for instance, in housing and in medical services.

Housing and slum clearance

A number of the larger towns had taken steps under Private Acts to clear some of the worst of their slum areas. Thus Liverpool Corporation obtained powers to do this in 1864, and in Glasgow the Improvement Trust carried out extensive schemes from 1870 onwards. Voluntary Housing Associations like the Peabody Trust in London also found it possible to build blocks of model dwellings to let at economic rents. Their efforts were reinforced by Octavia Hill's pioneer work in showing how scientific housing management could make blocks of property pay and improve housing standards. Under the Artisans' Dwelling Act of 1875 local authorities were given permissive powers to clear and rebuild insanitary areas. Birmingham Corporation, led by Joseph Chamberlain, used these powers to clear the slum area on which Corporation Street was built. The effectiveness of local authority intervention in the slum clearance and housing field was long delayed by the relative weakness of many authorities and their unwillingness to interfere with the interests of property-owning ratepayers. Following on the report of the Royal Commission on the Housing of the Working Classes in 1884–85, however, the Housing Act of 1890 consolidated and strengthened the powers of local authorities to regulate new building, demolish insanitary housing and engage in house building.

Efforts at effective replacement of the slums, however, whether by local authorities or by private bodies, came up against the obstacle of the cost of building houses of satisfactory quality. Houses built to replace cleared slums could not be let at economic rents which the displaced slum dwellers could afford, since they were mostly among the lowest income-groups. Thus the new houses tended to go to the better-off artisans rather than to those whose housing needs were greatest. Later it was to be accepted that the way to overcome this was to give subsidies, but the idea of subsidizing rents went against the deepest Victorian convictions of the dangers of encouraging improvidence and interfering with the market forces. For this reason public building on any great scale had to wait until after the First World War.

MEDICAL TREATMENT

With the spread of medical knowledge from the middle of the century there began to be a demand for more extensive facilities for hospital treatment than could be provided by the voluntary hospitals, which operated on a charitable basis. Hence the Poor Law infirmaries began to develop from merely being centres at which the more acutely sick paupers could be treated better than in the work-houses, into something like general hospitals, providing treatment for any of the acutely sick who could not afford to pay for it. This development was encouraged by the Medical Relief Disqualification Removal Act of 1885, under which those who took advantage of such treatment were no longer subject to the loss of rights associated with pauper status. Meanwhile the public health authorities had been developing hospitals for infectious diseases and for the mentally ill, so that a system of public hospitals was growing up alongside the voluntary ones. Provision was very uneven, however, being much better in the larger cities than in smaller towns or the country. Nor were there any similar developments in the field of family medicine. The services of the Poor Law doctors remained available only to those in direst poverty; others had either to pay doctors' fees, or rely on doctors' charity or the services of charitable dispensaries, or make use of voluntary sickness benefit clubs or friendly societies.

REALIZATION OF THE EXTENT OF POVERTY, AND CHANGING ATTITUDES TO IT

Public attitudes towards the causes of poverty and the methods required to deal with it were also beginning to change.

General living standards were rising among the prosperous artisans and the skilled workers, but especially among the middle classes. From the 'seventies this process was aided by the fall in food prices made possible by the railways, the steam ships and refrigeration plant, which were opening up the supply of cheap wheat from the United States and Canada, meat from the Argentine, Australia and New Zealand, and dairy produce from Denmark and New Zealand. Thus it came as a shock to realize the extent to which this prosperity was not shared by the mass of unskilled workers, whose earnings were still low and their employment precarious. Periodic trade depressions caused widespread distress, and attempts to relieve it by private charity, such as the Mansion House Fund of 1885–86, proved of little permanent value. However, demonstrations by the unemployed called the attention of the comfortable to the dimensions of the problem. So did the attempts to extend trade union organization from the skilled craftsmen to the unskilled workers, as marked by such episodes as the London Dock Strike of 1889, which aroused widespread public support for the dockers in their claim for a rate of 6d an hour. Similarly the rise of left wing political movements, such as the Independent Labour Party, the Fabian Society and the Social Democratic Federation, were symptomatic of the beginnings of a more active political concern over basic economic issues. Charitable

19

workers, such as those concerned with the various residential settlements sponsored by universities and similar bodies to work in the poorer areas of cities, also played a large part in arousing public awareness. Notable among these settlements was Toynbee Hall in Whitechapel where, under Canon Barnett, men like William Beveridge and R. H. Tawney began their careers.

Another factor which helped to arouse public concern was the revelation of the poor physical condition of many of the recruits who volunteered for service in the South African War of 1899–1902. The shock of this was so great that it led to the appointment of an Interdepartmental Committee on Physical Deterioration, which reported in 1904. Among other things, it recommended the general introduction of school meals for underfed children and a system of school medical inspection. This recommendation did much to make possible the general introduction of these services by the Liberal government which came to power in 1906.

The shock effect of these stirrings of concerned men became greater when more precise measurement of the extent and degree of poverty became possible through the early social surveys, pioneered by Charles Booth and B. Seebohm Rowntree. Booth, in his monumental survey of the *Life and Labour of the People of London*,[3] published over the years 1889 to 1903, but referring substantially to the years around 1890, found that some 30 per cent of the population of London were living at or below a poverty line represented by an income of around a pound a week. Rowntree, in the first of his three surveys of York, referring to the year 1899,[4] found a similar situation, with 28 per cent of the population living below the standard necessary for physical efficiency, whether because of lack of means, or because of inefficient use of means which were technically adequate by the stringent standards adopted for the survey. Rowntree adopted a poverty line based on the minimum requirements for bare physical efficiency, and those with incomes below this were held to be in primary poverty. Since this standard assumed that nothing was spent on items other than necessities, and that the housewife was expert in making the best use of her means, many with incomes above this level were in fact living in poverty conditions.

Figures like these made thinking people reconsider their attitudes. Poverty on this scale could not be realistically blamed on the personal improvidence, laziness or thriftlessness of the people concerned. It was becoming clear that, though these factors were only too likely to arise among those living under poverty conditions, the root causes must be seen rather in economic factors, such as the low rate of earnings of the unskilled and the irregular and casual nature of their employment, or social factors, such as the lack of adequate provision for those unable to earn owing to sickness, widowhood or old age. In particular, the mass of poverty among the old stood out, and voices began to be raised in favour of old age pensions; however, there were still many, as diverse as Octavia Hill and the officials of the Local Government Board, who feared anything that looked like giving doles to the poor.

THE CHANGE TO A MORE POSITIVE ATTITUDE

To sum up then, half a century's experience of the problem of an urbanized, industrial society was leading thoughtful people towards a more positive attitude to the role of the Government in promoting social welfare. The imperative problems of public health arising from uncontrolled urban growth had forced intervention to ensure provision of pure water and proper sanitation, to control standards of new building, to check epidemic diseases. Basic services such as elementary education and the care of the mentally ill had had to be introduced, and the inadequacies of the market were slowly forcing more public provision of housing, hospital services, and secondary and further education. The realization of the full extent of continuing poverty in a country enjoying riches and prosperity on a previously unparalleled scale was pointing in the same direction. Full realization of the implications for public action was slow in coming, and many strongly held misgivings had first to be overcome, but by the turn of the century the change of trend was recognizable.

One of the landmarks in this process of changing opinion was the Royal Commission on the Poor Law, which sat from 1905 to 1909, and carried out an exhaustive examination of the whole system of relief of those in need. The main recommendation of the majority of the Commission was that responsibility for the relief of the poor should be transferred from the special Poor Law authorities to the ordinary local authorities and, in order to get large enough units, that it should be given to the county councils and the councils of the county boroughs. They also recommended a system of unemployment insurance and of public works to provide employment in times of trade slump. But the public imagination was struck rather by the Minority Report, signed by Mrs Sidney Webb and four others. This denounced the Poor Law as a Destitution Authority concerned only to relieve destitution, not to discover and eliminate its causes. It called for the break up of the Poor Law and the transfer of responsibility for each class of needy person, children, the chronic sick, the feeble-minded, old people and the able-bodied unemployed, to the care of appropriate committees of the local authorities.

In fact, largely because of the hostility of the Local Government

21

Board, whose president, John Burns, had outgrown his radical past under the influence of his permanent officials, no immediate action was taken on the reports of the Commission. It was not until 1929 that responsibility for the relief of the poor was transferred to the ordinary local authorities. But the spirit of the Minority Report lay behind what actually happened in the development of the social security and welfare services in the first half of the twentieth century. As the particular needs of each class of people came to be recognized, special services were to be introduced, with the aim of removing them from the scope of the Poor Law.

Some of these developments had already taken place, with the introduction of Workmen's Compensation in 1897 and the development of public secondary education under the Act of 1902. Others were more or less contemporary with the Royal Commission, such as Old Age Pensions, in 1908, or school meals and the school medical service, and some followed shortly afterwards, such as National Health Insurance in 1911. These developments were piecemeal, and the measures introduced were often tentative, partial and inadequate, as we shall see in the next Chapter. They marked a decisive change of attitude, however. It was now becoming increasingly accepted that the Government's responsibility was not merely the negative one of intervening to prevent intolerable abuses. The Government also had an obligation to provide services in cash and in kind to help those in need to obtain a better life and to reduce the worst inequalities of opportunity. The foundations of the modern Welfare State were laid in the first decade of the twentieth century.

NOTES

1 The name derives from a meeting of the Berkshire magistrates held at Speenhamland, near Newbury, in 1795, at which this policy was adopted.

2 In Scotland, School Boards remained as education authorities up to 1918.

3 Charles Booth, *Life and Labour of the People of London*, complete edn (Macmillan, London, 1902).

4 B. S. Rowntree, *Poverty: A Study of Town Life, 1901*.

Chapter Three

DEVELOPMENT OF THE SOCIAL SERVICES, 1900–1948

As a result of the growing awareness of needs discussed in the last chapter, the first four decades of the twentieth century were to see the foundations of the Welfare State well and truly laid. A network of services grew up, in the fields of social security, health, welfare, education and housing, which went far to provide against the most serious cases of need and inequality. But social attitudes change slowly, and in spite of the shake-up of the First World War, there remained a legacy of suspicion of the harmful effects of increased public welfare activity and a resistance to higher taxation. Hence the services were never developed in a systematic and well-planned way; rather, there was a piece-meal introduction of specific services to meet the needs of particular groups of people as these came to be recognized as urgent. As a result, the social services as they existed in the 1930s, in spite of their remarkable growth since 1900, were still subject to strong criticism for their inadequacies. There were many gaps in their coverage and a great deal of overlapping between different schemes organized on different principles to serve restricted classes of people.

SOCIAL SECURITY

In the field of social security, the attempt to get away from the evils of the Poor Law led to the development of two different types of scheme. Some were based on the principle of social insurance, and others were based on that of social assistance, which still relied upon tests of need and means.

The name 'social insurance' came to be applied to services in which benefits were paid as of right to all those in the category of persons covered who had qualified by paying a minumum number of contributions. The benefits were at standard scales and, in the British system, at flat rates unrelated to income. This system became popular because it got away from means tests, yet appeared to be relating payments to contributions by the recipients and their employers; thus it seemed not to involve the indiscriminate payment of 'doles' by the State, which was still feared as encouraging improvidence. It was also acceptable because it seemed to be analogous both to private insurance schemes, providing cover against sickness, old age or death, and to the operations of sickness benefit clubs, friendly societies and trade unions on behalf of their members, which were all familiar.

In fact, social insurance bears little resemblance to private insurance. Risks can be pooled because contributions are compulsory, so that all can receive the same benefit for the same contribution. In the British case, the existence of a large Exchequer contribution made it possible to vary benefit rates and contribution rates as thought socially desirable, without too much regard for actuarial principles. In fact, the contribution was really only a disguised form of tax, earmarked for the support of a particular form of social service spending. In the 1920s, for instance, the Exchequer contribution amounted to between a quarter and a fifth of the total revenue of the National Health Insurance Fund and of the Unemployment Insurance Fund.[1]

Nor was social insurance something new or untried. It had been developed by Bismarck in Germany in the 1880s and in New Zealand in the 1890s. In Britain, however, the principle of the flat rate of benefit and contribution unrelated to income level became general, as did that of the tri-partite contribution by insured person, employer, and Exchequer. In Western Europe, and later in North America, income-related contributions and benefits became more common and in general, contributions from the State were less important, and those from the employer more important, than in Britain.

The piece-meal approach to the problem of social security had the result that, over the years, four separate schemes of social insurance came into being in Britain.

National health insurance This was introduced by Lloyd George's National Insurance Act of 1911, and came into operation in 1912–13. This provided for a limited scale of flat-rate weekly cash benefit to insured persons in case of sickness. It also provided for the free services of general practitioners and the supply of drugs. It did not cover dependants, except for a cash maternity benefit for wives of insured persons. It covered most manual employees,[2] and non-manual employees up to a certain income level. This was originally £160 a year; it was raised to £250 in the 1920s and to £420 after the Second World War.

Unemployment insurance An experimental scheme, confined to certain industries, was introduced in 1911; for provision of social insurance against unemployment was a new and untried field with little previous voluntary experience to draw on. It was extended to cover munition workers during the First World War. In 1920 a new scheme was introduced, covering all manual employees with certain exceptions, together with most non-manual employees up to the same income level as for National Health Insurance. The main employments excluded were teachers, local government officers, civil servants and railway clerks, whose liability to unemployment was thought to be negligible, and agricultural workers and indoor domestic servants, whose incomes were thought to be too low for them to afford the contributions. In addition, the banking and insurance industries were allowed to run separate schemes, giving the same rates of benefit for much lower contributions, paid entirely by the employers; they could afford to do this because of their low unemployment liability. It had been intended to encourage other separate occupational schemes of this sort, but these were the only two which came into being.

The scheme provided benefits at rates higher than those under National Health Insurance and included dependants' allowances for a period of up to six months. During the heavy unemployment of the 'twenties, the problem of the long-term unemployed who had exhausted their insurance benefit rights soon became a serious one. At first they were allowed to continue to draw benefit; this put the Unemployment Insurance Fund heavily into debt. In 1931 financial liability for the long-term unemployed had to be taken over by the Exchequer and payments to those who had exhausted benefit rights became subject to means tests.

Agricultural unemployment insurance A special system of unemployment insurance for agricultural employees was eventually introduced in 1935. It had much lower rates of contribution, geared to farmworkers' lower wages, and gave rather lower benefit rates than the general scheme. The lower liability to unemployment made possible a more favourable actuarial relationship between contributions and benefits.

Widows, orphans and old age contributory pensions A contributory system of pensions was introduced in 1925, contributions being covered by a single stamp for health and pensions insurance. Pensions were provided without a means test to insured persons and their wives at the age of 65,[3] without any condition of retirement from work. The rate originally was ten shillings a week, or twenty shillings for a married couple. Benefits were also provided for the widows and orphans of insured persons. The classes covered by the scheme were much the same as for National Health Insurance.

The social insurance schemes were, however, limited in their coverage, excluding for instance the self-employed, the non-employed and non-manual employees above a certain income level. They also provided limited rates of cash benefit unrelated to the needs of particular families, and available only to those who satisfied standard conditions. As the problems of other groups of people came to be recognized, it was therefore found necessary to extend and make more liberal the social assistance type of service, which provides benefits more closely related to the needs of particular cases, subject to test of means.

The first and decisive development in this field was the introduction of the **Old Age Non-Contributory Pension** in 1908. This gave a pension, originally with a maximum of five shillings (25p) a week, later raised to ten shillings (50p) to old people at the age of 70. It was subject to a means test, but this was much less stringent than under the Poor Law, since it disregarded small items of means and did not involve destitution; nor did it call on relatives for support or repayment. It did not involve any loss of civic rights. Small though the pension was, it did more than anything to raise the status of old people, who now had an assured income of their own which made them an asset to their family instead of a liability.

Twenty years elapsed, however, from the report of the Royal Commission before any change was made in the set-up of the Poor Law. Eventually, in the general reforms of local government in 1929, the separate Poor Law authorities were abolished and relief of the poor was transferred to the ordinary local authorities (the county councils in England and Wales, and the counties and the large burghs in Scotland). The name 'Poor Law' was replaced by that of Public Assistance and the administration became a good deal more liberal and sympathetic though, until 1940, it was still conducted under the household means test, under which the means of all members of a family were deemed to be pooled.

Later on, a number of other Assistance-type services came into being. The problem of the support of the long-term unemployed was eventually tackled in 1934 by introducing a system of **Unemployment Assistance.** Under this, benefit was given subject to a means test administered uniformly on a nation-wide basis by the Unemployment Assistance Board; the able-bodied unemployed in general ceased to be the concern of the Public Assistance authorities. This eased the very heavy burden on the local authorities in those areas where unemployment was extensive and prolonged, though the stringent application of the household means test, reflecting concern at the cost of the service, caused a great deal of resentment and hardship.

The rise in the cost of living in the Second World War caused problems to old people with limited means; to save them having to have recourse to Public Assistance in growing numbers, a special system of **Supplementary Pensions** was introduced in 1940. These were administered under means tests by the Unemployment Assistance Board, which was renamed the Assistance Board and also made responsible for the needs of those who had suffered loss or damage through the war. At the same time, the household means test gave way to an individual means test, under which only the means of the applicant, his wife or her husband, and their dependant children were to be considered as pooled; older children living at home and working were regarded as making only a fixed contribution to the support of their parents.

In the case of industrial injuries the procedure followed before 1948 was that of placing the liability on the employer. Employers have always been liable at common law for payment of damages in those cases where injury could be shown to be due to their negligence, but there were many cases of disabling injury where this could not be done. Proof of negligence was made more difficult by the legal doctrine of common employment, under which it was a sufficient defence for an employer to show that an accident was due to the negligence of a fellow-employee of the injured person.

The remedy adopted under the Workmen's Compensation Acts of 1897, 1900 and 1906 was to place a limited, statutory liability on the employer to pay compensation even in cases where no negligence could be proved. The maximum weekly amount payable was normally half the previous average earnings, subject to an overall maximum, with the option of settling for a lump sum in certain cases. The system had the disadvantage that the claimant had to show that the accident arose out of, and in the course of, his employment; therefore in contested cases success still depended on a legal action brought by the injured workman against his employer or the employer's insurance company. He was thus apt to be at a disadvantage, even with the aid of his trade union. There was also often pressure on a claimant to accept a lump sum; by paying a few hundred pounds the employer might be saved weekly payments over many years. Such agreements had to be approved by the court, to protect the claimant's interest, but cases nevertheless arose of a lump sum being accepted and perhaps speedily lost in an unsound business venture. Nor were employers obliged by law to insure against their liabilities, except in a few industries like mining. Most did insure, but there was always the risk of a small employer being unable to meet his liabilities for payment. It was for such reasons as these that, following Beveridge's recommendations, Workmen's Compensation was replaced in 1948 by the present system of Industrial Injuries Insurance.

Medical Services

Medical services also were being extended during this period along a number of different and sometimes conflicting lines.

So far as personal medical care was concerned, the biggest development was the general practitioner service, introduced in 1911 as part of the scheme of National Health Insurance. This had serious limitations, however; it only covered insured persons and not their dependants, and it did not cover hospital or consultant treatment, nor dental and ophthalmic treatment, except in certain cases where the insured person belonged to an Approved Society which gave additional benefits. Those who were not covered by the 'panel', as it was called, still had to pay doctors' fees, except in so far as they were able to get medical attention through membership of voluntary sick-benefit clubs. In the last resort they had to use the free service available under the Poor Law and later under Public Assistance.

Meanwhile the local authorities were also beginning to take a more positive responsibility for the medical needs and welfare of certain groups of people. Thus the School Medical Service was set up in 1907 as part of the educational system, to inspect and if necessary treat pupils who could not profit from their education because of health defects. In the previous year the education authorities had also become responsible for providing school meals to children who needed them. Just before the First World War the local authorities became responsible for the care of the blind, tuberculous and mentally deficient in their own homes. They also gradually developed services for the welfare of mothers and young children, including maternity and child welfare clinics and the provision of health visitors to advise mothers in their homes. These services, at first partial and experimental, received statutory recognition in the Maternity and Child Welfare Act of 1918, and also in the Notification of Births Act of 1915, which made notification of births to local health authorities compulsory throughout the country.

Under the local government reforms of 1929, the former Poor Law infirmaries were taken over by the local authorities. They were mostly transferred from the Public Assistance Committees of each authority to the Public Health Committees and reorganized as local authority general hospitals. Thus, with the infectious diseases hospitals and mental hospitals which went back to the nineteenth century, they formed part of a local authority hospital system parallel to, and quite independent of, the voluntary hospitals. The local authority service, however, was not popular with the medical profession, who tended to fear interference with their professional freedom; hence these hospitals tended to suffer in prestige in comparison with the larger voluntary hospitals.

The voluntary hospitals varied enormously in size and prestige, from the great teaching hospitals of London and the major provincial cities, through the sizeable hospitals in the medium-sized towns to cottage hospitals in country towns staffed by local general practitioners. They all tended to operate with very small full-time medical staffs and to depend heavily on the voluntary services of consultants. Some of them had substantial incomes from endowments and contributions, whereas others were in chronic financial difficulties. Treatment was still on a semi-charitable basis, with patients making contributions according to their means. There was a big development of voluntary weekly contribution schemes, often based on workplaces, which entitled contributors to free treatment and ensured a regular flow of income for the hospitals.

Education

In England and Wales the main development of the period was the building up of the local authority secondary schools under the powers of the Education Act of 1902. In most cases these schools remained partly fee-paying, so that the main benefit from them was the opening up of secondary education on a wider scale to middle-class boys and girls for modest fees. They also provided a proportion of free places to 'scholarship' pupils from the elementary schools, on the basis of an attainments test at the age of 11; this thus opened up an educational ladder, even if a fairly narrow and steep one, to the bright boy or girl from a working-class home. Under the financial stresses of 1931 the system of free places was replaced by one of special places subject to parental means test, but along with it went a wider opening of secondary school places to all those eligible on grounds of ability. The proportion of elementary school pupils who were able to pass on to secondary schools, though still low, tended to rise considerably, e.g. from 56 per thousand in 1914 to 112 per thousand in 1929.

The so-called 'Fisher' Education Act of 1918 finally raised the school leaving age to 14 for all without exceptions and gave permissive powers for its extension to 15 and for the creation of nursery schools. It also envisaged a general system of part-time day continuation classes for young workers up to 18, though this, as well as the raising of the leaving age, were casualties of the Geddes economy axe on public spending in 1921. In fact, financial stringency throughout the inter-war period prevented the ideals of the Fisher Act being carried into effect, but the period was not without developments in the educational field. In the 1930s the fall in the birth rate reduced the number of pupils and thus enabled more to be spent per pupil. Class sizes were reduced and teaching methods much improved, especially in infant and primary classes. Under the influence of the Hadow Committee (1926), which accepted the principle of secondary education for all, considerable progress was made in transferring pupils over the age of 11 to specialized senior schools, which were intended to form the nucleus of future secondary provision. By 1939 two-thirds of all pupils of this age had been so transferred. Provision for higher education was also being extended, with local authorities beginning to give scholarships to universities, supplemented by State scholarships, and development of technical colleges. The Government also began to give financial help direct to the universities, through the University Grants Committee, established in 1919.

In Scotland public education was already more highly developed, with an extensive system of publicly supervised endowed secondary schools, a rate of university attendance per thousand of the population twice that of England and Wales, and a largely graduate teaching profession. In 1920, for instance, expenditure per pupil in Scotland averaged £10·5 per year as against £8·5 in England and Wales. The Education (Scotland) Act of 1918 replaced the local School Boards by *ad hoc* education authorities in each county and city; these were in turn replaced by the county councils and the councils of the four cities in 1929. It also provided for the voluntary schools owned by certain religious denominations to be taken over by the education authorities, while retaining complete religious freedom. Developments in the inter-war years followed a similar pattern to those in England, with a growth of intermediate schools paralleling that of senior elementary schools in the south, but there were similar limitations owing to financial stringency.

Welfare services

Concern for health and education naturally led to a wider concern for the general welfare of the sick and disabled, and of children and their families. Hence many of what have now developed into separate welfare services arose out of the health and education services; this was so in the case of the care of the blind, tuberculous and mentally deficient in their own homes, and school meals, and the supervision of school attendance. Other services arose out of the relief of the poor, as in the cases of care of old people in their own homes or in institutions, and the care of children in need of support, either at home, or in special Children's Homes, or by boarding out. There was also a development of services more specifically concerned with children's welfare. Thus the Children's Act of 1908 abolished imprisonment of children and set up remand homes and juvenile courts. This concern was carried further by the Children and Young Persons Act of 1933, which extended responsibility to young persons up to the age of 17 and laid down the principle that the courts concerned with young people should have regard specifically to their welfare, in proper cases by removing them from undesirable surroundings. In this it reflected the opinion of the day, though subsequent experience has tended to lay more stress on the part which the family can play in helping children in trouble. Various strands were thus coming together to form the services which later would be recognized as welfare services.

HOUSING

In the field of Housing the First World War marked a decisive change in the role of the public authorities. Up till then their intervention had been confined by and large to the clearance of some of the worst slum areas; the success of this had been hampered by the inability of slum dwellers to pay economic rents for replacement housing.

During the war it became obvious that uncontrolled rise of rents would cause hardship, and so in 1915 rents of all but the largest houses were frozen. Rent control in one form or another has continued ever since. In the inter-war years permitted increases were granted, but the lower-valued houses remained under control. New building virtually ceased during the war, but population continued to grow, so that there came to be an acute housing shortage; in view of the promise of 'homes for heroes' in the 1918 election campaign the Government had to do something about housing. Minimum standards of what was desirable for new houses had risen, while building costs rose sharply in the years of rising prices up to 1920. Hence it became clear that housing could not be provided at an economic rent within the capacity to pay of those with lower incomes.

Thus the principle of local authority building of houses to let at subsidized rents was established as a general practice by the Housing Act of 1919, and has continued to be the basis of public housing policy ever since. The actual forms of subsidy have, however, changed over the years.

The original Addison Subsidy of 1919, under which the local authorities were to make good the deficiencies of housing in their areas, and the Treasury bore the cost of any deficit above the proceeds of a penny rate ($\frac{5}{6}$ of a penny in Scotland) proved too costly, and a limit was placed on the number of houses to be built under it. It was followed by more limited subsidies, usually based on a payment

31

of so much per house for a number of years, as under the Chamberlain Act of 1923, which placed the emphasis mainly on private building, and the Wheatley Act of 1924, under which large-scale local authority building again took place. Up till the 'thirties building costs remained high and private building could make relatively little contribution to housing needs.

In the 1930s building costs fell, because of lower prices, lower interest rates and greater efficiency among large-scale builders. This led to a big development of private building of relatively cheap houses, mainly for sale to owner-occupiers, aided by easy availability of mortgages from the growing building societies. This building boom was more marked in the prosperous areas of the South and Midlands than it was in depressed areas like north-east England; in particular it never really got going in Scotland, except to a limited extent around Glasgow and Edinburgh. The Scottish tradition of low spending on housing had been accompanied by a proportionately greater extension of local authority building. Thus not only was total house building relatively less in Scotland, with new building over the years 1919–39 amounting to 28 per cent of the housing stock existing in 1911, as against 52 per cent in England and Wales, the proportion of public and private building was different also. Whereas in England and Wales it was roughly 70 per cent private and 30 per cent local authority, in Scotland these figures were reversed, with 70 per cent local authority to 30 per cent private; moreover a bigger proportion of total private building consisted of houses subsidized under the Chamberlain Act.

As a result of the private building boom, the governments of the 'thirties tried to concentrate local authority building on to slum clearance and the relief of overcrowding. A five year programme for clearing the slums was announced in 1933, involving a quarter of a million houses. It was followed in 1935 by a national census of overcrowding, under which 341,000 houses in England and Wales were found to be affected. Both of these programmes were conservative in the standards they adopted and hence under-estimated the extent of the problem. Nevertheless, though some authorities did better than others, only about half of the declared slums had been cleared by 1939.

The inter-war years were thus marked by very large-scale house building. Local authorities built more than a million altogether, of a much higher standard than the pre-1914 housing which they replaced. Private enterprise built over two million, mostly in the 'thirties; many of these were within the reach of the better-paid manual workers. Movement into new houses led to a good deal of 'filtering up' of those less well-off into those vacated. By 1939 there were more than enough houses available in total for all but the poorest groups, though they were not always in the right places. The hard core of the housing problem, however, had not really been tackled. Local authority rents, even though subsidized, were still too high for the means of the worst off, who remained crowded into the poorest types of property. Slum clearance lagged behind, especially in the larger towns, and meanwhile much older property on the fringe of the slum category was deteriorating and creating new slums. On top of this unresolved situation were to come the effects of the Second World War, with its six years' cessation of house building and its intensive damage by bombing.

By 1939, Britain had developed a system of social services as good as that of any country in the world at that time. It had grown up empirically with little coherent planning, but certain underlying principles can be distinguished. In the field of social security, the movement was towards a system of social insurance which provided minimum basic incomes for those who could not earn, owing to old age, sickness or unemployment, together with provision of social assistance on less deterrent terms than under the old Poor Law for those who were not covered by insurance. In the case of the services in kind, the principle was coming gradually to be accepted that the Government had to provide a minimum of basic education and health services, with some provision for more equal access to services above the minimum, as well as subsidized houses for those with low incomes who could not pay economic rents.

Nevertheless, this provision had many limitations, which were vigorously pointed out by those working in the various fields at the time.

It was not comprehensive in its coverage This was the result of the way in which the services had grown up, by the piece-meal introduction of new measures to meet the needs of different groups as they were recognized. Thus, while all manual employees and non-manual employees up to a certain income level were insured against sickness from 1911 and for pensions from 1925, unemployment insurance was less comprehensive, excluding several groups of non-manual employees, as well as domestic servants and (up to 1935) agricultural workers also. Non-manual employees above the exemption level, the self-employed and the non-employed had no cover, except for very limited facilities for becoming voluntary contributors.

In the medical field, insured persons were covered for general practitioner services, but not their dependants, and not those who were ineligible for health insurance. In education, while elementary schooling was available to all up to 14, secondary schooling was still mainly limited to those who could pay fees or obtain a limited number of scholarships. Access to higher education was still more limited. In the case of housing, it is more debatable how wide public provision should be; building by local authorities was in principle limited to the provision of houses for the working classes, and in practice the poorest and worst housed could not afford even subsidized rents on new houses.

The benefits provided were limited In the social security field, the amount of financial benefit paid was still very limited. Under National Health Insurance, the weekly payments were not intended to be more than a help in tiding over sickness, for they amounted to only 15s (75p) a week for men for the first 26 weeks, raised to 18s (90p) in 1942, and a reduced rate of 7s 6d (37½p) a week (raised in 1942 to 10s 6d or 52½p), for a further period, with no allowance for dependants. Rates for insured women were lower. Similarly, the Old Age Pension remained at 10s (50p) a week, or 20s (£1·00) for a married couple, until it was raised to 26s (£1·30) in 1946. Unemployment Insurance was slightly more generous, since it had to provide an allowance for the maintenance of dependants, but during most of the 'thirties for instance, the rates were 17s (85p) for a man, 9s (45p) for an adult dependant, and 3s (15p) for a child dependant. Similarly the standard Unemployment Assistance benefit, as introduced in 1934 subject to a means test, was 24s (£1·20) for a man and wife, with allowances of 3s (15p) to 5s (25p) according to age for children. Various social surveys of the 'thirties made it clear that those dependent on social security benefits would not have sufficient income to keep them above a reasonable poverty standard, such as that adopted by Rowntree for his survey of York in 1936.

Similarly, the medical benefits obtainable under National Health Insurance in general covered only the services of a general practitioner and the supply of drugs. They did not include hospital treatment, the service of consultants, dental and ophthalmic treatment, nor the supply of surgical appliances. There was, however, the further anomaly that those who belonged to Approved Societies which had a surplus at the quinquennial valuation of their assets might be entitled to a range of additional benefits which others could not get. These did not normally include hospital treatment, but covered most of the other things mentioned, and often also the use of convalescent homes maintained by the Societies. Thus equal social insurance contributions brought with them unequal entitlement to benefits, depending on whether the insured person belonged to a society whose members were unduly sickness-prone or not. This links up with the question of anomalies in administration of the services, which was also a cause of much criticism.

The administration was often unduly complex and costly The piece-meal growth of the services meant that separate administrative structures had to be set up for each of them and consequently their administration was often unduly complicated and costly. For instance, the non-contributory Old Age Pensions were administered by the Board of Customs and Excise, since this was the only body which had the necessary network of local offices at the time when they were introduced. National Health Insurance, in view of its pioneering nature, was given an exceedingly complicated structure, in order to enlist the co-operation of all the various bodies already interested in the fields covered. Centrally, the scheme was administered first by four Insurance Commissions and then, from 1919, by the Ministry of Health and corresponding bodies in Scotland and Wales. In each major local government area the medical benefits were administered by insurance committees, on which the doctors were represented. The cash benefits were, however, administered by Approved Societies, which could be formed by such bodies as trade unions, friendly societies and insurance companies which were already providing sickness cover. The Societies had to be non-profit-making and constitutionally under the control of their members. This system got the co-operation of these bodies and enabled their agents, who were already in touch with a large number of homes, to be used to check on eligibility for benefit. It proved to be very costly form of administration, however, since most of the Societies were nation-wide and hence there was a great deal of overlapping of agents of different societies covering the same areas to make house-to-house visits.

Such a division of functions was not followed for later schemes. The Unemployment Insurance Scheme of 1920 was administered by the Ministry of Labour through the Employment Exchanges, as was the agricultural scheme of 1935. The Contributory Pensions were administered directly by the Ministry of Health and the corresponding Scottish and Welsh departments, without the involvement of the Approved Societies. Similarly, the introduction of Unemployment Assistance in 1934 and Supplementary Pensions in 1940 meant that these two services were operated on a uniform basis throughout the country, whereas Public Assistance remained subject to control by local authorities, with varying conditions and benefit rates. In fact, one of the great anomalies arising from the existence of separate systems separately administered was that conditions of eligibility for benefit, duration of benefit, disqualifications and similar details varied often for little apparent reason between the different schemes.

In the field of medical services there were similar complications. These were notably between the general practitioner service under National Health Insurance and that under Public Assistance; between the clinics and the domiciliary services being developed for various groups such as school children, mothers with babies, the blind, tuberculous and mentally deficient; and the various general practitioner and hospital services. These were to cause confusions which were carried over into the tri-partite structure of the National Health Service after 1948.

The underlying concept was still a limited and partial one In general, the concept underlying the services was that of making special provision for the minimum requirements of those groups recognized as being in particular need. Providing a basic minimum income for all who were unable to provide for themselves, or a basic minimum of equality of access to education and medical treatment, were not included. It was a marked improvement on the nineteenth-century Poor Law attitude, reflecting both the higher general standard of living and the acceptance of a more active and positive role for the Government in social welfare. But further development was hindered, both by the scale of the poverty created by the unemployment of the 1920s and 1930s, and by continued uneasiness about further extension of public spending.

Financial orthodoxy still accepted that the Government must balance its budget; hence if trade depression reduced revenues, spending must be cut back also. Thus in 1931 the financial crisis was met by reductions in Government spending, including unemployment benefit rates, in spite of unemployment reaching two and half million. It was not until 1936 that Keynes' 'General Theory of Employment, Interest and Money' made deficit spending in slump conditions academically respectable, and it was not in fact adopted in the 'thirties in the country of its conception. Similarly, there was a considerable resistance to the possible effects of the taxation (which a permanently higher level of spending would entail) on incentives to private enterprise. There was also a continued fear of the effects of too generous treatment of those less well off on self-reliance and self-help. Thus, although the deficiencies in the services were well known and well documented by studies published at the time, further progress towards overcoming them was slowed down by a general feeling among those in authority that there were strict limits to what the country could afford.

Public expenditure in total in the later 1930s was about 25 per cent of the gross national product, with social service expenditure running at about 11 per cent, or rather less than half of the total. This was quite a change from the 1890s when total public expenditure was about 12 per cent and social service expenditure about 2½ per cent of GNP, respectively. The First World War had been a decisive watershed, both in revealing social needs and making society more critical of its shortcomings. People also got used to the idea of the Government doing more, and to paying higher rates of tax to pay for it. But it was to take the further upheavals of the Second World War to carry this process of re-thinking and re-assessing a stage onward. A crucial part in this was played by the Beveridge Report and it is to the 'Beveridge Revolution' that we must turn in the next chapter.

Table 2 summarizes the growth of the main forms of social service spending, relative to the national product, over the inter-war period.

TABLE 2 *The main forms of social service spending in the inter-war period*[4]

Year	1920	1929	1933	1938
GNP at current prices, £m.	6,070	4,628	4,141	5,294
Social service expenditure at current prices, £m.				
Education	97·4	108·0	107·5	138·9
Health	48·8	69·0	72·2	98·9
Social security	212·8	207·5	268·7	278·2
Housing	52·8	53·5	45·8	80·3
Total	411·8	438·0	497·2	596·2
As percentages of GNP at current prices				
Education	1·6	2·3	2·6	2·6
Health	0·8	1·5	1·8	1·9
Social security	3·5	4·5	6·5	5·3
Housing	0·9	1·2	1·1	1·5
Total	6·8	9·5	12·0	11·3

The figures of expenditure and of national product at current prices are, of course, affected by trends in the general level of prices. Thus the big drop in current price GNP between 1920 and 1933 reflects entirely the fall in the price level; real GNP was in fact some 10 per cent higher in 1929 than in 1920, and the same in 1933 as in 1929.

Similarly, the rise from 1933 to 1938 is affected by the slight rise in prices over this period, though real GNP in fact rose some 20 per cent during these years. Nevertheless the percentage figures show a considerable rise in total social service spending relative to national product, and in the main subdivisions, especially in the earlier years. The high percentage in 1933 reflects in particular the relatively heavy spending on social security at the depth of the depression. Social security spending was falling relative to a rising national product during the revival of the later 'thirties, whereas the other services were rising proportionally, or at least remaining constant.

Thus by 1938 we were spending over $2\frac{1}{2}$ per cent of our national product on public education, nearly 2 per cent on health services, $1\frac{1}{2}$ per cent on publicly-financed housing and nearly $5\frac{1}{2}$ per cent on social security.

NOTES

1 In 1914 the Exchequer contribution to National Health Insurance in Great Britain was £5·7 million out of a total revenue of £23·2 million. In 1928–29 it was £6·9 million out of £25·1 million for National Health Insurance and £11·8 million out of £42·3 million for Unemployment Insurance.
2 Certain types of employment pensionable by government departments, local authorities and railway companies could be excluded.
3 The age of eligibility for women was reduced to 60 in 1940.
4 Based on A. T. Peacock and J. Wiseman, *The Growth of Public Expenditure in the United Kingdom* (Oxford University Press, London, 1961); 2nd edn (Allen and Unwin, London, 1967), Tables 10 and A-2.

Chapter Four

THE 'BEVERIDGE REVOLUTION'

THE REAPPRAISAL ASSOCIATED WITH THE SECOND WORLD WAR

It is not surprising that the Second World War led to a profound rethinking and reorganization of Britain's social services. It has often been pointed out, notably by Lady Hicks[1] and by Peacock and Wiseman,[2] that public spending in Britain has not increased steadily over the present century, but rather that there have been two big jumps accompanying the two World Wars. This reflects the working of what have been called the inspection, displacement and concentration effects.

Wartime upheavals in normal living make a society more introspective. It looks at itself more self-critically, and all sorts of social evils, which those with experience may have pointed to in vain for years, now come vividly before the public and appear intolerable. This is the inspection effect. Wartime also gets people used to the Government doing much more and, perhaps more important, gets them used to a level of taxation for war purposes much higher than would previously have been thought tolerable. This is the displacement effect. Thus after the war the level of taxation and of government spending, though they fall from the wartime peak, are permanently displaced to a higher level than before. The concentration effect reinforces this by concentrating financial responsibility for the provision of services to a greater extent on to the central authorities as against the local authorities. This can be by the transfer of services, the setting up of new central services, or the increased financial dependence of local authorities on central Government grants.

In the longer span of history, the First World War was probably a more decisive breakthrough in these respects than the Second, for it came with shattering effect after many generations of apparent social stability. Public expenditure, which in the years just before 1914 had been about 12 per cent of the national product, and reached over 50 per cent by 1918, fell back in the 'twenties to between 25 and 30 per cent, rising rather higher in the 'thirties. The standard rate of income tax, 1s 3d (6½p) in the pound in 1913, reached 6s (30p) in 1920 and in the inter-war years never fell below 4s 6d (22½p). The wartime experience of growing government intervention in the working of the economy got people used to the idea of governments spreading their influence into fields which would have been thought quite inappropriate before.

So far as the development of the social services is concerned, however, as we saw in the last chapter, the First World War had the effect rather of accelerating an evolution along lines already begun before 1914, than of bringing about a decisive break into a new form of growth. Moreover, in the 'twenties the reaction from wartime spending and the desire to get back to pre-1914 normality had the effect first of cutting back public spending and then of inhibiting its expansion.

On the other hand, the Second World War came on top of a long experience of the evils of large-scale unemployment and a growing realization of the inadequacies of the social services as they then were. The disturbances of wartime brought about a more acute awareness of the needs of society, dramatically illustrated by the episode of the evacuation of mothers and children from the large cities and other vulnerable areas in September, 1939. This had the effect of bringing home by first-hand experience to the comfortable middle classes of the reception areas just what the implications of slum conditions and low incomes were for family life and standards. Similarly, the needs of war work by married women, together with rationing and the disruption of households, led to the general introduction of school meals, with orange juice and cod-liver oil for the very young, to ensure that the nation's children were properly nourished. The prospect of large-scale air-raid casualties made it imperative to bring together the voluntary and local authority hospitals into a unified Hospitals Emergency Service. The desire to help those most vulnerable to wartime hardships led to the introduction of Supplementary Pensions for the old in 1940.

At the same time, the Government was forced to organize more and more aspects of the economy and of society for the successful prosecution of the war. Hence came consumer rationing, controls over materials and increasingly over prices and production, controls over imports and foreign exchange, government trading in key products, conscription and direction of labour, increased taxation and savings drives to drain off the inflationary increase of money incomes. This control was exercised very successfully, by and large. Hence government action was generally accepted as an expression of the national will to a common effort for victory.

It was natural that those who had experienced the Government's success in organizing the nation's efforts for war purposes, while at the same time extending the welfare services, should come to feel that much more could and should be done on a return to peace.

Hence the latter part of the war saw plans being made for fundamental improvements in the social services and in the national use of resources. These included the series of reports on the planning of land use and the distribution of industry associated with the names of Barlow, Uthwatt and Scott[3]; the various physical plans for the redevelopment of urban areas, such as the Abercrombie Plan for Greater London[4]; the proposals for a National Health Service; the Butler Education Act of 1944, and the Government's acceptance of responsibility for full employment in the 1944 White Paper on Employment Policy. Most significant of all, since it became a kind of symbol of the expected new age, was the Beveridge Report on Social Insurance and Allied Services,[5] which came out in November, 1942.

THE BEVERIDGE REPORT

Although it arose out of the work of an Inter-departmental Committee of civil servants, the Report as it appeared was the work of Sir William Beveridge himself, and only his name appeared on it. It was owing to his vision and grasp of the opportunities of the time that it did not merely recommend the extension and improvement of the existing social insurance schemes, but rather their replacement by a single new and comprehensive scheme. Moreover, social insurance was seen as only part of a wider series of welfare measures, which were to be the community's weapons against the 'Five Giants'. It was primarily the weapon against the giant of Want, but those of Disease, Ignorance, Squalor and Idleness had equally to be combated.

Written as it was in this spirit, and coming at the turning point of the war, at the time of Alamein and Stalingrad, the Report became a symbol of the country's aspirations for a better society to be achieved after victory was won, and its principles were to be accepted far beyond the field of social security which was its immediate concern.

Beveridge's essential recommendation was the replacement of the existing National Insurance schemes by a single, comprehensive system of social insurance covering virtually the whole population. Thus the better-paid non-manual employees, the self-employed and the excepted employments would all be included. It was to be based on flat-rate benefits and contributions, as the existing schemes were; Beveridge maintained very strongly that it was not the State's business to provide benefits of higher than subsistence level. If people wanted these, they should make use of voluntary insurance. He also felt that a system of flat rates would make for a greater sense of participation in common rights of citizenship, with all paying the same and entitled to receive the same, irrespective of income. Hence

41

there would tend to be a more responsible use made of the service. Benefits were, however, intended to be adequate for minimum subsistence. The tri-partite system of contributions by insured person, employer and Exchequer was also to be retained.

Contributions were, however, to be divided into three classes, employed, self-employed and non-employed, with different contribution rates and benefit entitlements. Thus the contribution of the self-employed would be less than the total contribution for each employed person, taking employee's and employer's share together (though larger than the employee's share alone), but he would not be eligible for unemployment benefit, because of the difficulty of adequate checks against abuse. Beveridge recommended that the self-employed and the non-employed might be made eligible for training benefit, should their source of livelihood come to an end, on condition of undergoing an approved form of training. This was never in fact adopted. The non-employed—i.e. those of independent means—would pay less still, but they would not be eligible for unemployment benefit, sickness benefit, nor maternity benefit, since their incomes were not affected by these contingencies.

In all, Beveridge distinguished six categories of people with distinctive needs; these were the employed, the self-employed, the non-employed of working age, housewives, dependant children and retired persons. Benefits were to be provided appropriate to each class of need and would include unemployment benefit, training benefit, sickness benefit, retirement pensions, maternity benefits, widows' and orphans' pensions and a funeral grant, with dependants' allowances wherever required. In addition, a system of industrial injury benefits was proposed for employed persons, to replace the existing system of Workmen's Compensation liability placed on the employers. There was also an optional proposal to set up a State system of industrial insurance, i.e. life insurance financed by weekly premiums. This was to replace that operated by insurance companies and mutual insurance societies, in which Beveridge felt that there were many abuses, arising out of both the costly collection of weekly premiums by house-to-house visits by agents, and the pressure on the agents to get more business.

Beveridge recognized that a system of social insurance making payments as of right to those satisfying contribution conditions could not cover all cases of need. It would have to be supplemented by a system of National Assistance making payments subject to test of need and means. This he recommended should be administered by his proposed Ministry of Social Security on the basis of uniform tests and scales of benefit. It would replace both Public Assistance administered by the local authorities and the various assistance services administered by the Assistance Board. He believed that once a comprehensive insurance scheme was in operation the scope for Assistance would be much reduced and would not involve more than some 25 million pounds a year. In this he was to be proved decisively wrong. This was largely because his assumption of insurance benefit rates adequate for subsistence was not accepted, but also because the post-war rise both in real earnings and in the cost of living meant that a flat rate insurance scheme never provided adequate benefits to catch up.[6]

Beveridge saw clearly that social security was only one part of the provision needed for an effective attack on the 'Five Giants'. In particular, the success of his proposals would depend on the fulfilling of three assumptions, involving action by the Government in other fields.

i The introduction of a system of family allowances to provide against poverty in large families, where the head of the family was working, and hence no benefit could be obtained from social security. The need for this had been made clear by many pre-war enquiries into social conditions which had brought out the extent of poverty among large families with only one earner.

ii The introduction of a comprehensive health and rehabilitation service available to all independently of the National Insurance scheme. This was necessary to provide effectively against ill-health as a cause of poverty. Thus Beveridge came down in favour of the growing body of opinion which supported an independent National Health Service rather than extending the eligibility and extent of medical benefit under the existing National Health Insurance, perhaps by including dependants or covering hospital and specialist treatment or dental and ophthalmic services.

iii The acceptance by the Government of the responsibility for maintaining a high and stable level of employment. Experience in the inter-war years had made it abundantly clear that widespread general unemployment caused poverty on a scale far too large to be dealt with by social insurance benefits or assistance payments. The work of Keynes had now shown the lines of policy along which the Government could use fiscal and monetary measures to maintain full employment, and Beveridge himself was to spell all this out more fully in his book *Full Employment in a Free Society*.[7]

THE CONSEQUENCES OF BEVERIDGE

The Beveridge Report struck the public imagination to such an extent that, in spite of initial hesitations over accepting such an ambitious scheme in the middle of the war, the Government was eventually obliged to commit itself in principle to implementing it. In its essentials it was to be embodied in the system of social insurance introduced by the National Insurance Act of 1946 which came into operation in July, 1948, and also of the unified National Assistance system introduced at the same time.

There were, however, some departures from Beveridge's proposals. The principle of subsistence rates of benefit was not adopted in practice; this had continuing consequences for the level of National Assistance which was found to be necessary in later years. On the other hand Beveridge had proposed that the full new rate of national insurance retirement pensions should only gradually be introduced for persons retiring after the scheme came into effect, and that existing pensioners should only receive the higher rates subject to test of need and means. This proved politically impossible, and in fact existing pensions under the 1925 Act were raised to the new level of 26s (£1·30) in 1946, before the new scheme began; those not covered by the 1925 pension scheme were made eligible for full pension after contributing for ten years from 1948. The result was to greatly increase the outlay on pensions relative to the income from contributions, assumed actuarially to be made over the whole insured life; this put a burden on the Insurance Fund which had to be met directly from the Exchequer. Less serious modifications included the abandonment of Beveridge's proposed training benefit for the self-employed and non-employed, and of his optional proposals for nationalizing industrial assurance.

Meanwhile parallel developments were taking place in other fields. In February, 1943, the Government accepted the principle of a comprehensive health service independent of social insurance; so the process of planning began which led to the National Health Service of 1948, and the fulfilment of Beveridge's second assumption. The first assumption found expression in the Family Allowances Act of 1945, which introduced allowances for second and subsequent children without means test or insurance contribution. The third assumption was accepted in principle in the White Paper on Employment Policy of 1944,[8] in which the Government pledged itself to use fiscal and monetary policy to maintain a high general level of employment. Although post-war experience was to place the emphasis on the need to restrain inflation rather than on the need to prevent unemployment, the acceptance of this responsibility nevertheless underlay a good deal of the continued confidence of businessmen in good business prospects; this has done much to retain a high level of activity.

In education, the Butler Act of 1944 embodied the principle of providing free secondary education for all pupils according to age, aptitude and ability, thus fulfilling the aspirations which had been so long delayed. Following accepted beliefs at the time, this was carried into effect through a system of selecting children for different types of secondary school, a method which later experience has found much to criticize. This was not laid down in the Act, however, but arose rather from the recommendations of the Hadow Committee of 1926 and the Spens Committee of 1938. The Act also provided for the raising of the school leaving age to 15 and this came into effect in 1947.

In housing, the policy in the early post-war years was to make the local authorities responsible for meeting the general housing needs of their areas, as well as making good wartime damage and arrears, and tackling the slums. For this purpose a general subsidy of a set amount per house for a period of years was given. Private building remained drastically limited and private rents remained controlled at 1939 levels.

There were also developments in the fields of government control over land use and the physical planning of local and regional development; this tended to take different forms for different problems, sometimes with little relationship between them. Thus local physical planning found expression in the Town and Country Planning Act of 1948. The Act carried considerably further the policies begun under earlier planning acts in laying upon local planning authorities the duty of drawing up comprehensive Development Plans for their areas, including those parts which were already built-up, and in giving them powers to make these effective. It also tried abortively to solve the problems of compensation and betterment by nationalizing development rights and levying a Development Charge on increments of land value arising out of change of use. Control of the location of industry was greatly extended through the inducements to invest in the Development Areas given under the Distribution of Industry Act of 1945 and through the restraints on development in congested areas, made possible by the system of Industrial Development Certificates required for new factories. Meanwhile a series of self-contained New Towns was being planned to make a more orderly movement of population and industry from the largest cities possible; they were also to serve as foci for development in some declining industrial areas.

Meanwhile, the welfare services were also being extended and becoming separated from health, education and poor relief. Following the Curtis Committee's report in 1946, which revealed many defects in the existing provision of care for deprived children, the Children Act of 1948 made mandatory the setting up of separate children's committees and departments by local authorities. It also imposed a statutory duty of receiving into care children whose parents or guardians could not satisfactorily provide a home for them on the local authorities. Welfare services for old people also began to be extended, particularly under Part III of the National Assistance Act of 1948. Under this act local authorities remained responsible for residential accommodation for the old, and under the National Health Service Act of the same year, they were empowered to provide home-helps and home-nursing services.

These new developments were to give rise to many problems and were to prove in some ways less appropriate than had been hoped to the new situation which developed in the post-war years. Yet they represented a considerable advance in the acceptance of greater government responsibility, not only in the provision of social services, but also in seeking to control and influence the level of economic activity and the use of the country's material resources in the interests of greater social benefit. Taken together, they amounted for the first time to what we have come to call the Welfare State.

So far as the form and spirit of the social services themselves were concerned, the guiding principle of these years was that of universalism rather than selectivism. In earlier years the tendency had been to single out different groups as the community became aware of their particular needs, and to set up special services to meet these needs. Now, following the spirit of Beveridge, the aim was rather to provide general services open to all, irrespective of income or social position, to be available on similar terms and conditions. This is the universalist aim, which sees the social services as a means by which the community provides benefits which all can equally enjoy as part of the rights of citizenship. It can be contrasted with the selectivist view, which sees the concern to provide special help to those who are in particular need, on terms which are geared to their need.

There was, however, a difference in emphasis between the social security services and those providing services in kind, such as education and medical treatment. In social security, pre-war experience of the need to eliminate poverty among those unable to earn led to stress being laid on the aim of providing a minimum subsistence income to all who could not provide for themselves, at rates as nearly as possible equal, having regard to such factors as the number of dependants. Hence all kinds of needs were to be covered, as far as possible, but all were to receive the amount appropriate only to their basic wants. This would be achieved mainly through social insurance, supplemented where necessary by social assistance.

In education and medical treatment, however, and also in the slowly-developing welfare services, the emphasis was coming to be not on minimum standards but on optimum standards. The pre-war services had been on a minimum basis. For instance, elementary education for all, with secondary education only for the highly gifted few who could pass the scholarship examinations; or a general practitioner service only to insured persons under National Health Insurance, and hospital treatment not provided for under the State scheme except as part of poor relief, or for special cases such as infectious diseases or mental illness. Now, under the Butler Education Act and the National Health Service, the accepted aim was to be to provide the appropriate type of secondary education free to all pupils according to age, aptitude and ability, and the appropriate type of medical treatment, without barrier of means, to all the sick according to their clinical needs. Competing national claims on limited resources were to mean that in practice there had to be political and administrative choices about how fast and how fully different types of educational and health service could be expanded; thus rationing by crowded classroom and crowded clinic replaced rationing by purse to some extent. However a change of principle had been made.

The history of the social services in the post-war period is largely that of how far the system inspired by the ideals of Beveridge has proved appropriate to the unforseeable changes and new needs of a society experiencing a rapid rise of incomes. In order to discuss these problems, we must first consider in more detail the characteristics of the system set up in the early years after 1945, and culminating in the great social security and health measures of 1948. This we do in the next chapter.

NOTES

1 Compare with U.K. Hicks, *British Public Finances, Their Structure and Development, 1880–1952* (Oxford University Press, London, 1954), Chap. 1.

2 Compare with A. T. Peacock and J. Wiseman, *The Growth of Public Expenditure in the United Kingdom* (Oxford University Press, London, 1961), Chap. 2.

3 Report of the Royal Commission on the *Distribution of the Industrial Population* (Cmd 6153, HMSO, 1940).
Report of the Committee on *Compensation and Betterment* (Cmd 6386, HMSO, 1942).
Report of the Committee on *Land Utilisation in Rural Areas* (Cmd 6378, HMSO 1942).

4 *Greater London Plan, 1944* (HMSO, 1945).

5 Beveridge Report, *Social Insurance and Allied Services* (Cmd 6404, HMSO, 1942).

6   This problem is discussed further in Chapter Five, pages 51 and 59–60, and in Chapter Six, page 97.

7   Beveridge, *Full Employment in a Free Society* (Allen and Unwin, London, 1944).

8   Cmd 6527, HMSO, 1944.

Chapter Five

GENERAL DESCRIPTION OF THE POST-1945 WELFARE STATE

Out of the principles of the Beveridge Report and the parallel developments of the wartime and early post-war years there arose a reconstruction of the social services, which had taken shape by 1948. In this chapter the main outlines of the system set up in these years will be described, and also the main ways in which they have changed and developed since. An appraisal of its limitations in face of the changing social and economic developments of the years since 1948 is left until the next chapter.

In this account we shall be concerned only with general descriptions and broad characteristics. The details of the organization of the individual services, such as who is qualified to benefit from them, what standards of services are given, who administers each type of service and how, rates of contribution and benefit and contribution conditions cannot be dealt with here. They are far too complex and far too fast-changing, and those who need them will need them in much greater detail than could be included in a general survey. They are referred to the more specialized studies listed in the bibliography.

We deal first with the services giving cash benefits, which together form the system of social security: National Insurance (General and Industrial Injuries), National Assistance (now Supplementary Benefit), Family Allowances and War Pensions. Following them are the main services providing benefits in kind; the National Health Service, Education, the Welfare Services, and Housing.

SOCIAL SECURITY

Following Beveridge, the new social security system took shape through the extension and generalization of the principles already accepted. Social insurance was relied upon to provide a basic, minimum income to those unable to earn, but it was extended, and made more uniform and comprehensive. Similarly, a uniform, comprehensive system of social assistance to meet those cases not covered by social insurance was introduced. In addition, there were two systems which provided more specialized benefits without either contribution conditions or test of means, namely Family Allowances and War Pensions.

NATIONAL INSURANCE

The main system of National Insurance, as introduced under the National Insurance Act of 1946 which came into operation in July, 1948, closely followed the pattern of organization envisaged by Beveridge. Its aim was to cover virtually the whole population with a single comprehensive system of social insurance; it intended to provide a minimum income in all the main cases of inability to earn for the insured persons and their dependants.

Three classes of contributor were distinguished; Class I (employed persons), Class II (self-employed) and Class III (non-employed). These had different entitlements to benefit, the self-employed not being eligible for unemployment benefit and the non-employed not being eligible for unemployment benefit, sickness benefit and maternity benefit. The main types of benefit covered were retirement pensions, sickness benefit, unemployment benefit, maternity benefits, widows' benefits, guardian's allowance (for orphans), the child's special allowance (for a child of divorced parents whose father subsequently dies), and the lump sum death grant to help meet funeral expenses. Of these, retirement pensions have been by far the most significant in terms of financial cost, accounting in recent years for some 67 per cent of the total. This is the inevitable result both of the growing numbers of men over 65 and women over 60 in the population, and of the fact that they tend to draw pensions continuously for many years. Sickness benefit comes next, accounting for 15 per cent of the total in 1970. The number of persons receiving it at any given time tends to average about a million over the year, though an influenza epidemic can send the total up spectacularly for a few weeks; on the other hand, most people only draw sickness benefit for short periods. This compares with a number of retirement pensioners, which has grown from 5·4 million in 1958 to 7·6 million in 1970. Unemployment benefit is a relatively small part of the total because of low post-war levels of unemployment; in fact it only accounted for 5 per cent of total payments in 1970, when unemployment rates were high by post-war standards. Widows' benefits in fact formed a somewhat larger part of the total.

In the case of widows, there were three different types of benefit. First, a widows' allowance paid to all widows for the first thirteen weeks, to cover the period of temporary adjustment; second, a widowed mothers' allowance payable to widows with dependant children; and third, a widows' pension which was only payable to widows who were over 50 either at the husband's death, or when the widowed mothers' allowance ceased. In other words, the widow under 50 without dependant children was regarded as able to earn her own living after a temporary period of adjustment, provided she was fit. If unfit, she became eligible for sickness benefit.

In the case of maternity benefits there were, for most of the period, two types; a lump sum grant payable to all mothers to cover the extra costs of equipment and so on, and a maternity allowance for a period of eleven weeks before confinement and six weeks afterwards. The latter was payable only to women insured in their own right, to compensate them for loss of earnings. Married women have the option, if employed, of contributing at the full rate to become entitled to unemployment, sickness and other benefits in their own right, or of paying only insurance against industrial injuries and relying for other contingencies on their husbands' entitlement to benefit for his wife as a dependant.

Until fairly recently the system of contributions and benefits was entirely a flat rate one, with a three-fold contribution from insured person, employer and Exchequer, following the British tradition. It is, however, inherent in a flat rate system that benefits must be limited. If an actuarial relationship is to be retained between contributions and benefits, any increase in benefit rates must mean an increase in contribution rates, and these must be limited to what the lower income groups can bear without undue hardship. Hence it is not possible under a flat rate system to provide benefits which form a satisfactory proportion of the earnings of those higher in the scale. In more recent years a beginning has been made with departures from the flat rate principle, under the graduated pension scheme of 1961 and the earnings-related supplements to sickness and unemployment benefit introduced in 1966. The proposals of the Labour Government's National Insurance Bill of 1970 in fact represented a complete departure from it.

Beveridge had intended that the basic rate of pension should, however, be adequate for minimum subsistence, and the figures he suggested, of 24s (£1·20) a week for a single person and 40s (£2·00) for a married couple, plus dependants' allowances, were intended to secure this on the assumption of a cost of living after the war 25 per cent above that of 1939. The actual rates introduced under the new scheme (26s (£1·30) for a single person and 42s (£2·10) for a married couple) were not in fact adequate for subsistence in 1948. Although they were based on the official cost of living index, which in 1946 was 31 per cent above 1939, this was artificially kept down by the overweighting in it of basic foodstuffs, whose price had been held down by subsidies; prices had, in any case, risen further by 1948. Since then benefit rates have been raised many times. Overall, their rate of increase has more than kept pace with the rising cost of living, though sometimes they have lagged behind and later jumped ahead.[1] In fact, the rise in real national insurance benefit rates has kept up with the average rise in real earnings. But they started in 1948 at a very low level relative to average earnings, and this gap has not been reduced. In fact, with the rise in money incomes, it has risen in absolute terms, though not in percentage terms.[2]

In theory, the finances of the National Insurance Fund were based on what is known as the Full Funding principle. That is to say that the actuarial relationship between the rate of total contribution in respect of insured persons and the rate of benefits enjoyed by them was based on the assumption that contributions over the entire insured life from the age of 16 to retiring age were invested and accumulated at compound interest to produce a flow of income sufficient to meet the average total of benefits received. This is the assumption on which commercial life insurance is based and it underlay all previous social insurance schemes. It is, however, unrealistic for a number of reasons.

First, no one has in fact contributed to the present scheme from the age of 16 through to retirement age, nor even to the old contributory pension scheme, since this was only introduced in 1925 and in any case involved much lower contributions and benefits. Yet full retirement pension at the new rates could be drawn by all those who were in the old scheme and new entrants in 1948 could draw full pension after ten years' contributions. Thus the assumed actuarial basis was undermined from the start, and a large additional Exchequer contribution was provided to meet this extra burden, which was made more heavy by the growing numbers of old people in the population. The effect was, however, offset to some extent by the fact that the rate of unemployment proved to be very much lower than the 8 per cent figure originally assumed in the actuarial calculations on the basis of pre-war experience. Nevertheless, from 1958 onwards there began to be an annual deficit in the National Insurance Fund which, it was estimated, would have reached £475 million a year by 1979-80, had its finances continued on the same principles. This was one reason for the introduction of the Graduated Pension Scheme in 1961, for this produced an immediate increase of revenue from the graduated additions to contributions, while involving increased benefit commitments which were deferred for many years.

Secondly, each time benefit rates were increased, although contribution rates were raised accordingly, it was only possible to raise them from that date and not to increase the back contributions to the level actuarially appropriate to the new benefit rates. This could be offset in part by loading the contributions with a higher increase, but the flat rate system limited the extent to which this could be done without putting an undue burden on lower incomes.

Thirdly, as a matter of practical administration, it has never been possible to invest all the contribution revenue as it came in and accumulate it at compound interest. The total amount is far too great for this to be done without completely disrupting the market for government securities and playing havoc with the Government's ability to use the buying and selling of such securities in pursuit of monetary and debt-management policies.

Hence, in practice, what is known as the Assessment Principle is followed; current payments of benefit are made out of current income from contributions and only the surplus, if any, is invested in government securities to produce a small flow of additional revenue. The use of the additional graduated contribution income, under the 1961 scheme to balance the growing burden of current pension payments, was an explicit recognition of this change of principle. It was accepted more fully in the financial basis of the comprehensive graduated scheme proposed in the 1970 Bill.

Moreover, the existence of an Exchequer contribution which can be varied as required, and the fact that contributions by insured persons and employers are compulsory, mean that the strict actuarial relationships between premium and benefit rates essential to commercial insurance do not apply to social insurance. Risks can be pooled between all the contributors in each main class, for those who are more favourable risks cannot exact more favourable terms as they can in the commercial insurance market. Hence all can be made to pay the same rates of contribution for the same benefits. The terms can be slanted to favour the lower income-groups relative to the higher ones, or in any other way that is thought appropriate. If there is a deficit, this can be met by altering the Exchequer contribution. Hence in practice benefit rates are varied as thought desirable on grounds of social policy, to help those thought to be most in need. Contribution rates need not be adjusted on strict actuarial principles, but can be used to raise the necessary revenue in what is felt to be the most equitable way. In other words, social insurance contributions are really a special form of tax; they are found to be acceptable as a means of meeting part of the cost of social security benefits, rather than being in any way analogous to insurance premiums.

National Insurance has long been one of the costliest elements in the social services, largely because of the heavy cost of retirement pensions. The total expenditure had reached £1,000 million by 1960–61 and by 1970–71 was £2,724 million, or over 6 per cent of the gross national product. All but a small proportion of this, however, represented a transfer of income from taxpayers and contributors to beneficiaries and did not involve using up real resources.

Industrial Injuries

Again following Beveridge's recommendations, the general insurance scheme was accompanied by a separate scheme, covering employed persons only, of benefits for industrial injuries and industrial diseases. This replaced the liability of employers under the Workers Compensation Acts to compensate employees for accidents arising out of, or in the course of, employment, and for certain specified industrial diseases. It did not, however, remove the liability of employers at common law to compensate employees in those cases where negligence by the employer could be proved. In fact, this responsibility was strengthened by the removal of the defence of common employment, under which liability could formerly be avoided when the accident was due to negligence by a fellow employee. The change reflected experience of the disadvantages suffered by employees when they had to rely on taking legal action against their employers in the event of injury, as discussed in Chapter Three. It was felt to be more satisfactory to enable them to claim a social insurance benefit as of right. In fact, in the case of industrial injuries there are no minimum contribution conditions to be satisfied before a claimant is eligible, as there are in the case of the main National Insurance scheme.

Three main types of benefit are given. Injury benefit is paid for a maximum of 26 weeks at a flat rate higher than that for National Insurance sickness benefit, plus dependants allowances.[3] If incapacity continues beyond this period, disablement benefit is paid, the amount depending on the extent of disablement as assessed by a medical tribunal; this is on a sliding scale, beginning with a lump sum for disablement of under 20 per cent, up to a weekly amount of £11·20 from October, 1972, plus dependants allowances, for injuries assessed at 100 per cent. Supplementary payments can be made in cases of unemployability or special hardship, for hospital treatment, or where constant attendance is required. Widows and dependants are paid on similar, but more generous terms than under the main insurance scheme, including entitlement to a small pension even in the case of widows under 50 with no dependant children. Widows are also entitled to any earnings-related supplement which they would have been entitled to under the main insurance scheme.

The total cost of Industrial Injuries insurance has been fairly small, only about £126 million even in 1970–71, but the existence of two systems of benefit for sickness and injury has caused considerable anomalies. A man or woman who is injured at work, or contracts an industrial disease, has tended to receive more generous treatment than if he had been knocked down by a car in the street, or suffered from an ordinary illness.

NATIONAL ASSISTANCE

Beveridge's recommendation that there should be a single, comprehensive system of social assistance, making payments on a test of need and means on a uniform basis, bore fruit in the introduction of National Assistance in 1948. His advice was departed from, however, in that the National Assistance Board remained separate from the Ministry of National Insurance, though responsible to its Minister. It was in fact the old Assistance Board in extended form, having taken over the public assistance responsibilities of the local authorities so far as cash payments were concerned, as well as the care of those formerly eligible for unemployment assistance and supplementary pensions. This formal separation of responsibility for social assistance from that for social insurance proved to have disadvantages. This was seen especially in encouraging a reluctance among old people to apply for National Assistance to supplement their retirement pensions, because the Board's offices had unwittingly acquired some of the stigma of the old Poor Law. Hence in 1966 the two were to be more closely integrated, when National Assistance was replaced by Supplementary Benefits administered by a Commission forming part of the Ministry.

Under the National Assistance Board, with its network of local offices, uniform scales and conditions of benefit were established. Standard income scales were fixed, representing a minimum subsistence income for families of different sizes; they were revised from time to time to take account of rises in the cost of living and also in general living standards. The usual practice was to pay the difference between the means of the applicant and his or her direct dependants and the standard scale applicable, disregarding certain minimum means. In addition a rent allowance was paid which normally covered the actual rent. Special higher scales applied to the blind and tuberculous, and special discretionary payments could be made in cases of exceptional need, whether for weekly allowances for special food or extra heating, or lump sum allowances to meet capital needs such as replacement of bedding or furniture. On the other hand, in cases such as those of low-paid wage earners with large families, the scale payments to which the family were entitled, should the man be unable to earn through sickness or unemployment, might well exceed his normal earnings. In such cases, should he apply for Assistance, the wage stop would be applied and he would not be paid any more than the amount of his normal earnings, in order to prevent any deterrent effect on his willingness to work.

National Assistance came to play a much larger part in the social security system than Beveridge had expected. This was largely because the standard rates of National Insurance benefit were not fixed at the subsistence level, which Beveridge had advocated. The National Assistance scale rates, which represent society's standard of what is the minimum acceptable income level at any particular time, have for most of the period since 1948 usually been only a little below the National Insurance rates, even before allowing for rent, and sometimes even higher. Since actual rent is normally paid, a person or family with no other source of income than National Insurance benefit was almost always likely to be below the income level to which he could be raised by National Assistance, unless he had very low payments to make for housing. Those people whose housing expenditure was heavy, or who had other exceptional payments to make, would be still further below the level guaranteed them by the NAB.

The great bulk of National Assistance payments were in fact made in supplementation of inadequate insurance benefits, especially old age pensions, but also to widows and the chronic sick. In 1966, the last year of the separate National Assistance Board, the total amount of grants came to £314 million. In June of that year there were 2,005,000 weekly payments being made. Of these 1,218,000, or 61 per cent, were in supplementation of retirement pensions, and a total of 1,543,000, or 77 per cent, were in supplementation of some form of social security benefits, including a small number who, not being eligible for National Insurance pensions in 1948, continued to receive the non-contributory pension of 1908, at its post-war rate of 26s (£1·30) a week.

By 1970–71, with considerable increases in scale rates, the total expenditure on Supplementary Benefits had risen to £618 million, or rather less than 1½ per cent of the gross national product. The total number of weekly payments was 2·7 million, of whom 64 per cent were still retirement pensioners. Thus social assistance under test of means, far from being an exceptional measure to meet those cases who had special needs or who for various reasons were not eligible for social insurance, has continued to be the service on which reliance is placed to see that those with little means other than social security are brought up to the minimum standard accepted as socially necessary.

FAMILY ALLOWANCES

Family allowances were the first part of the new system of social security to come into effect, being introduced under the Family Allowances Act of 1945, and paid from 1946. There were two main motives behind their introduction. The first was the extent of poverty among families with large numbers of children and only one earner, as revealed in many pre-war social surveys and stressed by Beveridge in his first assumption for a satisfactory social insurance system. The second was a demographic motive, for there had been considerable concern in pre-war days over the fall in the annual number of births, and fears that this was becoming too low for the existing generation of parents to replace themselves.

For these reasons the allowances were paid to all families with two or more children, at a flat rate per child for all children other than the first. The first child was excluded on the ground that almost all families would want, and could afford, to have at least one child. But whereas Beveridge had proposed that the rate of the allowance should be the same as that proposed for dependant children under National Insurance, and had suggested a rate of 8s (40p) a week (based on a cost of living 25 per cent above that of 1938) the allowance when first introduced was only 5s (25p) a week, though this was raised to 8s (40p) a week in 1952. In 1956 the amount for third and subsequent children was raised to 10s (50p). Following the growing evidence of continued poverty among large families of low-paid workers, the rates were raised steeply in 1968, to 18s (90p) for the second child and £1 for third and subsequent children. The allowance is normally paid up to the minimum school leaving age of 15, but up to 19 where young people are still at school or serving apprenticeships.

The object of the allowance is to benefit the family as a whole and it is normally paid to the mother. It is not subject to a means test or contribution conditions. It is liable to income tax, though the effect of this is more than offset for families liable to the standard rate of tax by the children's allowances deductible from taxable income under income tax law. In order to preserve the principle of freedom from means test and at the same time to confine the benefit of the increased allowances of 1968 to those who needed them, provision was made for the income tax children's allowances of those liable to pay the tax to be reduced to the extent necessary to claim back from them in increased tax the amount of the extra family allowance they received.

Family allowances in Britain are on a comparatively modest scale compared with those in some other countries such as France. Until the recent increases they did little to reduce poverty among large families with only one low-paid earner, who receive no benefit from other forms of social security. It is often pointed out that there are in fact numerous other benefits for families in kind, such as free school meals, milk and welfare foods, maintenance grants for secondary school pupils and, in some cases, free clothes. But most of these are subject to means test and in some cases the conditions and extent of availability vary greatly between different local authorities. They are all limited in scope and cannot fully make up for an income inadequate to keep a family out of poverty. On the other hand, the income tax children's allowances, which are much more generous than the family allowances, mainly benefit the better-off.[4]

Nor would allowances at this level have had as much effect in encouraging larger families (had that still been appropriate) as the much higher French family allowances appear to have done in the post-war years. In fact, although the number of births fell from the post-war peak of around a million a year in 1946–48 to a minimum of 789,000 in 1955, it was always well above the 1930s figure of not much more than 750,000. From 1956 onwards it rose again steadily to a new peak of 1,015,000 in 1964, though it has since tended to fall slowly but steadily to 903,000 in 1970. The reasons behind these fluctuations are uncertain and include changes in the proportion of women married, in the age of marriage and in family spacing, so that it is not clear how far they reflect changes in family size. They suggest, however, that there is little ground for any fears about the size of families being too small for replacement, and in fact the Registrar-Generals' population projections suggest an increase of the population of the United Kingdom from 55·8 million in 1970 up to a figure which may be as high as 66 million by 2000. Too much weight cannot be put on such projections, since the assumptions on which they are based have often been proved wrong in the past. However, in view of the country's problems in housing, town planning, road traffic, pollution and so on they have led many to think that the need may be rather to discourage large families than to encourage them.

The total cost of family allowances rose slowly over the years to about £100 million in 1966–67, but the increases of 1968 raised it sharply to £318 million for 1968–69 and £365 million in 1970–71. This was about 0·9 per cent of the gross national product. About 6½ million allowances were being paid to 4 million families.

WAR PENSIONS

War pensions are like family allowances in that they are paid without a means test or contribution conditions. Although they are not part of the regular social security system, being regarded as a form of compensation for those who have suffered injury or bereavement in wartime active service, they are in some cases an alternative form of benefit, and in others an additional form of benefit for those in certain types of need.

The war disablement benefit is very similar to the industrial injuries disablement benefit, which was modelled on it. There is a basic regular payment, the amount of which depends on the degree of disablement as assessed by a medical tribunal. For a private or equivalent rank with 100 per cent assessment the pension had been raised in October, 1972 to £11·20 a week with smaller weekly amounts for lesser assessments down to 20 per cent, below which there is a lump sum payment. Additional payments are made for dependants, and also for unemployability, constant attendance and certain other contingencies. There are also additions according to rank for ex-NCOs, warrant officers and officers. There is also a system of pensions for widows and orphans, on similar terms to those for industrial injuries, but varying with the rank of the husband.

Thus war pensions, like industrial injury benefits, give higher incomes than are available under ordinary National Insurance. In some cases, a war pensioner can also draw National Insurance benefits. For instance, he can normally receive unemployment benefit, sickness benefit or retirement pension for himself, provided he can satisfy the contribution conditions, though not if he is receiving the unemployability supplement. He cannot, however, receive the full amount of the NI benefits for his dependants in addition to war pension dependants' allowances, but only enough to make up the value of his war pension allowances to the NI level, should that be greater.

The number of people who benefit from war pensions is of course a diminishing one since the great bulk represent the casualties of the two World Wars. At the end of 1968, however, there were still over 409,000 people receiving disablement pensions, and about another 150,000 pensions being paid to widows, orphans and parents of those killed. The total cost of war pensions in 1970–71 came to £134 million, or 0·3 per cent of the gross national product.

Total expenditure on social security in Britain has tended to rise faster than the national product. By the calendar year 1970 the total spent on all the above services came to £3,908 million, or over 9 per cent of the gross national product at factor cost. In 1960, when the amount spent was £1,488 million, this had represented only 6½ per cent of GNP.[5] The rise reflects the growing proportion of old people in the population[6] and the desire to ensure that those who could not earn might share rather more fully in the rise in real earnings enjoyed by those at work. Because the system was based on flat rate benefits, not initially intended to guarantee a subsistence level, and supplemented by payments according to test of need, it did not guarantee that all those who could not earn adequately were kept out of poverty, as we shall see.

All but a small proportion of this expenditure represents a transfer from contributors and tax-payers to beneficiaries and so does not involve any using up of real resources. It does, however, represent a considerable redistribution of income; hence it has marked effects on the patterns of consumption and of saving, and on incentives to work, save and undertake business enterprise. The need to raise revenue on this scale, and the large-scale contractual expenditure obligations it involves, are also a complicating factor in the Government's exercise of fiscal policy to regulate the economy. These economic effects must be considered further in Chapter Seven.

Further details of rates of social security benefits and social insurance contributions as from October, 1972, are given in the Appendix to this chapter.

SERVICES IN KIND

The post-war period also saw a comprehensive reorganization of the main social services providing benefits in kind. We shall deal in turn with the National Health Service, the educational system, the local authority welfare services and finally with housing.

THE NATIONAL HEALTH SERVICE

After prolonged negotiations with the various interests concerned, the principle of a comprehensive system of medical services available to all, independent of National Insurance, found expression in the National Health Service as introduced by Mr Aneurin Bevan in July, 1948.

Technically there are two separate services, in England and Wales, and in Scotland; the former is under the Secretary of State for Health and Social Security (before 1968 under the Minister of Health); the other is under the Secretary of State for Scotland, working through the Department of Health for Scotland. The differences between them, however, are only minor. In Northern Ireland the organization is rather different, though the principles are the same.

The organization of the National Health Service reflects the varied historical development of the various branches of the medical services. To bring into being a unified hospital system involved the integration of the voluntary and the local authority hospitals. Local authority areas, such as those of counties and county boroughs, or large burghs in Scotland, were too small to be suitable units on which to base a hospital organization capable of making full use of all the specialized hospital facilities. There was also great objection on the part of the staffs of the voluntary hospitals to the idea of coming under local authority control. Hence it was natural to set up a regional organization for the hospitals responsible directly to the two Ministries, with Regional Hospital Boards having control over the hospitals in their regions. There are fifteen regions in England and Wales, and five in Scotland. Within them the day-to-day management of groups of hospitals comes under Hospital Management Committees or, in Scotland, Boards of Management. These bodies consist of men and women appointed by the Minister after consultation with certain bodies; their members serve in their personal capacities, not as representatives, and they obtain their funds direct from the Parliamentary vote of the Ministry. In England and Wales, but not in Scotland, the teaching hospitals, that is those with medical schools, are separately controlled by their own Boards of Governors directly responsible to the Minister.

In the field of general practitioner services, the nucleus of an organization already existed in the Local Insurance Committees under which the 'panel' service under National Health Insurance had been operated. Therefore the general practitioner medical, dental and ophthalmic services, with the supply of drugs on prescription, were placed under Executive Councils in the areas of each local health authority, or sometimes for two adjacent authorities. These represent the Ministry, the local authority, and the doctors, dentists and pharmacists practising in the area.

The local health authorities, i.e. the county council and county borough councils (or in Scotland the councils of large burghs), lost their hospitals. However, they retained their maternity and child welfare clinics and their responsibilities for the provision of midwives and health visitors, though in some cases what had previously been permissive powers were replaced by duties. They also have the duty of providing a home nursing service and arranging for vaccination and immunization, as well as responsibilities for the care of persons suffering from mental illness and defect, and for the blind and the tuberculous. They also have wide powers in connection with the prevention of illness. In England and Wales they were made responsible for the ambulance service and were intended to become responsible for the setting up of health centres. In Scotland, where many local health authorities are very small, these two services have remained with the Secretary of State. In addition, the local authorities had other services in the health field which are not formally part of the National Health Service, notably the school medical service; these are in the hands of the education authorities, which are not always the same bodies as the local health authorities.

Thus there arose a tripartite structure, and given past history and the organizational needs of the different services, it was probably inevitable that this should have happened. It has, however, been much criticized for separating various forms of medical care which should be operated in close conjunction. For instance, in many smaller towns where the general practitioners had been able to treat their own patients in the local cottage hospital, this now became part of a separate hospital service, to which general practitioners no longer had direct access. In maternity and child welfare cases, the mother and her baby would normally be under the care of her general practitioner, of the hospital in which she had the baby and of the local authority clinics and health visitors, yet these came under three different controlling bodies. In the case of old people, mental patients, the blind and the tuberculous, the hospital boards were responsible for their treatment in hospital or at out-patients clinics, but the local authorities were charged with their domiciliary care, or their care in residential institutions. More generally, the separation of the general practitioners from the hospitals was held to be reinforcing the trend, already strong with the growing specialization of medicine, for the devaluation of the work of general practitioners, so that they felt themselves to be merely a kind of filter, separating out the more serious cases for treatment in hospital and giving only routine care to minor ailments.

This problem of separation was made more difficult by the failure to develop the health centres, for it was intended that these should be the means of bringing the three branches of the Service together. The hope was that under one roof in each area there would be grouped surgeries used by local general practitioners, out-patients' clinics from the local hospital and the local authority's maternity and other clinics, all serviced by a common staff of receptionists, nurses, radiologists and secretaries. The pressures of national financial stringency prevented these centres being developed, with the result that the three branches have gone ahead over the years in providing their own facilities.

Yet it is doubtful whether such a complex service could have had a simple form of organization, and some form of sub-division of the various branches had to be adopted. The alternative principle often advocated is that of setting up unified bodies covering all branches of the service on the basis of local areas. This foundered in 1948 on the three rocks of the unwillingness of the doctors to come under the local authorities, the small size of local authority areas, and the desire not to separate the local authority health services from the welfare and other services closely connected with them. This proposal was revived with the Government's Green Paper on health service reorganization of 1968, which envisaged areas larger than those of the present local health authorities, but smaller than hospital regions. Since this must be considered with the more general question of the re-organization of local government and its role in the social services, we shall return to it in the last chapter.

The cost of the National Health Service has tended to rise faster than was expected before it was introduced. In the early years this was largely due to the backlog of unsatisfied demand from those who had not previously been able to afford treatment, especially in the case of the dental and ophthalmic services, where there had formerly been very few facilities for those who could not afford fees. Dentists, opticians and ophthalmic out-patients' clinics had a rush of demand which took some time to catch up, and there was much public criticism of free glasses and false teeth, as of alleged lavish prescribing of free aspirins and cotton wool. The Guillebaud Committee, reporting in January, 1956, found, however, that although the money cost of the NHS had risen fast, there had been little change in its real cost in relation to the rising national product up till then. In fact, when allowance was made for the introduction of prescription and other charges in 1952, the net cost to the public funds had actually fallen in relation to GNP.[7] Most of this early backlog of demand was undoubtedly genuine. It always seemed inherently unlikely that many people would submit themselves to the dentist if they did not need treatment, nor wait hours in out-patients' clinics unless they felt they needed attention, just because it was all free.

More recently, the rise in costs has reflected the rapidly rising real cost of the steadily more sophisticated forms of medical treatment being developed, especially hospital treatment involving intensive care and the use of expensive drugs and equipment. In common with all forms of social service needing the intensive use of skilled man-power, it also reflects the need to compete in the salary field with industry and commerce, which are much better able to offset higher salaries by rising productivity. Nevertheless, the cost of the National Health Service, as it falls on the public purse, is still a relatively small share of the national product. The 1970 total of £2,089 million was only 4·9 per cent of GNP, at factor cost, though ten years earlier it had been only 3·8 per cent.[7]

Of total current expenditure in 1970, the hospital service accounted for about 61 per cent, with the general practitioner services taking 25 per cent and the local authority services 10 per cent; the remainder was accounted for by various central charges such as administration.

In capital expenditure the hospitals were much more predominant, accounting for over 85 per cent of the total.

The rapid expansion of demand in the early days of the Service and the rapid rise in real costs more recently both highlight one of the essential features of services in kind like the National Health Service. It is open-ended in the sense that once the principle of a basically free service is accepted, there is little or no limit to what could be spent on providing improved medical care, given that the resources in equipment and skilled man-power could be made available. Yet resources, both human and material, for the health services have to be sought in competition with many other uses, both in the public sector, such as education, housing and the welfare services, or private, such as the demands of industry and commerce for technical skills and specialized equipment. We cannot provide all we would like of all these services.

Since we have to choose, and since the community has decided no longer to rely on rationing by purse to determine what types of medical services should be provided and who should get the benefit of them, this means that in practice a political choice has to be made as to how much we can afford to spend on the service in total, and on each branch of it. So far as the bulk of the services are concerned, this means ultimately that the Minister must urge the needs of health expenditure against the competing claims of other ministers in the Government, subject to the over-riding decision of the Chancellor of the Exchequer as to how much can be afforded in the light of the stresses and strains on the national economy. In the case of the local authority services, a similar decision has to be made by the local council, though it is strongly influenced by how far increased health expenditure is taken into account in fixing the Rate Support Grant, out of which a large part of their spending is financed.

Since the resources available for the health services, as for other types of use, are never enough for all that could be done, rationing by purse is inevitably replaced to some extent by rationing by waiting time. This is waiting time to get a hospital bed in non-urgent cases, waiting time to get an appointment with a doctor, or, very often more crudely, long periods of waiting in doctors' surgeries or out-patients' clinics.

There has also been a certain tendency to find ways of re-introducing the price element. Thus part of the cost of dental and ophthalmic treatment is met by standard charges on the recipients, remitted only in cases of need; prescription charges have several times been imposed, removed and re-imposed. Revenue from charges in 1970–71 however, was estimated at only £63 million, or about 3 per cent of total expenditure on the Service. To a limited extent private provision continues to be available for those able and willing to pay for it, and although very few people have opted to be private patients of general practitioners, a sizeable number are prepared to pay for private advice from consultants, or treatment in the private wards of hospitals or in private nursing homes. Such private facilities have been very limited, but speedier treatment in more congenial surroundings is felt to be worth high fees, and this choice has become easier for many through the spread of medical insurance schemes.

Such developments give rise to serious issues of how far the ideal of a free service available to all, implicit in the Beveridge Report, is appropriate at a time of rising incomes and limited resources, and how far there should be further reliance on charges and private services for those who can afford them. These must be more fully considered later.

EDUCATION

The Education Act of 1944, introduced by the then Mr R. A. Butler, and the corresponding Scottish act of 1946, marked a similar milestone towards the establishment of what was intended to be a single State system of equal educational opportunity. The ideal of secondary education for all, put forward in principle in 1918 and long deferred, was now explicitly accepted, and all children were to receive education suited to their age, aptitude and ability, without any barrier of means. The minimum school leaving age was to be raised to 15, and this was achieved in 1947. It was hoped soon to raise it further to 16, though this did not prove possible until 1972–73.

The organization of the public education system did not then appear to need to be remodelled drastically, as did that of the health service, since the great bulk of the nation's children were already in the hands of the local education authorities, acting under the guidance of the national Education Departments. Indeed, it was largely because of this that the secondary school system was allowed to develop on a selective basis, since this arose naturally out of the existing structure of schools, though it also reflected prevailing beliefs about the reliability of using tests at the age of eleven plus to decide which type of education was most suited to particular children.

Hence in England and Wales the former county and county borough secondary schools were developed as grammar schools for what were regarded as the more academic pupils, the few existing junior technical schools became secondary technical schools for pupils with academic ability but a technical bias, while the former senior elementary schools became secondary modern schools for the less academic majority. In Scotland the situation was more complex, for in many areas there had developed a parallel system of secondary schools for the more able taking pupils up to leaving certificate level, and other schools giving shorter secondary courses from which brighter pupils could be transferred if they were to continue in academic education. Here, too, however, a system of selection between senior and junior secondary schools tended to develop, analogous to the English grammar and modern schools.

Given the belief that children could be selected at eleven plus in this way, on the basis of the measurement of what was taken to be innate ability, it was held that equality of opportunity was ensured so long as all those who had the ability to profit from the more academic type of education, leading to certificate examinations, got the chance to do so. But in practice the extent of provision of grammar school places for secondary entrants varied very greatly between education authorities, from 20 per cent or less in some cases, up to 50 per cent or so in others, especially in some of the Welsh counties. So that opportunities to enter the type of school which increasingly formed the gateway to the professions and other skilled non-manual jobs, as well as to higher education, tended to vary greatly according to where the pupil lived. This was always a less serious problem in Scotland, where opportunities for pursuing an academic type of education were less restricted.

On top of this, however, there has been growing criticism of the principle of selection at eleven plus, on grounds both of the un-reliability of the selection tests used and of the continuing adverse affects on the performance of those children selected for what were regarded as 'inferior' schools.

The education service has been under even more strain from ex-panding demand than the health service. In part this reflects popula-tion trends. The post-war bulge in births, reaching a peak in 1947, left a legacy of increased numbers of children whose passage through the school system caused strain at successive levels from the early 1950s onwards. After a few years lull, the more sustained rise in the birth rate over the years 1954–64 caused a further increase in numbers spreading through the primary and into the secondary schools, to be followed in the late 'sixties by a drop in primary school entrants. The total number of children aged 5–14 in the United Kingdom, which in 1951 was 7·0 million, had reached 8·1 million by 1961 and 8·8 million by 1970.

On top of the 'bulge' and the later more sustained rise in births came what has been called the 'trend'. This is the tendency for a larger proportion of those over the minimum school-leaving age to stay on in full-time education, remaining at school until they are 16, 17 or 18 and increasingly going on to further or higher education. Whereas as late as 1951 only 10·3 per cent of young people aged 15–18 in England and Wales were attending State schools, and in Scotland 7·9 per cent, by 1961 these percentages were 13·5 and 14·3 respectively; by 1970, they were 23·8 and 27·0. Taking the United Kingdom as a whole, in 1961 38·8 per cent of the 15-year-olds were still at school, and 4·1 per cent of the 18-year-olds. By 1970 the proportion of 15-year-olds was up to 69·0 per cent and that of 18-year-olds up to 6·7 per cent. The age groups in between had moved proportionately. There were, of course, considerable variations, with more boys staying on than girls, and higher proportions in Southern England than in Northern England.

The number of students in full-time further and higher education has also grown greatly. The total numbers in universities, teachers' training colleges and full-time courses in further education institutions was about 163,000 in 1954–55. By 1962–63 this had grown to 330,000, and by 1969–70 the corresponding total was about 665,000.

Thus there has been a disproportionate growth in the most costly forms of education, for the latter years of secondary school cost much more per pupil than the early years or primary education, and further and higher education are much costlier still per student. This is a reflection of the smaller classes, the more highly qualified teachers and the costly equipment required. The 'trend' has therefore done a great deal to push up educational costs.

On top of this has come pressure to improve the quality of education, to reduce the average size of classes, still excessively large in many cases, especially in primary schools,[8] to improve the training of teachers, to replace old and inadequate buildings with modern ones, and to improve equipment and facilities. In addition, teachers' and other salaries have had to be raised to keep up with the general rise of money incomes. It is not surprising, therefore, that public spending on education has tended to rise much faster than the national product. The total rose from £401 million in 1951 to £861 million in 1960; it reached £2,592 million by 1970. As a proportion of the gross national product this represented a rise from 3 per cent to 4 per cent, to over 6 per cent.[9]

Against this background of the growing calls being made on the national resources to meet the demands of education, there has been continuing controversy over the methods of organization of secondary education. Experience of the working of the selective system has brought growing evidence that the assumptions on which it grew up are unrealistic. Selection at the age of eleven plus, it seems clear, is by no means as objective as was once thought, even when intelligence tests are combined in various ways with attainments tests, school records and teachers' reports. The standard of teaching received, the educational standard of the home background and the degree of parental interest and encouragement received have far more effect on a child's achievements in the tests than was realized. Limited grammar school provision in many areas has given a greater incentive to parents and teachers to push their children towards what is still thought of as success rather than merely classification. Testing of the subsequent achievements and intelligence test scores of children selected for grammar schools and secondary modern schools produces evidence that those who are selected for what are regarded as the 'inferior' type of school tend cumulatively to do worse than those selected for the 'better' schools. In particular, attention has been focused on schools in problem areas, whose pupils tend to suffer the worst effects of unfavourable home backgrounds, the worst buildings, the poorest teachers (with some notable exceptions) and a rapid turnover of staff.

Hence the advocacy of comprehensive schools, which take the whole secondary school intake of an area, and in which pupils of all types and levels of ability can be educated together. It is held that this is the best way in which the mistakes of early selection can be rectified, for it is much easier to switch pupils between classes within a school than from one school to another. It is also held to be the only type of organization that avoids the cumulative disadvantages otherwise experienced by those selected for what are regarded as 'inferior' schools.

On the other hand, the advocates of selection point to the needs of the more able pupils, which the traditional grammar schools are well suited to cater for, and to the danger that these will be less well catered for in a comprehensive school. They also point to the very large size which comprehensive schools must achieve if they are to offer the same range of advanced courses for their more able pupils as a good grammar school can now provide. They would also maintain that the system of full-scale comprehensivization produces a danger of selection by residence, since those parents who can afford to do so will choose to live in the areas where the schools are best.

Dangers of make-shift comprehensivization

Many of those who favour the comprehensive ideal in principle and look towards a general system of comprehensive schools as a long-run aim have been concerned about the dangers of hasty and make-shift comprehensivization. In order to comply with government requirements to produce a scheme for the re-organization of their secondary schools, some education authorities have amalgamated into comprehensives separate secondary schools sometimes a considerable distance apart and with buildings unsuited for their new purpose. This is largely because resources have not been available to build new schools planned for the purpose, in view of all the competing calls on the scarce means available for education. It is argued, however, that by so doing they have merely replaced several functioning existing schools by an amalgam which is not really a viable new unit.

In this connection, the role of the direct grant schools has become crucial. They receive grants from the central Education Departments as well as from the local authorities to whose pupils they provide free places. Hence they are able to combine the offering of low fees to those parents who want to pay for what they regard as a superior academic education with the provision of free education to some of the ablest pupils drawn from the local primary schools. Many of them certainly have attained extremely high academic standards, as evidenced by their success in getting university places for their sixth-form leavers, but this, it is alleged, is at the expense of creaming off the most able pupils from the local authority schools and thus depriving any comprehensive system of its top stratum of ability. Hence though the number of pupils in them has been relatively small, only about 1½ per cent of the total school population (though a higher proportion of the secondary population), they have had an importance out of all proportion to their size.

Finally, there are the independent schools, a category which includes everything from the most famous public schools like Eton, Harrow, Winchester and Rugby, through the whole range of public boarding schools,[10] down to preparatory schools and small private schools for junior pupils. They have continued to account for something like 5 per cent of the total number of pupils. Here again, the academic standards and social status of the more eminent of these institutions have given them an influence out of all proportion to their numbers, and rising incomes have meant that there have been enough parents who have been prepared to pay increasingly high fees to get for their children the advantages they are felt to bring.

The implications of these issues of educational policy and organization in terms of the meaning of educational opportunity, and the way in which public education should develop at a time of rising incomes and pressing demands for public expenditure must occupy us further in later chapters.

WELFARE SERVICES

We saw earlier that by the time of the Second World War the welfare services were beginning to be clearly differentiated from the services of health, education, poor relief and the administration of justice out of which they arose. Several developments of the early post-war years carried this process further. Because of their origins and relationship with other services, most of them have continued, however, to be operated by the local authorities, usually either by the health or the education authorities.

Following the report of the Curtis Committee, which had investigated the means of best providing for children deprived of a normal home life, the Children Act of 1948 considerably extended the responsibilities of local authorities for the welfare of children. Each health authority had to have a separate Children's Department under a Children's Officer, to take over all responsibility for all children in care in its area. The authorities were given the duty (not merely the power, as by earlier statutes) of enquiring into any case where there might be a child in need of care or protection. Under these provisions the care of children ceased to be a branch of public assistance and became orientated specifically towards providing for the welfare of the child in the best way possible, whether through children's homes or by boarding out with suitable foster-parents.

At the same time the National Assistance Act of 1948, which removed from the local authorities the responsibility for the financial relief of the poor, left with them the duty of providing for those who needed residential accommodation or welfare services in their own homes. The growing number of old people[11] has meant that the major part of these responsibilities have concerned care for the aged. Former public assistance institutions have been converted into old people's homes, though the success of this process is often hampered by the institutional bleakness of outmoded buildings. Smaller hostels have been opened both by local authorities and by voluntary bodies, and local housing authorities and voluntary societies have tried to provide housing suitable for old people who can live on their own. Local authorities have also developed services such as home helps, meals on wheels, social clubs, chiropody and so on for old people living in their own homes, sometimes directly and sometimes by giving financial aid to voluntary bodies. Their powers in these respects were much extended by the National Assistance Amendment Act of 1962.

Under the 1948 National Assistance Act the local authorities also have a duty to provide welfare services for the physically handicapped, including the blind, partially sighted, deaf, hard of hearing and the crippled. These include advice on occupational and personal problems, help in carrying out adaptations in the home, provision of social and occupational centres, teaching of handicrafts and other occupations, provision of holiday centres and outings. Much use is again made of voluntary agencies.

In other cases, welfare services are provided as part of the health or the educational responsibilities of the local authorities. Thus the work of the maternity and child welfare clinics and of the health visitors is as much welfare as medical in character, and that of the home-helps even more so, though all are technically part of the National Health Service. The same applies to the treatment of the mentally disordered and mentally handicapped in their own homes, and this is becoming increasingly important with the growing emphasis on treatment of mental illness and defect within the community instead of under custodial conditions in institutions. The education authorities have also developed an educational welfare service out of the old school attendance service, which is not now concerned merely with chasing up truants, but with the welfare of the school child in his home background.

Developments in the more enlightened and more reformative treatment of offenders, especially young offenders, have tended in the same direction. The probation service, as well as being an essential part of the administration of justice, has a large welfare element in its work and must inevitably be concerned with the family background of its clients. When children come before the children's courts, concern has come to be as much with their need for care and protection as with the need for deterrence and reform, and committal to the care of the children's authority may be an alternative to probation or committal to an approved school. Recent developments towards lowering the age of criminal responsibility for young people and replacing the juvenile courts by panels concerned with deciding the most suitable form of treatment for children in trouble will carry this process of extending welfare responsibilities a stage further. Under the Social Work (Scotland) Act of 1968 this change is now being introduced and it was also proposed for England and Wales in the White Paper 'Children in Trouble' (Cmnd. 3601, 1968).

The various services have each tended in the past to be specialized on one aspect of a family's life, such as health or housing or education, or on one group of its members, such as mothers and babies, or school children, or delinquents, or old people, or the handicapped. Increasingly, however, the dangers of an overlapping and conflicting approach to families by separate agencies are being recognized, and many of these problems are coming to be seen as concerned with the life of the family as a unit. There is thus a growing emphasis on

71

family casework, especially as applied to the needs of problem families, those which for various reasons are unable to cope with the stresses and strains of life, whether financial, emotional or physical. So far, family casework as such has been undertaken mainly by voluntary agencies, since it involves the kind of intensive care which local authorities cannot give to all the families in their area which might benefit from it. Local authorities are, however, increasingly contributing financially towards the work of these agencies and trying to use them in conjunction with their own services.

Because of their diverse origins, largely as ancillaries to other services, the welfare services have been slow in developing common professional standards and a common ethos. Whereas some branches have a well developed system of specialized training, notably medical and psychiatric social workers, probation officers and family case-workers, in other cases many of the existing staffs have had little training except on the job. Nevertheless, there has been a definite move to bring the various services together into a unified system which can deal in a more integrated way with all aspects of the needs of those in its care. This has gone further in Scotland, where under the Social Work (Scotland) Act of 1968, each local authority has set up a unified social work department under a professional head, bringing together the child care service, most of the welfare services, the probation service and the care of young offenders. Similar proposals were made for England and Wales by the Seebohm Committee [12] which reported in 1968; they have since been accepted by the Government. Under the powers of the Local Authorities Social Services Act of 1970, unified Social Service Departments came into being on 1st April 1971.

Problems arise, however, concerning the relationship between the social work departments and those responsible for closely associated services. Thus the work of medical and psychiatric social workers is intimately concerned with social welfare, but they form part of the hospital service since they are based on the hospitals. Health visitors are similarly part of the local authority health services and their work comes under the Medical Officer of Health. The educational welfare service likewise remains part of the educational system, since it is closely connected with the work of the schools. Similar difficulties have arisen in the case of the probation officers, whose work is inseparable from the administration of justice. The Scottish decision to place them under the new Social Work Departments has not yet been followed elsewhere, and has caused considerable controversy.

In spite of all these developments, the welfare services in total remain comparatively small. Total expenditure on the local authority welfare services in 1970 came to only £190 million, and if to this we add £174 million spent on school meals and welfare foods, that makes a total of £364 million, or 0·8 per cent of gross national product. This had, however, gone up from 0·6 per cent in 1958.[13]

HOUSING

The main outlines of the housing problem as it has developed over the post-war period were already clearly seen at the end of the war, as a result of the experience of the 1920s and 1930s.

The housing boom of the 'thirties had made it plain that the demand for houses among those with higher incomes would be met more and more by owner-occupancy, both of existing houses and of new houses built for sale, once private building could start again. The supply of newer and better quality housing to let would come to be even more in the hands of the local authorities, who alone were in a position to build and let at rents which those of low or moderate income could pay, because they could provide subsidies from their own resources and those of the Exchequer. The private ownership of houses to let was to become less and less an attractive economic proposition, the more so under strict rent control. Privately-owned rented houses were increasingly to become the oldest, poorest, least attractive and lowest rented group, but by and large they were to be available only to well-established tenants. Those who could not afford to buy houses, nor get themselves to the top of the local authorities' lists, and who were not sitting tenants of privately-owned rented houses, were more and more to become dependant on obtaining sub-let or nominally furnished accommodation, often at high rents and under unsatisfactory conditions.

The problem of the large stock of old and often run-down and inadequately equipped houses had also emerged. According to the White Paper on 'Housing in England and Wales' published in 1961 (Cmnd 1290), out of a total of 14·3 million houses and flats in England and Wales, the distribution by age was roughly as follows:

built

since 1945	3·3 million
between 1919 and 1939	4·3 million
between 1880 and 1915	3·0 million
before 1880	3·7 million

Most of those built before 1880, even if not officially slums, were unlikely to be in a satisfactory condition, while large numbers of those built between 1880 and the First World War, even if structurally sound, lacked modern amenities, such as baths, hot water supply

and indoor sanitation, and their environments were often un-
attractive.

The pre-war slum clearance and relief of over-crowding programmes had had little effect on the hard core of slums in the bigger
towns, whilst the years of neglect of maintenance and damage by
enemy action during the war had made it clear that the slum problem
was not a static one of a limited set of houses which needed replacement, but rather a dynamic one of older houses continuously
deteriorating into slums. Paradoxically, slum clearance itself still
tended to make this worse, for the poorest and worst housed who
could not afford even subsidized rents tended to be pushed into new
areas on the fringe of the old slums.

At the end of the war there was once again a serious housing
shortage. Hardly any houses had been built for six years. 200,000
houses had been destroyed, another 250,000 so badly damaged as to
be uninhabitable, and a further 250,000 needed large-scale repairs.
Millions of men and women were about to come home from the
forces and war work. Marriage and birth rates were high and families
were tending to split up into smaller units, so that housing demand
tended to rise faster than population. The building labour force had
been allowed to fall to a third of its pre-war size and was mainly
concentrated on war damage repairs, so that experience in house-
building had been lost.

Faced with these conditions, the Labour Government of 1945
adopted a policy of continued control over housing and of encouraging large-scale building of subsidized houses by the local
authorities. They were encouraged to build for the general needs of
their areas, not only to provide working class housing, as in the past.
Severe restrictions on building for private owners continued, limiting
it to priority classes like doctors and to a small percentage of the
annual quota of houses allowed to each housing authority. Rents of
all but the largest privately owned houses had been pegged at the
1939 level and continued to be limited to this level in spite of the steep
rise of repair costs. Rents of local authority houses were not controlled, but in practice they tended to be kept low, by pooling the
lower annual interest charges on the much cheaper pre-war houses
with the rising interest charges on post-war building, and by incurring
deficits on housing accounts which were made up out of the general
rates. This latter policy was followed particularly in Scotland, which
had a tradition of low rents.

The rate of building new houses recovered fairly quickly and
reached over 200,000 a year by the early 'fifties and over 300,000 a
year by the mid-'fifties. Nevertheless, the net result of all these
policies was to prevent the effective working of a free housing market,

which in any case would have been difficult in a situation of shortage; however, it did not effectively supersede it by any social service type of allocation of housing according to need. Local authority housing lists were long, and complicated points systems were evolved to grade the applicants in order, with the result that there was a delay of many years before all but those with the most urgent priority could get a council house. Those who could afford to buy houses had to add their demand to a static stock of older houses, with the result that the prices of second-hand houses rose sharply. With pegged rents and rising maintenance costs, ownership of rented houses became an increasing burden on their landlords, who were often small-scale owners in any case, with few resources. Hence, whenever houses became vacant, they were sold and new private tenancies were hardly to be had.

Sitting tenants of privately owned houses enjoyed low rents, pegged at 1939 levels, which in return were often for poor amenities and minimum repairs. Hence many old people held on to houses which were too large for them because they were paying low rents and could not get anything smaller or more suitable. Sitting tenants of local authorities and those who came to the head of the lists, or got rehoused because they were in a priority category, enjoyed good value at subsidized rents, with little relation to their incomes or sometimes to their housing needs. Those who could not afford to buy, because their incomes were not high enough to get a mortgage, and those who could not get themselves rehoused by the local authority, were reduced to renting make-shift so-called furnished accommodation, the rents of which were much less strictly controlled, or to doubling up with their families. This included many young couples, and many newcomers to an area; neither group had accumulated the necessary housing points. It also included many of the poorest and most insecure who never became eligible for council housing.

Faced with this situation, the Conservative governments of the years after 1951 tried to meet it by taking steps to restore a free market in housing. Thus building licensing was ended in 1954 and builders were free to build houses for private sale. To encourage this, attempts were made to confine local authority building to slum clearance and the relief of over-crowding. The subsidy ceased to be available in England and Wales for new houses from October, 1958, except for these purposes, though this policy had later to be abandoned. Under the Rent Act of 1957 an attempt was made to bring about a big increase in the supply of privately rented houses by a large scale measure of decontrol. All houses became decontrolled which had a rateable value of £40 or over in London and Scotland and £30 or over elsewhere (at the pre-war valuations which still prevailed at that time). Houses below these values which remained controlled, became decontrolled if they became vacant. Meantime, they were given a permitted increase of rent, of up to a new maximum level of from one and a third to two and a third times the gross annual value, according to whether repairs were done by the tenant or the landlord. In Scotland, where rateable values were then still on a local basis and hence very variable, a straight increase of up to 50 per cent was allowed.

The hoped-for effects on the supply of rented housing did not take place. The cost of repairs and maintenance was too high to make these increased rents attractive to landlords, while competition from subsidized local authority rents tended to keep rent levels down. Unlike industrial investment, investment in property receives no depreciation allowances against tax. Most landlords did not regard their houses as a business proposition, but rather as a burden to be got rid of as soon as possible, and thus houses continued to be sold as soon as they became vacant. Improvement grants, offered under the Housing Act of 1961, were used much more by owner-occupiers than by landlords, many of whom had not the resources to treat their property as a commercial investment. On the other hand, in areas of acute housing demand and limited supply, such as parts of London, decontrol opened the gateway to the abuses in the way of harassment of tenants and extraction of extortionate rents associated with what came to be called Rachmanism.

In spite of the growth of building societies and the development of alternative sources of loans from insurance companies and local authorities, owner-occupancy was not really a viable alternative for those with low incomes. Building societies will not normally grant mortgages where the monthly payments amount to more than a quarter of the income, and this kept them out of the reach of all except those above the average incomes level. Moreover, they normally advance only some 70 to 80 per cent of their valuation of the house, so that a substantial cash payment is needed, except in a few cases where the potential borrower can get a guarantee from an insurance company or a local authority, on which the societies are prepared to advance up to 90 or even 95 per cent. They are, however, much keener to lend on generous terms on new property than on old, and are wary in particular of the cheaper types of old property, which is likely to lose its value.

With the change of government in 1964, there was a shift back towards greater control and greater emphasis on public building. The Rent Act of 1965 re-introduced rent control in a more flexible form on unfurnished houses with a rateable value of up to £400 in London and £200 elsewhere (on the new, increased valuations). On the houses which became once more controlled fair rents can be fixed on application by either landlord or tenant to a rent officer, or by an appeal from the rent officer to a rent assessment committee. Rents are to be determined in relation to the rent of similar dwellings, on the assumption that demand does not greatly exceed supply; thus they are intended to reflect what a free market rent would be in the absence of excessive scarcity. For furnished property the procedure remains one of appeal to a rent tribunal for determination of a reasonable rent, and tenants of such property do not have the guarantees of tenure which tenants of unfurnished property enjoy.

Like the 1957 Act, the 1965 Act has not been as successful as its sponsors hoped. In the first place, houses which had remained controlled under the 1957 Act were excluded from the provisions for the fixing of fair rents, and remained subject to the 1957 maxima, though it was intended to include them in due course. Under the 1969 Housing Act, they can become eligible for rent fixing, but only in those cases where they have already been brought up to an adequate standard.[14] This situation has been highlighted by a number of cases, where landlords of limited means have had to keep houses in repair at costs far exceeding the controlled rents paid by their tenants; they have been unable either to displace the tenants, or to sell the property, since no one else wishes to take on such an obligation. On the other hand, in the case of houses of higher values which became subject to rent fixing under the 1965 Act, there is evidence that the procedures have been used more successfully by landlords seeking rent increases, or by the better-off tenants seeking decreases, than by the poorer and less knowledgeable tenants. The latter are most likely to be subject to unreasonable rents, because they find it hard to get alternative accommodation, and they are unlikely to take the initiative in appealing to the Rent Officer on their own. Moreover, furnished properties remain free from rent regulation and from the security of tenure guaranteed by the Rent Acts, except for tenants rights to appeal to a Tribunal if aggrieved. Many of those whose housing needs were greatest could only get furnished accommodation, and hence had little protection.

The need is to hold the balance between poor, ignorant tenants and unscrupulous landlords on the one hand, and between elderly and often poor owners of controlled houses and their sometimes better-off protected tenants on the other. Experience has shown that the free market cannot be relied upon to do this for both the supply of, and the demand for, housing are far too inelastic; more than fifty years of public control and action have made the market still more imperfect. But it has not proved easy to devise a workable method of replacing market control by administrative control.

The Government's aim was to encourage increased building, both by local authorities and for private ownership. To counteract the adverse effects on local authorities of the recent steep rises in long-term interest rates, the basis of the general subsidy was changed in the 1967 Housing Subsidies Act. Instead of being at a flat rate of so much per year for a period of years, as it had been in principle ever since the Chamberlain Act of 1923, it was in future to cover the difference between what the authority would have to pay in interest as the market rate of interest prevailing at the time of borrowing and what it would have had to pay if the market rate had been 4 per cent.

In the case of potential owner-occupiers, help was given in the same Act to those with lower incomes by the option mortgage scheme. Borrowers were given the option of either claiming their income tax relief on the interest payments on their loan, or of fore-going tax relief and having the rate of interest they paid reduced by 2 per cent, with a minimum of 4 per cent. In the latter case the difference is made up by a subsidy paid to the building society. This second option benefits those with lower incomes, who receive little benefit from the income tax allowance, because they pay little or no income tax, whereas in general those with higher incomes will gain from claiming the tax allowance.

Attempts were also made to encourage alternative sources of housing for those who could not afford to buy and could not get local authority rented houses. In particular, realization of the need to make better use of the large stocks of older houses and prevent their deterioration into slums led to greater emphasis on encouraging the use of improvement grants. Grants of up to 50 per cent of the cost of improvements have been available for some years, but under the powers of the Housing Act of 1969, the upper limits to the total amount of each grant were raised, and local authorities were em-powered to declare general replacement areas, within which land-lords would be encouraged to improve their properties with the aid of increased grants. Local authorities were given power to spend on improving the general environment in such areas. Grants could also be made to local authorities and to housing associations to buy houses for improvement and conversion.

Meanwhile, the financial stringency of the late 1960s, with the high interest rates and restrictions on credit and the curbs on government spending (necessary to divert resources into exports after devaluation in 1967) made it difficult to carry out the intended programme of increased building. The total number of houses completed annually in Great Britain, which rose fairly steadily from around 300,000 at the beginning of the 'sixties to over 400,000 by 1967–68, fell sharply by 1970 to a figure of 362,000, instead of increasing towards the target of 500,000.

By the end of the 'sixties the overall housing shortage of the early post-war years had been overcome, in the sense that the total number of houses equalled the total number of families seeking accommodation. There were severe imbalances, however, between different areas and different social groups. In the older industrial areas of Northern England, where population and industry were growing but slowly, there was an excess of housing, though its quality was often poor. In areas like London and the South-East or the West Midlands, where there was a rapid growth of industry and population, supply still could not catch up with demand. And those whose housing needs were greatest, such as families with young children, those with very low incomes, or immigrants, still found it difficult to get accommodation, except at high rents and under poor conditions, especially in the inner areas of large towns.

More than two million families had been rehoused through slum clearance since the early 'fifties, and except in the larger cities the problem of clearing and redeveloping the hard core of older slums seemed to be nearing completion. Meanwhile, however, much housing formerly of a good standard on the fringes of the old slums was in danger of deteriorating through sub-letting and the neglect of repairs, and thus creating new slums out of houses which could not be replaced by new ones for many years. It was being increasingly realized that there was a need for a thorough rethinking of housing policy, which had grown up piece-meal over the decades. In particular, the fact that the benefits of the large-scale public spending on housing subsidies (both positive through reduced rents, and negative, through income tax allowances) were not going to those whose means were lowest, or housing needs greatest, was leading to discussion of policies whereby subsidies could be attached to persons instead of houses. This was to find expression in the changes in policy announced by the Conservative Government in October, 1970, and embodied in the Housing Finance, and Housing Finance (Scotland), Bills introduced in 1972.

Housing is unique among the services in the field of the Welfare State in that capital expenditure is very important relative to current expenditure. Even in the public sector, the greater part of current expenditure is met out of prices to consumers rather than out of taxation. Total current-plus-capital expenditure on housing falling on the public authorities in 1970 came to £1,213 million, or about 3 per cent of the gross national product at factor cost. Ten years earlier the proportion had been only 2·2 per cent.[15] The 1970 total was made up as follows:[16]

79

	£ million
Gross fixed capital formation	815
Subsidies	317
Other expenditure (mostly capital grants and loans to individuals)	81
	1,213

The capital expenditure was incurred mainly by local authorities, but also by public corporations, such as New Town Development Corporations and the Scottish Special Housing Association; it was mostly financed out of loans. Subsidies included the Exchequer subsidy to the local authorities and other bodies, and also any deficits on local authority housing accounts met out of rates. Thus the total of £317 million of housing subsidies has to be compared

TABLE 3 *Public expenditure on the social services in the post-war period*

	Education	National Health Service	Local welfare services, child care	School meals, milk, welfare foods	Social security	Housing	Total
Total public expenditure—£ million							
1951	401	486	29	67	707	368	2,058
1960	917	861	58	85	1,488	490	3,899
1970	2,592	2,089	190	174	3,908	1,213	10,166
Percentage of gross national product							
1951	3·1	3·8	0·2	0·5	5·5	2·8	15·9
1960	4·0	3·8	0·3	0·4	6·5	2·2	17·1
1970	6·1	4·9	0·4	0·4	9·1	2·8	23·7

Economic classification of total social service expenditure—£ million

	Current expenditure on goods and services	Transfers and subsidies	Capital expenditure	Total	Current expenditure on goods and services	Current transfers and subsidies	Capital expenditure
					Per cent of total		
1951	897	775	386	2,058	43·6	37·7	18·8
1960	1,692	1,772	435	3,899	43·4	45·4	11·2
1970	4,199	4,684	1,283	10,166	41·3	46·1	12·6

Source: *National Income Blue Books*, HMSO.

with the £686 million total received by the local authorities in rents on their houses.[17]

Moreover, housing differs from the other services in that the role of the public sector is considerably smaller relative to the private sector. Thus in 1970, new capital formation in housing in the private sector amounted to £696 million, not much less than in the public sector. And as to current expenditure, it is estimated that households spent a total of £3,192 million in 1970 on rent, rates and water charges (though admittedly a large part of that was taxation), while occupiers spent £712 million on maintenance, repairs and improvements.[18]

Thus, in spite of the large-scale building of new houses and the rising expenditure on subsidies, the housing problems with which the period opened were not solved. In fact, as we shall see, in many ways they have got worse and the policy designed to tackle them has become more confused.

Such, in outline, were the main lines along which Britain's social services were reconstructed in the years after 1945, and the main modifications and developments which followed as the situation changed. How far have actual achievements lived up to the ideals of the Beveridge period? How far are those ideals still appropriate in the very different world of the early 'seventies? These are the questions to which we must address ourselves in the next chapter.

Table 3 summarizes the trends of expenditure on the social services in relation to the national product, over the post-war period.

NOTES

1   It has been estimated that between 1952 and 1965, personal disposable income per head rose by 144 per cent, whereas retirement pensions rose by 167 per cent for a single person and 160 per cent for a married couple. Compare with M. Lipton, *Assessing Economic Performance* (Staples, London), p. 190.

2   The basic rates of unemployment and sickness benefit from October, 1972, are £6·75 for a single claimant, £10·90 for a married couple, £2·10 for a first child, who gets no family allowance, £1·20 for a second child and £1·10 for other children, plus an earnings-related supplement on average earnings between £9 and £48 per week. Retirement and widows pensions are similar, though with higher childrens' allowances, and no earnings-related supplement, except for the small additional pension available under the graduated pension scheme. Further details are given in the Appendix to this Chapter.

3   From October 1972 the standard rates of injury benefit are £9·50 a week plus £3·70 for an adult dependant, £2·10 for a first child, £1·20

for a second and £1·10 for other children. Further details are given in the Appendix to this Chapter.

4 It was pointed out in 1958, for instance, that for a family which paid income tax at the standard rate, the family allowance for the second child was then worth only £13 18s 5d (£13·82) a year, and that for third and subsequent children £15 10s 0d (£15·50) a year. On the other hand, the tax reliefs were then worth £42 10s 0d (£42·50) a year for each child, including the first, if they were under 11, £53 12s 6d (£53·62½) for a child between 12 and 16, and £63 15s 0d (£63·75) if he was over 16 and still at school or college. For surtax payers the value would be even greater. (Quoted by M. Penelope Hall, *The Social Services in Modern England*, p. 24 from the *Manchester Guardian*, 11 January 1958.)

5 See Table 3, p. 80.

6 Persons of pensionable age, for example men of 65 and over and women of 60 and over, increased from 14·6 per cent of the population to 15·8 per cent between 1960 and 1970.

7 See Table 3, p. 80.

8 The official maximum class size in England and Wales is still 40 for primary schools and 30 for secondary. In Scotland, it is 45 for primary schools, 40 for the first three years of secondary school and 30 for subsequent years.

9 See Table 3, p. 80.

10 Some schools which are mainly boarding schools are, of course, direct grant schools, while some independent schools are primarily day schools.

11 Persons aged 65 and over numbered 5·5 million in 1951, or 10·8 per cent of the population. By 1970 this had risen to 7·1 million, or 12·8 per cent.

12 Report of the Committee on *Local Authority and Allied Personal Social Services* (Cmnd 3703, HMSO, 1968).

13 See Table 3, p. 80.

14 It is proposed that the principle of fair rents should be applied to controlled, as well as to uncontrolled, tenancies. Compare with the Government's proposals of Autumn 1970, as embodied in the Housing Finance Bill of 1972.

15 See Table 3, p. 80.

16 *National Income and Expenditure* (HMSO, 1971), Table 50.

17 Ibid., Table 42.

18 Ibid., Tables 51 and 23.

Appendix

National Insurance	Weekly rate £
Standard rate of unemployment and sickness benefits, maternity and widowed mother's allowances and invalidity, widow's and retirement pensions	
Single person	6·75*
Wife or other adult dependant	4·15*
(I.e. married couple, total	10·90)
Unemployment or sickness benefit	
Married woman (insured in own right)	4·75
Persons under 18 (insured in own right)	3·70
Widow's allowance (first 26 weeks of widowhood)	9·45
Widow's basic pension	2·03
Invalidity allowance payable with invalidity pension when incapacity began before age	
35	1·15
45	0·70
60 for men or 55 for women	0·35
Attendance allowance	
Higher rate (constant attendance day and night)	5·40
Lower rate (constant attendance day or night)	3·60
Old person's pension	
Wife	2·50*
Any other person	4·05*
Child's special allowance and allowances for children of widows, invalidity and retirement pensioners	
First child	3·30
Second child†	2·40
Other children†	2·30
Allowances for children of all other beneficiaries	
First child	2·10
Second child†	1·20
Other children†	1·10

* If the pensioner or dependant is 80 or over an age addition of 25p is payable.
† Family allowances are payable for second and subsequent children.
Source: *The 1972 Review of Social Security Benefits and Associated Charges* (Cmnd 4958, HMSO, May 1972).

Earnings-related unemployment and sickness benefit

In addition to the standard rates as quoted above, additional benefit is paid of one-third of the excess of earnings above £9 per week, with a maximum of £7—i.e. one-third of excess earnings in the range £9 to £30 per week.

It is intended that earnings-related benefit will eventually also be paid at a rate of 15 per cent on excess earnings in the range £30 to £48, but this will only take effect in the assessment of supplements based on earnings in the 1973–74 income tax year.

Industrial injuries	Weekly rate £
Injury benefit	9·50
Disablement benefit (100 per cent assessment)	11·20
Supplements—Unemployability	6·75
—Others	4·50
Industrial death benefit	
Widows—first 26 weeks	9·45
—over 50 at husband's death, or invalid	7·30
—under 50 at husband's death, and fit	2·03
Widower's allowance	7·30
Children's allowances—as for National Insurance, higher rate	
Dependants—as for National Insurance (unemployment or sickness)	

War pensions	
Basic 100 per cent disablement rate for a private	11·20
Allowances—similar to industrial injuries, but somewhat higher	
Death benefits—similar to industrial injuries, but somewhat higher	

Supplementary benefits—maximum rates	
Ordinary Scale	
Husband and wife	10·65
Person living alone	6·55
Other persons—18 and over	5·20
—under 18	1·90–4·05 according to age
Blind scale—higher rates—e.g. husband and wife,	
both blind	12·70
one blind	11·90

Non-householder rent allowance	0·70
(Householders get a rent allowance which is normally the actual rent paid)	
Allowance for attendance requirements—higher rate	5·40
—lower rate	3·60
Long term addition—aged 80 and over	0·85
—aged under 80	0·60

EXAMPLES OF WEEKLY RATES OF NATIONAL INSURANCE
CONTRIBUTIONS, INCLUDING INDUSTRIAL INJURIES AND
NATIONAL HEALTH SERVICE CONTRIBUTION

	Employed Person			Employer		
	Flat rate £	Graduated £	Total £	Flat rate £	Graduated £	Total £
CLASS I						
EMPLOYED MAN						
Contracted out						
Earnings £15	1·00	0·04	1·04	1·107	0·04	1·147
£20	1·00	0·16	1·16	1·107	0·16	1·267
£30	1·00	0·64	1·64	1·107	0·64	1·747
£40	1·00	1·11	2·11	1·107	1·11	2·217
£48	1·00	1·47	2·47	1·107	1·47	2·577
Not contracted out						
Earnings £15	0·88	0.30	1·18	0·987	0·30	1·287
£20	0·88	0·55	1·43	0·987	0·55	1·537
£30	0·88	1·02	1·90	0·987	1·02	2·007
£40	0·88	1·50	2·38	0·987	1·50	2·487
£48	0·88	1·85	2·73	0·987	1·85	2·837
CLASS I						
EMPLOYED WOMAN						
Contracted out						
Earnings £15	0·83	0·04	0·87	0·941	0·04	0·981
£20	0·83	0·16	0·99	0·941	0·16	1·101
£30	0·83	0·64	1·47	0·941	0·64	1·581
£40	0·83	1·11	1·94	0·941	1·11	2·051
£48	0·83	1·47	2·30	0·941	1·47	2·411

Not contracted out

Earnings £15	0·75	0·30	1·05	0·861	0·30	1·161
£20	0·75	0·55	1·30	0·861	0·55	1·411
£30	0·75	1·02	1·77	0·861	1·02	1·881
£40	0·75	1·50	2·25	0·861	1·50	2·361
£48	0·75	1·85	2·60	0·861	1·85	2·711

In addition, employers pay Redundancy Fund contributions (£0·063 man, £0·029 woman) and Selective Employment Tax (£1·20 man, £0·60 woman).

Class II

Self-employed

Man—£1·68
Woman—£1·40

Class III

Non-employed

Man—£1·33
Woman—£1·04

There are reduced rates of flat rate contribution in Class I and of total contribution in Classes II and III for boys and girls under 18.

Chapter Six

THE LIMITATIONS OF THE BRITISH WELFARE STATE

In Chapter Five we gave a general description of the social security and social welfare services of Britain as they were reorganized after the Second World War, and of the main developments in each service over the post-war period. Briefly, the aims with which the services were established were two-fold. So far as social security was concerned, they were to ensure that everyone had an adequate minimum income related to their needs, when they were unable to earn because of old age, sickness, disablement, unemployment, widowhood or other contingencies. So far as the services in kind were concerned, the goal was equality of opportunity in access to appropriate education, medical treatment, welfare services and housing.

Some of the problems which have arisen in the working of the individual services as they have developed have already been mentioned, as well as some of their limitations. It is now time to summarize these in the form of a critique of the relative success or failure of the British Welfare State in achieving its ideals. We begin by considering how far it has accomplished the two main aims mentioned above.

CONTINUANCE OF POVERTY AMONG CERTAIN GROUPS

Poverty is of course a relative thing. It means falling below the accepted standards of the country, period or social group to which one belongs. The numbers in Britain today who could be said to be in poverty by the standards of Britain in 1900, or still more by those of the underdeveloped countries of Asia or Africa today, would be small indeed. Few indeed are there who are absolutely destitute, in the sense of lacking food, shelter or clothing to keep them alive, or the financial means to buy them. Provision exists in principle to ensure that everyone with very few exceptions gets a minimum of cash through supplementary benefits. Those who lack this bare minimum are mostly those who for various reasons, usually of a personal character, have dropped out of conventional society and are driven to live rough.

Having said this it is nevertheless clear that by the standards of the 1970s there are many who must be said to be in poverty, in that they cannot share in the standard of living accepted as normal by the great majority of their contemporaries. For them, life is a constant struggle to make ends meet. The need to conform in some degree to accepted standards may make for real hardship as, when in order to pay the rent, old people or the mothers of fatherless families must skimp on food or heating.

Measurement of the actual numbers who are in poverty is always complicated by the need to establish a poverty line income, below which people can be deemed to be poor. It is clear that whatever may have been the case in 1899, or even in 1936, there is little value today in trying to lay down an absolute standard, based on minimum requirements for food, shelter, clothing, heat and light and so on, as B.S. Rowntree did for his York surveys. Once he was driven in 1936 to include conventional necessities in his Human Needs Standard, an element of judgment had already entered in. In practice the danger is that either one will make the poverty line very stringent in order to avoid any danger of over-estimating the extent of poverty, and will end up by under-estimating what in fact would be considered poverty by contemporary standards; or one will go to the other extreme so as not to under-estimate and adopt a very lenient standard and so include large numbers of those who might more appropriately be called hard-up, rather than poverty-stricken.

Perhaps the best course is to take as our standard the officially-accepted definition of what is the minimum income which everyone should be guaranteed; that is, the scales laid down for families of different sizes by the National Assistance Board or, since 1966, the Supplementary Benefits Commission. All those whose incomes fall below this level could fairly be held to be in poverty by the standards of the day. There are a number of complications about using these, however. In the first place, they do not include rent, since the actual rent is normally added to the allowance paid. In practice, actual rents vary very greatly, so that in estimating national figures an average rent must be added to the scale rates. This means that some of those who come below the standard, but whose payments for house-room are below the average will be reckoned to be in poverty when in fact they are not, while others whose incomes are above the standard, but who have to make exceptionally large payments for house-room will be reckoned not to be in poverty when in fact they are.

In the second place, the official scales are themselves raised from time to time to reflect increases both in the cost of living and in average earnings. Thus one is not using an absolute standard, but one which rises as circumstances change, though it tends to lag behind somewhat and then catch up. But this means that when the scale rates go up, this in itself increases the numbers recorded as being in poverty, on such a standard, for a number of people who were above the lower scale rates will fall below the higher ones, and if for any reason these do not then receive supplementary benefit, they will now come into the total. A large part of the problem, as we shall see, is that many such people in fact either do not claim these benefits or are not eligible for them.

Bearing these limitations in mind the numbers having incomes below those to which they would be entitled under Supplementary Benefits, including average rent, are probably the best indication we can get of the extent of poverty. Several estimates of these numbers have been made in recent years, and the evidence is summarized by A. B. Atkinson in his study of *Poverty in Britain and the Reform of the Welfare State*.[1] His conclusion is that, in the years 1960–67, anything between 4 and 9 per cent of the population, according to different estimates, had incomes below this level. If, as he suggests is likely, the proportion is nearer the upper than the lower limit, this would mean some 5 million people, though if we allow for sharing of income among households, including other earners whose income is not reckoned in with the means of applicants for benefit, the number whose actual living standard is below this poverty line is probably nearer 2 million.

Who were these people? Atkinson's review of the evidence suggests that about half the households concerned consisted of persons living alone and another quarter of couples with no children living with them. On the other hand some 12 per cent of the households included children, and these households accounted for over 30 per cent of the total number of people living in households with low incomes. According to Abel-Smith and Townsend, who analysed the Ministry of Labour's Family Expenditure Survey for 1960 in their book *The Poor and the Poorest*,[2] 37 per cent of the persons having incomes below the National Assistance scales had retirement or widows' pensions as their primary source of income; another 44 per cent had other forms of State social security benefit, such as sickness or unemployment benefit or National Assistance. However, at the same time 18 per cent had, as their primary source, earnings or other forms of private income.

This evidence makes it clear that the biggest bulk of those living below the poverty line in the 1960s were old people, living alone or as couples, and dependent on social security. They also included a number of others who were unable to earn, such as widows, deserted or divorced wives and unmarried mothers with young children, and the chronic sick and disabled. But there were among them a considerable number who were at work with low earnings. The Ministry of

Social Security enquiry into Family Circumstances in 1966 revealed 70,000 families containing 255,000 children with incomes below the National Assistance scales for the size of family concerned, even though the father was in full-time work.[3]

Many of these would be in poverty primarily because they were large families with only one relatively low-paid earner, so that the household income was less than the equivalent NAB scale rate for a family of that size. The problem is not entirely one of large families, however; whereas 34 per cent of the families in the Ministry's survey would not have fallen below the NAB scale (including average rent) if they had not had four or more children, on the other hand 42 per cent of the families had only two or three children, and 2 per cent had only one child.[4] This suggests that there is in Britain still a problem of low earnings in themselves, apart from that of large families. Thus Beveridge's assumption that earnings from work can always be relied upon to keep a single breadwinner household above the poverty line, provided there is not an unduly large number of children, is not always correct.

Why are the social security provisions of the Welfare State not adequate to prevent these cases of poverty? For the biggest number of cases, those where there is no earner, the main reason appears to have been a failure on the part of those who would have been eligible for National Assistance (or Supplementary Benefit after 1966) in fact to apply for it. Evidence suggests that this is most true of retirement pensioners, of whom there were some 3 million in 1964 with incomes below the assistance scale (including average rent), but only about half of them were receiving it.[5] In a few cases, they may have been ineligible because, for instance, they had savings above the permitted limit. Most of them probably failed to apply for it, either through not knowing that they would be eligible, or because of unwillingness to submit to investigation of their means, or to draw on what was still thought of as 'charity', with some of the stigma of the old Poor Law. There is some evidence also, on a lesser scale, of failure to claim assistance in the case of the sick and the unemployed, but very few cases among fatherless families, where, presumably, the pressure of urgent needs overcomes any reluctance.[6]

The replacement of National Assistance by Supplementary Benefits did a good deal to reduce the problem of failure to claim benefit to which the applicant would be entitled. Under the new scheme it was specifically laid down that those who satisfied the conditions were entitled to benefit. A long-term addition to the weekly allowance was introduced for those of pensionable age and others likely to claim benefit for long periods, in place of formerly discretionary allowances; the procedure for claiming was also simplified. In fact, the numbers receiving assistance increased dramatically, by some 20 per cent between September and December, 1966,[7] but this figure exaggerates the success of the new methods, since the increase in the rates of benefit simultaneously increased the numbers who became eligible for it.

On the other hand, in the case of heads of large families in low-paid occupations, if for any reason they ceased to be able to work and had to claim assistance, because, for instance they found their National Insurance benefit inadequate or had exhausted their insurance rights, they might well be subject to the wage stop. This means that if their average earnings when at work were less than what they were entitled to under the scale rates for assistance, they would not get their full assistance entitlement, but only the amount they would have earned at work. This in itself would ensure that their income could not reach the 'poverty line' level. According to the Annual Report of the Ministry of Social Security, 32,000 families were subject to the wage stop in November, 1967.[8]

In the case of those families where the head of the household is in full-time work, there was no entitlement to any social security benefit other than Family Allowances, and these were at a level too low to make much difference before the big increase of 1968. Even with this rise, Family Allowance for the third and subsequent children is still only about three-quarters of the Supplementary Benefit allowance for a child under 5, and less than half of that for a child aged 11 to 13. Where earnings are so low that there is likely to be poverty even if there are only two children, Family Allowance is even less adequate; where there is only one child, of course, it is not paid at all.

The evidence we have been reviewing shows that in the 1960s there was still a considerable amount of primary poverty in Britain, that is to say, poverty due to the lack of means adequate to secure what could be regarded as an appropriate minimum living standard under contemporary conditions. The biggest bulk of this was among those unable to earn, and especially among old people dependent on social security. It was also to be found to a smaller, but significant, extent among those who were earning, mostly where there was a large family, but even among some small families where earnings were exceptionally low. There is also a good deal of secondary poverty, caused by inability to make the best use of means that would be adequate to keep the family concerned above the 'poverty line' minimum. It is difficult to put any figure on this, but it is largely a question of 'problem families', which are so much the concern of the local authority and voluntary welfare workers; here, the stress of adverse circumstances combines with physical or emotional weaknesses to induce a situation of 'inability to cope'. Paradoxically, the rise in general living standards tends to make such cases stand out more clearly, for many families who formerly would have been concealed in the general mass of poverty, or in the unemployment of the inter-war years, now find their inabilities shown up by the general prosperity all around them.

The problem of secondary poverty is thus rather one of lack of opportunity than of lack of means and is often bound up with the effects of poor health or inadequate education. This leads us on to the second line of criticism of the achievements of the Welfare State.

FAILURE TO ACHIEVE EQUALITY OF OPPORTUNITY

It is obviously much more difficult to measure statistically the extent to which the Welfare State has succeeded or failed in this second objective of reducing inequality of opportunity through improving access to medical treatment, education, welfare services and housing.

In the case of medical treatment, the introduction of the National Health Service, making treatment available free or at nominal charges to the whole population, instead of only a limited service to a restricted number of employed persons before 1948, has undoubtedly greatly reduced the adverse effects of ill-health on opportunity. It has also removed a burden of anxiety about ability to meet doctors' bills or hospital charges, which in the past preyed heavily on many people of low or modest means. At the same time, as we have seen, while there is no difference in the quality of the medical attention available through the Health Service to the rich and to the poor, yet in many non-urgent cases it is possible for paying patients to see consultants or have operations more quickly and under more congenial conditions that they could have done under the NHS. The growth of the medical insurance schemes, such as the Nuffield Trust, is evidence of this.

The facilities available also vary between different parts of the country. In spite of restrictions on new practices in more favoured areas and inducements to doctors to go to less favoured areas, it is still true that there are more general practitioners in relation to population in the well-to-do residential parts of the country than in the less attractive industrial districts. In the case of hospital facilities, the limited investment in new hospitals since 1948 means that the geographical distribution of facilities still reflects differences in the development of voluntary hospitals in pre-National Health Service days; thus there are marked differences between areas in the number of beds for various kinds of specialized treatment in relation to the population.

In education, the development of secondary education for all under the Butler Act, the trend towards staying on at school later, and the rapid growth of higher education have meant that the gateway of opportunity to enter better paid occupations demanding academic training is now much wider than it was under the pre-1944 system of strictly competitive free places. Nevertheless the application of selective principles has tended to favour those from better-off and more educated homes. The eleven-plus system has tended to lead to a two-fold pattern of secondary schools, with 'superior' academic schools for those from middle-class home backgrounds, together with bright boys and girls moving upwards from working-class backgrounds, and 'inferior', more practical, schools for the bulk of children from working-class homes, who will go on in turn to become manual workers. This effect of polarization is seen more clearly at the higher education level, where limited places mean that selection for the universities and other high-prestige institutions must be primarily based on academic achievement. Paradoxically, in spite of the four-fold increase in the numbers of university students since before the war, the proportion of them whose fathers were manual workers was much the same (about 25 per cent), though this was less true of the technical colleges and the colleges of education, which have expanded even faster. Some would maintain that this is not unexpected, in that by a process of natural selection of abilities, one would expect manual workers' families to contain a smaller proportion of children of outstanding intellectual ability. The disproportion between the relative size of the different social groups and the relative proportion in which they provide recruits to higher education is, however, too great to be so simply explained. It is probable that differences in family and social background are much more important than differences in innate ability.

The Robbins Committee summed up the matter thus:[9]

The evidence presented so far may be summarized as follows. The proportion of middle-class children who reach degree level courses is eight times as high as the proportion from working class homes, and even in grammar schools it is twice as high. As has been shown, the difference in grammar schools is not chiefly due to lower intelligence, but rather to early leaving. However, it is not only in these schools that the wastage of ability is higher among manual working-class children. There is much evidence to show that, both before the age of 11 and in later years, the influence of environment is such that the differences in measured ability between social classes progressively widen as children grow up.

Even apart from the operation of the selective system, enquiries such as those of the Newsom and Plowden Committees have made it clear that differences in home background tend to be reinforced by

93

differences in the quality of school provision; the more socially-deprived areas tend also to have the poorest schools, with the oldest buildings, the poorest facilities and the most rapid turnover of teachers. Thus Newsom found that, whereas in all secondary modern schools taken together, 65 per cent of male teachers had held the same post over the previous three years, this proportion fell to 34 per cent in slum areas. Overall, at that time (the early 'sixties), 40 per cent of secondary modern schools still had seriously inadequate buildings, but in slum areas 79 per cent.[10]

The quality of educational provision also varies between richer and poorer authorities, and in particular between the older industrial areas of the north and the more prosperous south. A recent survey[11] showed that in the North-Western Region, for instance, 17 out of 23 local education authorities had rate incomes per child below the average for England and Wales in 1966–67, the shortfall in terms of the product of a penny rate ranging from 1s (5p) to 10s (50p). Similarly in Yorkshire and Humberside 12 out of 15 authorities were below the average, by similar amounts. On the other hand, in the South-East Region, excluding Greater London, all but one of the authorities had figures for penny rate product per child above the average, the excess ranging from 1s (5p) to 26s (£1·30). The main forms of expenditure, on teachers' salaries, students' grants, heating, lighting and maintenance and debt charges, are largely fixed by national standards, but the richer authorities can afford to spend more on books and equipment, repairs and improvements, out-of-school activities and nursery schools. Moreover, the older industrial areas, with their slowly growing or stationary population get fewer new schools than the areas of rapid population growth.

The welfare services are intended more specifically to minister to the needs of socially disadvantaged groups, or groups with special problems, such as old people, mothers with young children, children in need of care, the mentally and physically handicapped, or problem families. Hence their rapid expansion from very small beginnings has in itself done a good deal to reduce inequalities of opportunity. They are still on a comparatively small scale, however, relative to the problems they are intended to meet. Recent emphasis on the importance of community care, enabling old people and the handicapped to be cared for more cheaply and more effectively in their homes, rather than being isolated in institutions, has shown up how far from being adequate the welfare services still are to provide this effectively. Similarly, the problems of secondary poverty mentioned above, which are largely those of the emotionally handicapped and of the problem families, can only be tackled by patient individual and family casework, of a kind that demands trained and experienced man-power on a scale we have hardly begun to contemplate.

Moreover, in many of the welfare services the scale of provision is still permissive rather than mandatory; therefore authorities vary greatly in the extent and quality of the services which they provide, some being content to supply the basic statutory minimum and others doing much more.

In the case of housing the proper role to be played by the social service approach, as distinct from reliance on the commercial market, is still unclear and a matter of controversy. The element of personal choice of type, price, place and size of housing is greater than in the case of education or medical treatment. People are ready by and large to accept that the experts know best what kind of schooling is most suited to their children and what form of medical treatment is needed by themselves and their families. They are much less ready to accept that they should be allocated the kind of house the experts think suitable for them, if they have means to choose for themselves. The growing popularity of owner-occupancy is evidence of this. At the same time, experience has made it abundantly clear that private enterprise cannot provide new housing of acceptable standard to be let at economic rents which those with lower incomes can afford. Nor is it likely that the ownership of older houses to be let unfurnished to tenants can be made into an attractive commercial proposition, except for luxury flats and the like.

House building in relation to the population has varied greatly since the war between different parts of the country. It has been relatively high in the south-east, outside Greater London, in the Midlands and in East Anglia, which have had rapid population growth. It has been relatively low in the older industrial areas of northern England and in Wales, with their slowly growing populations and large legacy of old and obsolete houses, and slowest of all in Greater London where land is scarce and building costs high. Scotland has come off relatively better because of large-scale local authority building. Overall, 57 per cent of the houses built since 1945 have been in the public sector, but whereas in the south-east (outside London) the proportion was only 38 per cent, in Scotland it was 85 per cent. This reflects the Scottish tradition of low council house rents, the average local authority rent in Scotland in 1969 being 24s 1d (£1·20½) per week, as against 41s 7d (£2·08) south of the border.[12]

Continued intervention by the public authorities there must be then, yet the forms which this intervention has recently taken have not been very effective in reducing inequality of opportunity. Subsidies have been attached to houses, not to their occupiers, and hence their benefit has frequently been allocated with little reference to means or to housing needs. Apart from those who have been fortunate enough to be rehoused because of slum clearance schemes, many of those whose housing needs are most desperate have found it difficult to get access to local authority houses, because of the long waiting lists for all but the most urgent priority cases. Of course, the building of millions of modern, well-fitted houses and their letting at subsidized rents, has greatly improved the welfare of those who have been able to get them, and hence must have increased equality of opportunities, but they have not necessarily gone to those whose need is greatest, nor have the subsidies borne much relationship to incomes. This is the more true when account is taken also of the subsidy to owner-occupiers through the income tax allowance on mortgage interest and the abolition of Schedule A tax. The benefits of this have tended to go mainly to those with higher incomes, and the option mortgage scheme has only modified this slightly.

Similarly, the control of rents, and especially their pegging for so long at pre-war levels, while it benefited the sitting tenants, both accelerated the rapid decline in the supply of privately-owned rented houses and also kept many of them occupied by people for whom they were too large for their needs. On the other hand, the 'dash for freedom' implicit in the decontrol measures of the 1957 Rent Act was no more successful in improving the supply of houses. Experience in other countries, reinforced by experience of the introduction of rent regulation under the 1965 Act, suggests that some sort of control is essential while there are areas and types of housing for which there is a marked imbalance of supply with demand. The housing market is too imperfect, and has been subjected to control for too long, for the ideal of the restoration of a free market to be a viable one.

Those who saw the television play 'Cathy Come Home' had vividly brought home to them the extent to which the Welfare State could fail a not untypically unfortunate family in the housing field. Inequality of opportunity in the access to decent housing remains one of the most serious defects of British society.

A beginning was made in the rethinking of policy in the announcement in the autumn of 1970 that the principle of fair rents would be applied to all types of house, controlled and uncontrolled, privately owned and local authority owned, and that subsidies attached to houses would be replaced by rent rebates related to incomes. This is further discussed in Chapter Nine.

IS UNIVERSALISM STILL APPROPRIATE?

The continuance of considerable poverty and lack of opportunity in the generally prosperous Britain of the 1960s and 1970s has led many people to question the principles on which the Welfare State was based in the early post-war years. The two-fold aim of ensuring that all have enough income to keep them out of poverty if they cannot earn and that no-one is prevented by lack of education, medical treatment or adequate housing from realizing his potentialities has not been achieved. Is this because of an over-emphasis on the universalist ideal of providing uniform benefits and rights to all, irrespective of their means? Would it be more effective now to follow a more selective ideal, of providing services more generously to those in real need and less generously to those who are not?

It must be said first of all that universalism, as envisaged by Beveridge and his followers, has not so much been proved to have failed as not to have been fully applied. The comprehensive flat rate benefits introduced under National Insurance and Family Allowances were not in fact at the subsistence level envisaged by Beveridge and reliance has in practice been placed on means-tested assistance to bring their beneficiaries up to the minimum acceptable level, with the failures discussed above. The principle of selection on which secondary education was based proved to be unsound. In education generally, as also in the cases of the health services, housing and the welfare of the old and disadvantaged, the social, cultural and environmental obstacles to equality of opportunity between families of different backgrounds proved to be much more deep-rooted than was sometimes realized. In spite of the rapid rise of public spending on these services, it has not proved politically possible to spend enough to ensure that every child from a deprived, semi-literate background gets schooling of the quality available to the child from the comfortably-off professional home. Nor has it been possible to spend enough on the Health Service to ensure that every old person living on the pension, or every struggling family from the slums, gets medical treatment soon enough and continuously enough for perfect health. Still less have we been able to ensure that every family gets a decent house, and personal welfare services to cope with all its difficulties, especially those of the old and handicapped.

Nor is it only a matter of shortage of money, in the face of other calls on the public purse and the unwillingness of the public to support higher taxation. There have also been shortages of skilled labour of doctors, nurses, teachers, social workers and administrators, as well as of material resources such as bricks, concrete, timber and steel. In all of these, too, the social services must compete with other calls in a time of full employment.

This failure to achieve universalism in practice has led to further criticisms in principle, on the grounds that it is too costly. It involves diverting an ever-growing proportion of our national product from

97

income-receivers, both persons and business firms, through taxation and government spending, to social service beneficiaries. This has been more difficult in Britain, where the real national product has been rising relatively slowly, only averaging some $2\frac{1}{2}$ per cent a year of growth, as compared to twice this or more in most of the other Western European countries. There has thus been less natural buoyancy in tax revenue to provide the means for improved social services. It is also argued that we have a vicious circle here; the high taxation needed to finance social service growth, together with that so often needed in recent years to counteract inflationary tendencies in the economy, has itself been one factor inhibiting a faster rate of growth, because of its effects on incentives to work, saving and business enterprise. Exactly what force there is in these allegations is a matter of controversy, and we must discuss it further in the next chapter, but there is no doubt that they have influenced much public thinking.

It is a truism that a given volume of resources can be more effectively used in combating need and increasing opportunities, if they can be concentrated on those who can be identified as being most in need or most disadvantaged, rather than being dispersed over a much wider number, many of whom could afford to provide for themselves. The argument is about how far we can identify effectively those whose needs and disadvantages are greatest, and how far we can concentrate publicly provided benefits on them, without thereby bringing about off-setting costs, inefficiencies and inequities.

Thus it could be argued that the best way to combat the present-day problem of poverty, concentrated as it is on certain groups, such as the old, the chronic sick, fatherless families and families with only one low-paid earner, is not to attempt to raise basic rates of National Insurance benefit payable to all irrespective of means. Rather, it is to give more generous benefits, subject to test of need and means, to those who really need them, either by extending the present Supplementary Benefits scheme or by some alternative to it. This is the more true since we shall have to keep some form of means-tested assistance service in any case, to deal with exceptional cases of need, however generous the basic insurance scheme is.

But means tests have their disadvantages. Some people with real needs fail to be picked up by them, either because they do not apply for benefit, as so many old people have failed to do, or because they are not covered by the regulations. Moreover, the tests are not costless. They require trained and experienced man-power to operate them, and their administrative provisions are bound to be complex if they are to be flexible enough to deal with all types of case. In fact, there has grown up in Britain an exceedingly complex system of different means tests for all sorts of different services. Alongside the Supplementary Benefits scheme there are many others. Some are on a uniform national basis, like the means tests for students' grants, or the charges for prescriptions and certain other Health Service benefits. Others are administered purely locally, sometimes on bases which vary greatly between different local authorities, such as the tests for free school meals, school clothing, maintenance for secondary pupils, rates rebates and rebates for council house rents. Moreover, these means tests also impose a considerable, if unmeasured, cost on the claimants in terms of the time spent in filling up forms and waiting in public offices, as well as having to submit to enquiries into their means, which are not always of the most tactful. There is also the general anxiety about the results.

A further problem associated with the use of means tests is that they can give rise to what is in effect a substantial marginal rate of tax on extra income. If, as a result of an increase of earnings, a family experiences a reduction in the value of some cash benefit or benefit in kind which it has enjoyed, because a means test is applied, then the reduced value of benefit is equivalent to a tax on the extra earnings. Thus if, for instance, as under Supplementary Benefit, a man is able to earn an extra pound a week through part-time work, and if the result of this is that his allowance is reduced by a pound a week (as it would be if his income was already at the maximum level which is disregarded in calculating benefit entitlement), then this is equivalent to a marginal rate of tax of 100 per cent. If, as is the case of many of the free services, there is a cut-off income above which the benefit ceases altogether and the standard charge must be paid, the equivalent marginal rate of tax may be over 100 per cent.

It is because of these defects that attention has been given recently to devising ways in which help could be given to those in need in proportion to their need and means without the use of formal means tests. These usually involve the principle of negative income tax; that is to say, adapting the impersonal techniques of income assessment developed by the tax authorities to the purpose of paying benefits to those whose incomes come below a specified level, relative to family size, as well as to that of levying tax on those whose incomes come above it. By this means a smoother series of effective marginal rates of tax on rising incomes can be introduced, with the net benefits received from the State being progressively reduced as total income rises from a guaranteed minimum level towards a break-even point where no net benefit is received from the State, and net tax payments rising progressively as incomes rise above this point.

There have been many proposals along these lines. They mostly fall into two classes, though they may sometimes combine elements of both.

The Social Dividend type of scheme In these, a weekly Social Dividend is paid to all men, women and children, which is intended to replace both the present social insurance and assistance payments to those who cannot earn, as well as the present Family Allowances, and also the present deductions from taxable income allowed against income tax. All income other than this Social Dividend is then subjected to a proportional tax, irrespective of income level and with no deductions.

Schemes of Negative Income Tax In these, there remains a cut-off level, as at present, above which income tax is paid at proportional rates (with perhaps a surtax on the highest incomes), but the tax schedule is extended downwards below this level. Thus those below it not only pay no tax, but receive a positive cash payment, related to the difference between their actual income from work and property and some minimum level appropriate to their family size.

Further discussion of these proposals must wait until Chapter Nine, where future Welfare State policy is considered. It will suffice to say here that the Social Dividend type of scheme has the disadvantage of involving a much larger transfer of money through the Exchequer from taxpayers to beneficiaries and hence very heavy rates of tax. It also represents a more radical break from traditions both of social security and taxation. Both types of scheme involve considerable administrative problems, in extending the present income assessment system to millions of small income receivers who at present do not have to be assessed. Nor could they be flexible enough to deal with exceptional cases of need, such as people who have to pay very high rents, or meet heavy expenses arising out of sickness or disability, or losses through misfortune or disaster. Some type of means-tested assistance would still be necessary.

It is also argued that the Beveridge ideal of a minimum subsistence flat rate of benefits is no longer appropriate to a situation where the great majority of the population have achieved a standard of living well above this level. So long as the flat rate principle is adhered to, the level of benefit has to be kept down to that appropriate level of contributions within the reach of the lower-paid. This means that, for those with higher earnings, the drop in income if they cannot earn through old age, sickness or unemployment may be very great. There is thus a demand for earnings-related benefits, such as have been more common in Western Europe and North America.

It remains a matter of controversy, however, whether this demand should be met through a State system of earnings-related contributions and benefits, or whether, as Beveridge believed, it should be left to private provision through occupational pension schemes. This is especially true in the case of retirement pensions, for here the cost of providing a State scheme is very heavy and the alternative of occupational pensions is well developed. In this field there has emerged a clear difference of policy in Britain between the two main parties.

The Labour Party first put forward the idea of a National Superannuation scheme in 1957, with the aim of providing for all employees a system of pensions related to their own average earnings over their working life, the average level of earnings in the community, and the number of years they had contributed. This was to be financed by percentage contributions on earnings (up to a certain level) deducted by means of the Income Tax Pay-As-You-Earn system. In a revised and more fully worked out form, the plan was put forward in the White Paper on National Superannuation and Social Insurance, published in 1969,[13] and embodied in the National Superannuation and Social Insurance Bill; its progress through Parliament was cut short by the 1970 general election. Meanwhile they had introduced earnings-related benefits for sickness and unemployment in 1966 with graduated contributions and benefits over the income range from £9 to £30 a week.

The Conservatives, on the other hand, took the view that the main reliance for earnings-related pensions should be on occupational schemes, with the Government limiting itself to providing for those who could not take advantage of occupational pensions, particularly the lower-paid. This was the purpose of their graduated pension scheme, introduced in 1961. This provided a limited earnings-related supplement to retirement pensions,| intended to benefit mainly those with lower incomes, who are less likely to be able to get satisfactory cover from an occupational scheme. It was financed by graduated additional contributions over the income range of £9 to £18 a week, which incidentally brought in a much needed increase of income to the National Insurance Fund. Its terms were such that it paid those with incomes of over about £13 a week to be contracted out by their employers into a recognized superannuation scheme. Conservative policy is still to encourage occupational schemes, to make them more general and perhaps ultimately compulsory, and to ensure that pension rights are made transferable when changing from one employer to another. They also aim to provide a more elaborate State scheme than that of 1961 for the benefit of those who for any reason are not covered by a recognized occupational scheme, particularly those whose pay is too low for them to be able to get attractive enough terms without State subsidy, or who change their jobs too frequently to be likely to be eligible for full benefits under a scheme connected with their employers. They propose to maintain and improve the basic flat rate pensions and to meet the rising cost of these by going over to a general system of graduated contributions.

These two lines of policy reflect different underlying beliefs in the role of the social services and the nature of the Welfare State. In part these coincide with the distinction between universalism and selectivism, but in part they cut across it. We must explore these differences more fully in Chapter Nine before considering the present proposals in more detail.

In the fields of health services and education, costs have risen rapidly without apparently catching up with needs. The real costs of the services rise, for they employ skilled and expensive man-power and costly and elaborate equipment, and lack the scope for easy increases in productivity to be seen in industry and commerce. The numbers and proportion of young people and of old people in the population are rising, and they are the groups which make the biggest demands on these services. Standards of what is acceptable service is also rising; we are less content now to tolerate slum conditions in our schools and hospitals. Many have therefore been led to conclude that adequate expansion depends on encouraging more private spending. If those who can afford to do so, it is argued, can be encouraged to pay for their own hospital treatment, or for their own children's secondary schooling, this will set free resources to enable the State to spend more on providing medical treatment and schooling for those who cannot afford to pay.

This argument is bound up with further arguments about the desirability of encouraging freedom of choice among families who can afford to exercise it, as to what type of medical treatment or what type of education they prefer. It also reflects a belief that a more efficient use will be made of resources for the general public welfare with a greater reliance placed on the market and the price system, as against allocation by administrative decision.

These matters too must be explored further in Chapter Nine, but it must be pointed out that the issue of how, and how far, to encourage greater use of the price system and the market is by no means a clear-cut one. If one introduces a means test, above which free services are no longer to be supplied, there is the problem of where to fix it and how to avoid hardship to those who come just above it, and now have to pay for the service. Experience suggests that some who would have been eligible for the free service will be put off applying for it, if they have to undergo a means test, while others whose incomes are just too high to qualify may fail to get services which they badly need but cannot afford. If those of moderate means are expected to pay for education and medical treatment, they will expect tax reliefs to compensate, and this will reduce the revenue available to extend the services to those less well off. There is also the danger of creating two different standards of service, a superior one which is used by those who can afford to pay for private treatment or education, and an inferior public one used only by the poor. Experience with public and private hospitals in the United States suggests that this danger is only too real.

In housing the whole question of what should be the respective roles of the private market and the public service elements is much more confused. Within the sphere of public action as it has developed, however, there has also been a call for a more selective approach. In particular, there is a concern that the benefits of subsidies from public money should go to those whose means are lowest and whose housing needs are greatest. Hence there are moves to ensure that subsidies are attached to persons rather than to houses, and go to those who cannot afford economic rents for decent housing, whether they live in local authority or in privately owned houses. Many local authorities are moving in the same direction within their own sphere, by working towards a system of charging economic rents on their houses and granting rent rebates according to income.

In spite of all these criticisms it would be generally accepted that in a fundamental sense universalism is still valid. The State has accepted an obligation to provide a universal minimum both of income for those who cannot earn, and of access to basic services, like education, medical treatment and housing, without which any approach to equal opportunity is impossible. The experience of the last twenty years shows that we have not fully achieved this. Nevertheless, as more of the population rise well above this level, experience also suggests that a more selective approach becomes both necessary and desirable.

There is considerable disagreement, however, as to the right blend of universalism and selectivism to be applied, if the welfare problems of today are to be effectively met. There is also disagreement on the related issue of how extensive the role of collective provision through the State should be, as against private provision through the market. This reflects fundamental differences of belief as to the nature and role of the Welfare State in the Affluent Society.

Before we explore these further in Chapter Nine, we must get the position about the economic factors affecting the Welfare State clear, in particular the economic implications of the recent rapid growth of spending on the social services. This we do in Chapter Seven. It is also useful to compare the way in which the social services have developed in Britain with what has happened in countries of a similar social and economic background, notably those of Western Europe and North America. This is the subject of Chapter Eight.

NOTES

1 University of Cambridge, Department of Applied Economics, *Occasional Paper 18* (Cambridge University Press, 1969), pp. 37–38.
2 B. Abel-Smith and P. Townsend, *The Poor and the Poorest* (G. Bell and Sons, London, 1965), Tables 21 and 22.
3 Ministry of Social Security, *Circumstances of Families* (HMSO, 1967).
4 Atkinson, op. cit., p. 83.
5 Ibid., pp. 55–56.
6 Ibid., p. 42.
7 Ibid., p. 62.
8 Ibid., p. 93.
9 Report of the Committee on *Higher Education* (Cmnd 2154-I, HMSO, 1963); Appendix I, p. 46.
10 Ministry of Education, *Half Our Future* (HMSO, 1963), pp. 246 and 21.
11 George Taylor, North and South: the Education Split, *New Society*, (4 March 1971), pp. 346–48.
12 John Wareing, 'The Two Nations: How Housing Varies', *New Society* (21 January 1971), pp. 97–99.
13 Cmnd 3883, HMSO 1969.

Chapter Seven

THE ECONOMICS OF THE WELFARE STATE

In this chapter we shall be concerned to work out the economic implications of the Welfare State. What are the effects on the way in which the nation gets its living, of the diversion of such a large proportion of our national product from the incomes of individuals and firms to the recipients of cash benefits and services in kind, through taxation and the social services?

First, we trace in more detail the ways in which expenditure on the social services has grown, in the present century, and especially since 1945, relative to both the national product and to Government expenditure. Then we look at the expenditure on the different branches of the social services and the ways in which this is financed. This leads on to a discussion of the main social, economic and political factors lying behind the rising trend of expenditure and of whether there are any counteracting factors. From this we go on to discuss the extent of the redistribution of incomes involved, and its consumption, savings and investment and on incentives to work and to undertake business enterprise.

THE GROWTH AND DISTRIBUTION OF SOCIAL SERVICE EXPENDITURE

Table 4 shows the trends in total public expenditure, and the main categories into which it can be divided, as percentages of the gross national product. It includes all forms of Government agency, central Government, local authorities and specialized bodies such as the National Insurance Funds and the hospital boards, but not the nationalized industries, except for current or capital payments made to them from the Exchequer. It also includes both current and capital expenditure. Table 5 shows total public expenditure and gross national product, at current and at constant 1900 prices, and the indices of each in relation to 1900; it thus enables a measure to be made of real expenditure.

Total public expenditure as a proportion of gross national product at factor cost has risen from about 9 per cent in 1890 to 50½ per cent in 1970. This last figure is subject to some qualification, for as public expenditure rises, it becomes more important to be clear how one is

TABLE 4 *The main branches of public expenditure as percentages of national product*

	Admini-stration %	National debt service %	Law and order %	Overseas services %	Military defence %	Social services %	Economic services %	Environ-mental services %	Total of all services %
1890	1·1	1·6	0·6	—	2·4	1·9	1·3	0·3	8·9
1900	0·8	1·0	0·5	0·1	6·9	2·6	1·9	0·6	14·4
1910	1·0	0·9	0·6	0·1	3·5	4·2	1·8	0·7	12·7
1920	1·2	5·4	0·5	—	8·6	6·8	3·3	0·4	26·2
1928	1·1	6·7	0·7	0·1	2·8	9·6	2·6	0·7	24·2
1938	1·1	4·0	0·7	0·1	8·9	11·3	2·9	1·0	30·0
1950	1·5	4·4	0·7	1·5	7·2	18·0	4·9	0·8	39·0
1955	1·1	4·2	0·7	0·5	9·6	16·3	3·2	1·1	36·6
1961	0·9	5·2	0·8	1·0	7·1	17·6	7·1	3·0	42·8
1968	0·9	5·2	1·2	0·9	6·7	23·5	9·4	4·1	52·1
1970	1·1	4·9	1·2	0·8	5·7	23·7	8·2	4·4	50·4

TABLE 5 *Government expenditure and gross national product at current and at constant 1900 prices*

	Total Government expenditure				Gross national product			
	At current prices £m	At constant 1900 prices £m	Indices 1900=100 Current prices	Indices 1900=100 Constant prices	At current prices £m	At constant 1900 prices £m	Indices 1900=100 Current prices	Indices 1900=100 Constant prices
1890	131	133	47	47	1,472	1,508	76	78
1900	281	281	100	100	1,944	1,944	100	100
1910	272	264	97	94	2,143	2,057	110	106
1920	1,592	565	567	201	6,070	2,168	312	112
1928	1,095	555	390	198	4,523	2,289	233	118
1938	1,587	851	565	303	5,294	2,829	272	146
1950	4,539	1,195	1,616	426	11,636	3,024	599	156
1955	6,143	1,309	2,188	466	16,784	3,505	863	180
1961	10,440	1,859	3,718	662	24,391	4,241	1,255	218
1968	19,122	2,657	6,810	946	36,686	5,012	1,887	258
1970	21,564	3,018	7,674	1,074	42,819	5,995	2,203	308

Source: Peacock and Wiseman, *The Growth of Public Expenditure in the United Kingdom* (Oxford University Press, 1961), Tables 9 and 12; and *National Income and Expenditure* (HMSO, 1971).

defining it. The definition used here comprises both current and capital expenditure, including loans and grants to the nationalized industries and to the private sector. Thus in the 1950s and 1960s it includes a considerable amount of capital formation by, for instance, the electricity, gas and coal industries, the railways and the air corporations; equivalent capital formation in pre-war days when these industries were privately owned is not included. As far as current public expenditure is concerned, about half of it consists of transfers, such as social security benefits and interest on Government securities; hence it involves no actual using up of productive resources. Public expenditure on goods and services in 1970 was only 21 per cent of the gross national product, and total public current expenditure (including subsidies and transfers) was 39 per cent.

One other qualification must be made. Following Peacock and Wiseman,[1] public expenditure has been related to gross national product at factor cost, that is to say, the value of the productive resources used in producing the product; this excludes from the total the value of indirect taxes, but adds back the value of subsidies. If gross national product at market price is used, which includes indirect taxes but excludes subsidies, the value of the product is considerably increased, especially for recent years when indirect taxes greatly exceed subsidies. Public expenditure thus forms a smaller proportion of this total, e.g. 43 per cent in 1970 as against 50½ per cent.

Over the period up to the Second World War we see in the relationship of public expenditure to national product the results of the inspection and displacement effects discussed in Chapter Four. Thus there is a jump in the proportion in 1900, associated with Boer War military spending, and a drop thereafter to a level which in 1910 is nevertheless above that of 1890. During the First World War the proportion rose sharply owing to military spending, reaching a peak of 52 per cent in 1918. In the inter-war years it was displaced permanently upwards, settling down at around 25 to 30 per cent of GNP, more than double the pre-1914 level. During the Second World War it again rose steeply, reaching 73 per cent in 1944, and was again displaced to a new, higher post-war proportion of around 35 to 40 per cent. By the 1960s, however, a new trend appears to have set in towards a more steady peacetime rise from 40 per cent up to 50 per cent or more, though there is a slight declining of this rise from 1968 to 1970, reflecting the deflationary curbs to expenditure growth in those years.

Within the total of public expenditure the relative importance of the different main functional categories has changed. The more traditional functions, such as law and order and administration, have remained at a constant low proportion of the rising national product. Defence spending has fluctuated proportionally according to the world political situation. It was a low proportion of national product (some 2 to 3 per cent) in the pre-1939 times of peace, such as the 1890s, the 1900s and the 1920s. It was a considerably higher proportion in 1900, owing to the Boer War (7 per cent), in 1920, in the unsettled aftermath of the First World War (7 per cent), in 1938, owing to preparations for the Second World War (9 per cent), in 1950, in the aftermath of the Second World War and on the outbreak of the Korean War (7 per cent), and still more in 1955 in the aftermath of Korea ($9\frac{1}{2}$ per cent). By the 1960s it had settled down at about 7 per cent of GNP; it has since fallen to below 6 per cent.

The biggest absolute and proportionate increases have come in the social services and, to a lesser extent, in the economic and environmental services. Social service expenditure was only $2\frac{1}{2}$ per cent of GNP in 1890 and still only 7 per cent in 1920. By 1938 it was 11 per cent and by 1950 16 per cent. Since then it has risen steadily, to reach 23·7 per cent in 1970. Economic expenditure, on aid to industry, regional development, agricultural policy, publicly financed research and the like has also shot up, from only 3 per cent of GNP as late as 1938, to 8·2 per cent in 1968. Environmental expenditure, on such items as road building, public health, land drainage and coast protection, parks, libraries, museums and art galleries has similarly risen, from less than 1 per cent to 4·4 per cent.

The cost of national debt service relative to GNP has fluctuated under the influence of the large-scale borrowing of the two world wars and changes in prevailing monetary and credit conditions and general price levels. It was low before 1914, high in the 'twenties following the heavy borrowing at high interest rates during the First World War, and the subsequent falling prices, but lower in the 'thirties with the fall in interest rates. It was still comparatively low after the Second World War because the massive borrowing was done at low rates of interest and prices then rose, but it was higher in the 'sixties when interest rates rose and the Government became a net borrower to meet the needs of the nationalized industries.

The rise in the share of the national product passing through the hands of the Government and its agencies is thus due mainly to the growing part played by the State in providing social services. It also reflects its growing intervention to regulate the economy and provide services to industry, and the growing need to control and improve the environment of a crowded urban community. It reflects the bigger role which the State plays in the economy of all the developed, urban countries, for similar figures can be found for the countries of Western Europe and North America.

Table 5 enables us to relate these figures to the changes in the size of the national product. In terms of current prices, we see what look like astronomical rates of increase, with the national product having multiplied in value over 20 times since 1900 and total public expenditure having multiplied 76 times. But, of course, the greater part of this increase reflects the fall in the value of money. Adjusted for rising prices, the real national product in 1970 was about three times that of 1900 and real public expenditure was about ten times its level at the turn of the century. Owing to the difficulties in measuring price changes over such a long period, when the make-up of the national product has changed greatly, these estimates are of course only very approximate.

CAN PUBLIC SPENDING ON THE SOCIAL SERVICES CONTINUE TO GROW FASTER THAN THE NATIONAL PRODUCT?

By the 1960s it was looking as if a new trend had set in, towards a rapid growth of public spending particularly on the social services, relative to national product, even under peacetime conditions. Was this a purely temporary phenomenon, or must it be expected to continue? How far, and how fast, can it continue without undue strain on the economy?

The comparison between the fairly constant proportion of public spending to national product in the 'fifties and the steady rise in the 'sixties was to some extent misleading. During the later 'fifties, after the end of the Korean War and of the acute phase of the Cold War generally, it was possible to run down defence expenditure. This freed resources for a rise in social service spending, without the need for a rise in the total share taken of the national product. Thus in both 1953 and 1963, total public spending was about 40 per cent of the national product, but whereas in 1953 defence spending was 11 per cent of GNP and social service spending 13 per cent, by 1963 defence spending was 7 per cent and social service spending 16 per cent. From the early 1960s, with the growing costliness of sophisticated modern weapons, defence spending tended to rise in total and proved difficult to contain as a proportion of GNP without drastic reductions in commitments, which were eventually undertaken by the Labour Government in 1967–69. Social service spending, on the other hand, continued its steady rise.

FACTORS LEADING TO A RISE IN SOCIAL SERVICE SPENDING

The main factors which have led to a rise in social service spending relative to national product in recent years can be classified as follows.

110

Demographic factors

Population has risen faster than was expected earlier. This in itself has increased the demand for housing, education, medical services and so on. More especially, there has been a disproportionate rise in the age groups which make the heaviest demands on the services, the old people and the young. Between the censuses of 1951 and 1966, for instance, the total population of the United Kingdom went up by 7 per cent, but the numbers aged 19 and under went up 16 per cent, and those aged 65 and over went up 21 per cent. This was the result of the falling death rates of recent decades, which allowed larger numbers of people to reach old age, and of the higher birth-rates especially of the late 'fifties and early 'sixties. Young children and above all old people make above average demands on the health and welfare services, while young people of course make the biggest calls on education. The growing numbers of old people have also led to a rising level of payments for retirement pensions and supplementary benefits. These trends must be expected to continue, as the following figures make clear.

Estimated percentage increase of population, 1970–81[2]

Age group	Per cent
0–19	9
65 and over	15
Total population	5

The burden of dependancy and education on the social services will continue to grow.

Increased take-up of the services

Not only have the groups which make the most use of the services tended to grow fastest, but there has been a tendency to make greater use of the services by those entitled to them. This has been seen most dramatically in the 'trend' towards greater numbers of young people staying on at school after the minimum leaving age and going on to further and higher education, as discussed in Chapter Five. In the health services, the establishment of comprehensive treatment facilities under the NHS itself tended to bring this about, as more people took advantage of the treatment to which they were entitled. The extensions of the welfare services for the old and handicapped and for families in difficulties have had the same effect and it has been part of the duties of those responsible for such services to encourage greater take-up of them. In social security there have been consider-able efforts to ensure that those dependent on National Insurance benefits, especially old people, make full use of any supplementary benefits to which they are entitled. These efforts have not been completely successful, as we have seen, but they have increased the rate of take-up considerably. The more comprehensive provision of retirement pensions under National Insurance has also induced more men to retire and draw their pensions as soon as they are entitled to, so that the proportion of people of pensionable age who are drawing pensions is rising. Similarly, the number of claims for sickness benefit has been rising, and though the average number for any given year is affected by the incidence of such things as major influenza epidemics, a three year average of the annual averages for monthly figures shows a rise of 10 per cent between 1958–60 and 1968–70.

Rising standards

On top of increased numbers and greater take-up have come rising standards of quality in the services. Social security benefits, especially for the old, have to be increased as the average level of real incomes rises, even if they do not rise fast enough to reduce the gap between earners and non-earners. In education, there are pressures to reduce the size of classes, increase specialization and improve buildings and equipment, as well as to raise the school leaving age. In the health services, new and more costly treatments are constantly being developed and there are demands here also to improve staffing and facilities; there may be some offset in that a new, expensive drug may cure a patient more quickly and thus reduce the length of time he has to be treated and maintained. In particular, major costs must be incurred for building new schools and hospitals.

In the last chapter we discussed the widespread criticisms of the failure of the social services to achieve equality of opportunity but this criticism is itself part of a concern to achieve higher standards. The inspection effect, which in the past tended to operate really strongly only during the shake-up of a major war, now seems to operate much more continuously. Public opinion is more actively and continuously concerned about the quality of the social services and about the social evils which still have to be remedied. In this it is stimulated by the highly vocal pressure groups of those professionally engaged as teachers, doctors, nurses and social workers, or concerned with the organization and administration of the services. There has also been a growth of voluntary organizations concerned to further the development of one or other of the services or to campaign against their deficiencies. Some of these, like Shelter in the housing field, or the Child Poverty Action Group, have been particularly successful in striking the public imagination by a blend of propaganda and practical action. Enquiries, both official and non-official, constantly bring the facts of the situation before the public and highlight the needs which could be met by further spending.

Real rising costs

The real cost of providing the social services also tends to rise relative to that of other types of goods and services. They are labour-intensive and they make use of trained and skilled professional labour. There is little scope for offsetting rising salary costs by greater productivity, as in industry and commerce. Indeed, improvements in the quality of the services may involve what appears to be a reduction in 'productivity' in the crude sense, in that it means fewer pupils per teacher, fewer patients per doctor or nurse, fewer clients per social worker. No doubt there is scope for improved productivity in the proper sense, by making a more effective use of scarce technical skills while giving a better service, through using more equipment, or more ancillary labour from secretaries, teachers' aides, hospital domestic staff, and so on. Attempts to assess this are difficult, however, since there is no measurable product and in particular the quality of the service given can vary very greatly in ways which are very difficult to quantify.

Yet the social services must recruit staff in competition with industry and commerce and must match the salaries which they can pay, or at least not fall too far behind. In many cases this is made more difficult because these services were built up on the relatively cheap and abundant supplies of unmarried female labour, from the very large generation of spinsters of the inter-war years. The rise in the marriage rate has now dried up this source and as the older ladies retire there is difficulty in finding women able and willing to give lifetime service for often poor rewards.

Lagging growth of the real national product

The strain of meeting the demands for more spending on the social services arising out of the above factors, has been made worse by the relatively slow growth of the British national product, compared with that of the Western European countries. Relatively slow growth means that there is less scope to meet higher public expenditure out of an automatic increase of tax revenue generated by rising incomes; hence, extra expenditure means higher tax rates. On top of this, relatively slow growth has been bound up with the balance of payments problem and the need to restrain domestic inflation. During the years between 1964 and 1967, taxation was kept high in order to damp down home demand in an effort to protect the balance of payments and the parity of the pound. After November 1967, this deflationary policy was continued for several years in order to make devaluation work by diverting resources into exports. This in turn slowed down the growth of the real national product still further, so that over the years 1964–69 it grew by only 2 per cent or so a year.

Counteracting factors

It was factors such as these that lay behind the tendency for public spending on the social services to outstrip the growth of the national product in the 1960s. Were there any forces tending to work the other way?

First, there is the belief, mentioned in the last chapter, that as the general standard of living rises, there ought to be less need for social services providing benefits to all irrespective of means, and more scope for encouraging individuals and families to meet their own need through the market. This has been put forward very strongly in recent years, notably by the school of liberal economists and political writers associated with the Institute of Economic Affairs. It is part of a wider debate on what should be the principles and future organization of the Welfare State, at which we hinted in the last chapter, and which must be discussed in more detail in Chapter Nine. With the change of government in June, 1970, these views became more influential. Up to the present, however, they have had little practical effect in restraining spending, as against the strong pressures mentioned above.

Secondly, what about resistance to higher taxation, which did so much to slow down the growth of social service spending in pre-1939 days? Can we assume that the displacement effect now operates continuously as well as the inspection effect, and that public opinion is willing to accept higher taxes as a reasonable price to pay for more and better services? The years from 1964 onwards certainly saw a fairly steep rise in taxation, with an increase in the standard rate of income tax, increases in the newly-introduced corporation tax, rises in purchase tax and the duties on tobacco, drinks and petrol, and the introduction of selective employment tax and capital gains tax. National Insurance contributions and local rates also rose. Total tax revenue, including National Insurance contributions, rose from 33 per cent of the gross national product in 1964 to 45 per cent in 1970. The reason for this was in large part the desire to maintain and improve the standard of the social services in the face of the growing demands made on them by population trends and increased take-up, but it also reflected the need to pursue a deflationary fiscal policy to protect the balance of payments. The Conservatives won the 1970 election on a programme which included the reduction of taxation; in the years that followed, taxes have been reduced fairly steeply in order to refloat an economy faced with heavy unemployment. Thus the level of taxation depends mainly on the policy of the government in power and its judgment as to political exigencies and priorities.

Thirdly, the slow rate of growth of the economy and the need to divert resources into exports to ensure a balance of payments surplus, led from 1968 onwards to deliberate attempts to restrain the rate of growth of public spending, and that necessarily means restricting social service spending. In the National Plan of 1965, it had been expected that public spending would grow at a rate of $4\frac{1}{4}$ per cent a year in real terms, as against a hoped-for rate of growth of the real national product of 3·8 per cent. In fact, over the years 1964–69, public expenditure rose at an average real rate of nearly 6 per cent a year, while national output rose by less than 3 per cent. In 1968–69 the planned rate of growth of public spending was drastically cut to 1·6 per cent in real terms, and the projected rates over the following three years were between $3\frac{1}{4}$ and $3\frac{1}{2}$ per cent annually, with social service spending planned to rise rather faster, at $4\frac{1}{2}$ per cent a year.[3] After the change of government, the projected rate of increase in total government spending was revised in January, 1971, to 2·6 per cent, with the rates for the social services averaging an annual increase of 4·1 per cent.[4]

Thus in the early 1970s there are signs that changes of attitude towards the social services and economic stringency may combine to curb the rate of growth of expenditure on them. In view of the growing numbers of old and young people in the population, their growing willingness to take up their rights more fully, and the growing awareness of deficiencies in the standards of the services, it is unlikely that these factors will do more than modify a rising trend. Too many people are aware nowadays of the plight of the old people and others who are still in poverty. Too many are aware of the problems of homelessness and slums, and of the need for better educational opportunities for all. There is a growing emphasis on the need for community care and the role of the welfare services in it. There is little likelihood that spending on the social services will not grow further.

THE MAKE-UP AND THE SOURCES OF SOCIAL SERVICE EXPENDITURE

What are the effects on the working of the economy of this large-scale redistribution of resources and income through taxation and social service expenditure? Before we can discuss this, we must trace in more detail how the money is raised and how it is spent.

Table 6 shows how the various forms of social service spending were divided in 1970–71 as between current and capital expenditure, expenditure by the central Government and its agencies, and by the local authorities. This latter division can, however, be misleading, since a large part of local government expenditure is financed by grants from the Exchequer and most of this money comes from the general Rate Support Grant and is not allocated between different services. Table 7 therefore shows the main source of the local authorities' current revenues for 1970, taking the average of all authorities together.

In the case of education, the biggest bulk of spending, both current and capital, fell in the first place on the local authorities, though this is of course taken account of in fixing the Rate Support Grant. That part which fell directly on the central Government went mainly on the universities and certain other national institutions. The National Health Service was something of a contrast, with the biggest bulk of the expense falling directly on the national Exchequer, which pays for the hospitals and general practitioner services. On the other hand, the local welfare, child care and school meals services, much smaller in total, are the responsibility almost entirely of the local authorities. The cost of the various forms of social security, which is entirely current expenditure, in contrast again, is borne entirely by the central Government, partly from the National Insurance Funds and partly directly from the Exchequer. Housing is different again. Most of the expenditure falls on the local authorities, and their capital expenditure greatly exceeds their current expenditure, which is shown here net of receipts from rents and Exchequer subsidies.

As measured by the immediate source of expenditure, then, the overall picture in 1970–71 was that the local authorities were responsible for 29 per cent of the current expenditure on social services and for no less than 83 per cent of the capital expenditure. These proportions have not changed much in recent years, for seventeen years earlier, in 1953–54, the corresponding percentages were 24 for current and 89 for capital spending. The local authorities' high proportion on capital account is because housing and schools, the two biggest fields of capital formation, fall in their sphere. Most

TABLE 6 *Consolidated social service expenditure, 1970–71 (£ million)*

	Central Government			Local Authorities			Combined Authorities		
	Current	Capital	Total	Current	Capital	Total	Current	Capital	Total
Education	327·4	110·6	438·0	1,958·4	306·7	2,265·1	2,285·8	417·3	2,703·1
National Health Service	1,802·5	146·1	1,948·6	206·5	20·1	226·6	2,009·0	166·2	2,175·1
Local welfare services	—	—	—	95·5	19·9	115·4	95·5	19·9	115·4
Child care	6·4	0·8	7·2	72·2	6·3	78·5	78·6	7·1	85·7
School meals, milk and welfare foods	45·3	—	45·3	137·4	—[5]	137·4	182·7	—	182·7
National insurance and industrial injuries	2,849·9	—	2,849·9	—	—	—	2,849·9	—	2,849·9
War pensions	133·9	—	133·9	—	—	—	133·9	—	133·9
Supplementary benefits	618·8	—	618·8	—	—	—	618·6	—	618·8
Family allowances	365·3	—	365·3	—	—	—	365·3	—	365·3
Housing	227·6[1]	−2·6[2]	225·0	121·6[3]	897·3[4]	1,018·9	349·2[3]	894·7	1,243·9
Total social services	6,377·1	254·8	6,632·0	2,591·6	1,250·3	3,841·9	8,968·5	1,505·1	10,473·8

Source: *Annual Abstract of Statistics, 1971*, Tables 38, 39 and 40.

[1] Housing subsidies. [2] Loans to building societies and housing associations *less* repayments. [3] Expenditure *less* receipts from rents and subsidies. [4] Including public corporations. [5] Included in education.

TABLE 7 *Average source of local authority revenues—current account 1970*

	Per cent
Grants—general	40·9
specific	3·9
Rates	33·3
Rents	18·5
Interest and profits	3·4

Source: *National Income and Expenditure, 1971*, Table 42.

of this capital formation is financed by borrowing, about half of it from the Exchequer via the Public Works Loans Board, and about half of it direct from the market. On current account, as Table 7 shows, local authorities in total raised a bigger proportion of their revenue from Exchequer grants than they did from rates. This was an average figure for all authorities. Some of the higher areas got a smaller proportion than this of their revenue from the Rate Support Grant, since they did not share in the deficiency element which went only to authorities with a below-average rate product per head. On the other hand, the poorer ones got higher proportions, ranging up to 80 per cent or more of their revenue in the case, for instance, of some of the Highland counties.

When it comes to the ultimate raising of revenue from the public, therefore, the central Government is in a much more predominant position than appears from looking merely at who spends the money. So far as current spending is concerned, this is because the central Government has most of the more expansive forms of taxation, such as income tax, corporation tax, customs and excise duties and selective employment tax, as well as National Insurance contributions. The local authorities' only tax, the local rate, has the disadvantage of not producing an automatic increase of revenue as incomes rise. If rate revenue is to be increased, there must either be a revaluation of property or a rise in the rate in the pound. It is also very regressive and hence can be a severe burden to poorer families if it has to be raised. Nor does it take account of the number of earners in a family, and hence it bears heavily on families with young children, or retired couples.

So far as capital expenditure is concerned, although most of it in the social service field is done by the local autorities, the Treasury keeps a tight control over it. New loans have to be sanctioned by the

Government department responsible for the service concerned, and it in turn has to work within the Government's capital programme. The terms on which the authorities can borrow are also controlled and at times of financial stringency, when the Treasury is trying to restrict the supply of money and credit, they can be forced to borrow at high rates of interest and often only for short terms.

THE EXTENT OF REDISTRIBUTION OF INCOME

How far is it possible to measure the extent of the redistribution of incomes through social services and the taxation needed to pay for them? The Central Statistical Office produces an estimate of this for each year, based on information obtained from the Family Expenditure Survey; the results usually appear in the February issue of *Economic Trends*.

The limitations of such a survey must be borne in mind. It is based on a sample of some 7,000 households and most of the information about them covers only a short period of time. The range of error may therefore be considerable, especially for some of the smaller groups classified by income level and family composition which are included in it. On the taxation side, the survey takes account of personal income tax and surtax, employees' and employers' National Insurance contributions, local rates, selective employment tax, and customs and excise duties both on consumers' goods and on intermediate goods bought by manufacturers. These are allocated on the basis of the records of household expenditure, with an allowance for the under-reporting of expenditure characteristically found in the case of tobacco and drinks. It does not include corporation tax, which does not fall directly on households, nor estate duty and capital gains tax, which are treated as taxes on capital, not on income. On the benefit side, it includes direct benefits in cash, such as social security payments, and in kind, such as education and medical treatment, but the only indirect benefit included is housing subsidies.

A large part of total public expenditure goes on services such as defence, administration, police, museums, libraries, parks and roads, the benefits of which it is difficult to allocate between individuals on any but an arbitrary basis. These are excluded from the survey as are those forms of expenditure on aid to industry and so on which benefit business rather than households. Since the total of unallocated expenditure is greater than that of unallocated taxation mentioned above, over the community as a whole there is a net deficit of taxation on households over benefits to households. Moreover, in allocating the direct benefits in kind certain assumptions have to be made. In the case of education, children at each of eight main types of educational establishment are assumed each to receive benefits equal to the average expenditure per child by the State for that kind of establishment. Similarly, in the case of the health services, it is assumed that the total value per head of all services received is the same for all persons in each of six categories into which the population is divided, so that benefits to the healthy will be over-estimated and those to the less healthy under-estimated. The only exception is for maternity services, which are separately allocated.

Moreover, since the allocation of the indirect taxes on goods and services was based on the family consumption patterns revealed by the Family Expenditure Survey, it is affected by the serious under-reporting of expenditure on some items, especially tobacco and alcoholic drinks, which is always found in such surveys. An allowance has to be made for this. It is also assumed that the full burden of indirect taxes is passed on to the consumer in the form of higher prices. In practice the extent to which this happens depends on the relative price elasticities of demand and supply for the commodities in question. However, since the main revenue raisers among these taxes fall on goods of inelastic demand, this is perhaps not too unrelastic.

Bearing in mind these rather sweeping assumptions, the following conclusions can nevertheless be drawn.

The combined effect of all the taxes and benefits considered is to give a very considerable redistribution of net income from larger incomes to smaller ones, and, within each income range, from smaller families to larger ones. To take some examples from the 1970 Survey.[5]

For a household of one adult with no dependants, the percentage original income enjoyed after payment of tax and receipt of benefits ranged as follows; between 178 per cent of original income where this was between £260–315 per year (or 398 per cent where it was below £260) and 65 per cent where the original income was £3,104 and over per year.

Break-even point, where allocable benefits equalled allocable taxes, came in the original income range of £460–559.

For two adults with no children, the variations were between 245 per cent of the original income where this was from £260–315 (or 409 per cent where it was below £260) and 63 per cent where the original income was £3,104 and over.

Break-even point came in the income-group £559–676.

For two adults with two children the variations were between

120

117 per cent where the original income was £816–988[6] and 73 per cent where the original income was £3,104 and over. Break-even point came in the group £988–1,196.

For two adults with three children the variation was between 128 per cent where the original income was £816–988[6] and 74 per cent where it was £3,104 and over. Break-even point came in the group £1,196–1,448.

The greatest proportional benefits of all came to the households of one, two or three adults without any children in the lowest income ranges, roughly from £260 a year to £816. This is because these categories consist largely of retired people living on social security benefits, or to a smaller extent of the chronic sick and disabled, who are in a similar position. Thus the action of the State has the net result of providing these people with an income, however inadequate, whereas without it they would have little or no income at all. The conditions shown in the survey for families of this composition are thus not typical of the position of households of one or two adults who have not retired.

These generally progressive effects on income distribution were due to the incidence of direct taxes and direct benefits, both in cash and kind. This was very favourable both to lower income groups and to larger families within each income group. Indirect taxes, on the other hand, were in total mildly regressive as to incomes, though indirect benefits from housing subsidies were mildly progressive. Within the total of direct taxes, income tax and surtax are progressive, but national insurance contributions regressive. Within the total of indirect taxes, local rates, tobacco duty and beer duty appear to be regressive, as do taxes on intermediate goods. The duties on spirits and hydrocarbon oils, however, and purchase tax on final goods, appear to be mildly progressive. The somewhat shaky assumptions on which these estimates of incidence are based must be remembered.

Overall, therefore, these estimates indicate that the British Welfare State, in spite of its deficiencies, has done quite a lot to redistribute command over goods and services in favour of those whose need is greatest, the lowest income groups and the large families. This is done mainly through the incidence of the benefits of expenditure on social services in cash and kind. These go mainly to groups which cannot earn, such as the old people, or to those which make the most use of health services and education, which are the families with children and, again, the old people. The overall effect on income distribution of the taxation system is probably neutral, since the progressive effects of income tax and some of the indirect taxes are offset by the regressive effects of other indirect taxes and of local rates and National

Insurance contributions. In fact the redistribution is mainly between the working population, irrespective of income, and those who cannot earn, and between those with small families and those with large.

ECONOMIC EFFECTS

What are likely to be the main economic effects of this massive redistribution of income through taxation and Government expenditure on the social services? Many of them are of a type which is difficult to measure, so that no quantitative summing up of positive and negative elements can be attempted. They can, however, be treated under the three main headings of investment in the country's human capital, improvement in the quality of life, and repercussions on the efficient working of the economy.

INVESTMENT IN HUMAN CAPITAL

Most forms of social service expenditure provide, in varying degrees, not only consumers goods but also investment goods. In other words, they do not only provide benefits to those who immediately enjoy them, in the form of a capacity to get more out of life, because of better education or health, or the maintenance of spending power. They also improve the productive capacity of those who receive them and enable them to make a larger contribution through their work to the national product.

This is particularly true of educational spending, for the use of modern techniques demands a steady rise in the educational level of the labour force to make use of them. Increased education in turn reacts by promoting the development of more productive techniques. It is also true of spending on medical treatment, which makes people fitter and hence able to work more effectively, and also of spending on housing and welfare services, in varying degrees. It can also apply to income maintenance, especially in the case of payments to families with children to rear, though it is less true in the case of social security payments to the permanently dependant population, such as the retired and the chronic sick. Indeed, this is a case where the social benefit of adequate income for those who retire or are unfit to work may have to be secured at the expense of some loss of output, if workers are encouraged to retire earlier, or those who are unfit are encouraged to give up trying to work.

Experience has made it abundantly clear that, with the pressure of more urgent needs, poorer families are most unlikely to spend adequately on education for their children, or on medical treatment for themselves and their families, if these are left to be provided through the market. They may also be unable to get housing of a quality adequate for their full efficiency, except at prices they cannot afford. A public system of education and a national health service without barrier of means therefore have the result of making possible the development of the potentialities of many of these from poorer families, which would otherwise have been largely lost to the community. Housing subsidies, free welfare services and income maintenance to families have similar effects.

Indeed, it is one of the main criticisms of the British educational system that this is not yet done on a scale adequate to offset the disincentives of adverse home background and social environment. This is particularly true in the case of the majority of young people who leave school at fifteen, from the secondary modern schools. But the increased numbers staying on at school in recent years and entering various forms of full-time further and higher education are an indication of what has been achieved.

The part played by educational factors in accounting for the growth of the national product has received considerable emphasis in recent years. It is clear that output has increased more as a result of greater productivity (that is greater output per unit of input of labour and capital) than it has as a result of increases in the numbers of the labour force or even the physical volume of capital in the form of machines, plant or buildings. The labour force in Britain in particular has grown very slowly in recent years, at a rate of only about 0·5 per cent a year, and the stock of physical capital has grown at about the same rate. Yet the national product has grown at an average rate of some 2 to 2·5 per cent a year.[7]

The contribution of educational factors to growth of output takes two main forms; increases in the educational standard of the labour force, and advances in the general state of scientific and technical knowledge, which makes possible more productive methods and improved organization. They are obviously closely connected, for a higher standard of education is needed both to make possible the research and development out of which technical progress comes, and to apply the new methods to production. Attempts to measure their relative importance can only be very approximate, for all the estimates which have been made depend on many unverifiable assumptions. A rough idea of their magnitude can be gained from the figures of E. F. Denison. For the United Kingdom over the period 1950–62 he estimates that the higher educational standard of the work force accounted for something like 12 per cent of the growth of the real national product; advances in knowledge accounted for something over 30 per cent.[8]

No similar attempts have been made to quantify the contribution of improved health, housing or welfare services to greater productivity.

These are likely to take longer in having their effects and such effects are less likely to be separately measurable. Nevertheless, their cumulative contribution to productivity over the years must be considerable.

IMPROVEMENT IN THE QUALITY OF LIFE

The provision of social services, whether in kind or in cash, is of course a redistribution of consumption opportunities as well as a form of investment. Those who gain increased cash income or free or subsidized services can be presumed to receive an increase of welfare and satisfaction. Against this must be set the reduced satisfaction of those whose net income is reduced by the increased taxes needed to pay for them. In varying degrees, these are in most cases the same people, in that almost all families get some benefit from the social services and pay some taxes, so that it is the distribution of the net benefits relative to payments with which we are concerned. In addition to the redistribution of private benefits enjoyed by individuals and families, there is also a large element of social benefit involved, in that the community takes a political decision that social welfare will be enhanced if services like education, medical treatment, welfare services, housing and social security are made available to a greater extent and with a different distribution than would result from the market.

No strict scientific assessment of the overall effects of these redistributions can be made. So far as individual gains and losses of satisfaction are concerned, it is not possible to add up and compare the experiences of the gainers and losers, since this involves interpersonal comparisons of satisfaction for which there is no scientific foundation. No one can say objectively that a poor family gains more in satisfaction from free schooling and medical treatment or family allowances than a rich family loses in satisfaction through having to pay surtax. Nor can anyone measure the extent of the social benefit to the community at large of more general access to education and medical treatment or public provision for old people. The justification must always be a social and political one, in terms of the community's accepted standard of values. The very existence of the Welfare State is evidence that in Britain, in the second half of the twentieth century, such a redistribution is accepted as desirable in principle. The community accepts that it is desirable to seek to guarantee a certain level of income to those who cannot reach that standard by their own earnings or investments, and to try to ensure that all can get education, medical treatment or welfare services appropriate to their needs.

Controversy arises, however, over the means by which such a

policy is to be carried out, over how far it should be carried and over how far it has been effective in achieving its declared aims. Thus the Welfare State in Britain is criticized, as we have seen, because poverty and inequality of opportunity still exist in the early 1970s to a much greater extent than was expected at the time of the post-war changes. There is difference of opinion over how far the State should go in providing public services for all as against relying on the market as far as possible. There is difference of opinion also as to how the services should be paid for, e.g. how much out of taxation and how much out of charges on the better-off, how far the taxes used should be such that they put the burden of payment mainly on higher incomes or spread it more generally. Such controversies reflect differences of judgment as to social values within the context of the general acceptance of the Welfare State.

The process of trying to secure greater equality in enjoyment of the quality of life is a cumulative one, for the social services also reduce the obstacles to equality of opportunity. Improved education widens the gateway to more highly skilled, better paid and more satisfying employments, especially in the white-collar occupations and the professions. Improved health, welfare services and better housing have a similar effect. In all these fields there has been undoubted progress, especially over the longer period. Non-manual workers rose from 19 per cent of the labour force in 1911 to 34 per cent in 1961, and while in earlier decades the biggest part of this increase represented a growth in the number of clerical workers, often relatively poorly paid and doing comparatively routine jobs, more recently the most rapid growth has been in managerial, administrative, professional and technical occupations. These changes reflect changes in the structure of industry and trade, with technical development reducing the demand for manual workers relative to that for technicians and salaried professionals. The expansion of the educational system has enabled the supply of persons with the necessary skills to expand to meet the demand.

EFFECTS ON THE EFFICIENCY OF THE ECONOMY

A redistribution of net income on this scale has effects not only directly on the welfare of those who gain or lose, but also indirectly through the reactions of the gainers and losers in the performance of their economic functions as consumers, savers, workers and undertakers of business enterprise. Four main aspects of these need to be discussed further, namely

  effects on the general level of demand
  effects on incentives to work

effects on the supply of savings
effects of incentives to business enterprise

Effects on the general level of demand

The general effect of social service expenditure is to increase the income available in cash and in kind to the lowest income groups and the largest families. This we saw above was the result largely of the provision of cash incomes through social security to groups such as the retired, widowed and chronic sick which otherwise would have little or no earned income, and of the provision of educational and medical services which give a disproportionate benefit to old people and to families with young children. In so far as these services are financed out of the proceeds of income tax, this effect is reinforced. However the regressive incidence of other forms of tax, such as indirect taxes, local rates and National Insurance contributions, tends to work against it.

A redistribution of income in favour of the least well-off groups in the community and those with the most calls on their resources will tend to raise the average propensity to consume. Those groups which benefit will have a high tendency to use their extra income for consumption, rather than saving, since they have many unsatisfied needs and little margin for saving in any case. Most of the income received from retirement pensions and supplementary benefits, for instance, is spent on consumption. Those at this level of income will be dissaving rather than saving, and though the social security benefits may mean that they have to dissave less, they will also mean that they can consume more, and may still have to draw on any savings they have to make ends meet. The benefits in kind, such as education and health services, though they include an element of investment in human capital, also represent an additional claim on the country's real resources of manpower and materials in order to provide a current service. Hence they are similar in their effects on the economy to a rise in consumption.

Thus the net effect of a rising rate of public spending on the social services is likely to be inflationary in the short period at any rate, and in so far as the expenditure is financed by taxation on higher incomes, this effect is likely to be increased by the adverse influence of such taxation on the level of private saving. At a time when there is a tendency for the total level of demand in the economy to be inadequate to ensure full employment of productive resources, as in the inter-war period, the imparting of such an inflationary bias to public spending would be desirable. However, at that time, the level of spending on social services was not in fact high enough to offset the very strong deflationary trends in the economy. Since the Second World War, when on the whole the overall trends have tended to be inflationary, with the level of demand tending to outstrip the growth of productive capacity, the inflationary bias imparted by social service spending has been an additional problem. A balance has to be struck between the social aim of providing adequate minimum incomes to those who cannot earn, and adequate equality of opportunity to those less well off, on the one hand, and the need to restrain government spending in the interests of general economic policy on the other. This is the more true now that social service spending forms such a large part of total public expenditure.

Effects on incentives to work

In so far as social service spending leads to disincentives to work, this would make the overall economic problem more difficult. It would mean that increased inflationary pressure was accompanied by a slackening of the rate of growth of output to meet the demand. Disincentives to work might be held to arise from both sides of the equation, from those who receive benefits, especially cash benefits, without having to work for them, and from those who pay taxation, especially on marginal income received from doing extra work or undertaking more responsible positions.

So far as receipt of benefits by those not having to work for them is concerned, most of the recipients are in any case unable to work for an adequate income, because of old age, sickness or unemployment, or because they are mothers with young children and no breadwinner. In borderline cases, dangers of exploitation are guarded against by the retirement rule for pensioners (with the incentive of higher pensions to those who defer retirement), the need for a medical certificate in the case of sickness, or the need to sign on at the labour exchange in the case of unemployment. The avoidance of disincentives to work is also the rationale for the wage stop as applied to the level of supplementary benefit that can be drawn by those with habitually low earnings when at work.

At the margin there are undoubtedly disincentive effects. The earnings rule discourages pensioners from taking on part-time work which pays more than a certain amount, for otherwise the extra earnings would be liable to what is in effect a severe rate of tax through the reduction of pension entitlements. Men with large families and poor earning prospects may be encouraged to stay on supplementary benefit rather than actively seek work, since any work they could get would not give them an increase of net income which would outweigh the higher living costs and greater effort involved; moreover, should they later lose their jobs, they might become subject to the wage stop. Once again we have to strike a balance between being reasonably generous to those in need at the expense of some possible abuses, or taking precautions against disincentives at the expense of being unduly harsh to those in genuine need.

In the case of taxation, the disincentive effect is usually considered in relation to income tax, where the system of allowances and varying tax rates means that the rate of tax charged on additional earnings is higher than the average rate over the whole income. Since the abolition of the reduced rate in the 1970 Budget, any taxpayer who is liable to pay at all is charged at the standard rate (at present 38·75 per cent) on the total of his marginal earnings, less the earned income allowance of two-ninths. This means that he pays an effective marginal rate of about 30 per cent. From April, 1973, the earned income allowance disappears and there will be a basic rate of 30 per cent, with a surcharge of 15 per cent on investment income of over £2,000 a year. His average rate of tax over his whole income will be further reduced by the reduction of his taxable income through the personal, marriage, children's and other allowances. In the case of the higher salary earners, who are subject to surtax, the marginal rate on extra income will of course range up to much higher levels.

It is argued that high marginal tax rates will be a deterrent to doing overtime, or taking a job with a higher salary, since the extra net earnings after tax will not compensate for longer hours or greater responsibility. The taxpayer has a choice between more income and more leisure or more freedom from responsibility. The effect of the tax is to reduce the amount of net income which has to be foregone in order to have more leisure or more freedom from responsibility; hence it gives an incentive to substitute leisure (or freedom) for income. This is what is known as the substitution effect, and its strength is influenced by the marginal rate of tax. But the tax also reduces the total amount of net income below what it would otherwise be and hence gives a counteracting incentive to work longer, or harder, or to accept more responsibility, in order to earn a higher gross income and so keep the same net income after tax. This is what is known as the income effect, and here it is the average rate of tax which is the crucial factor.

It is very doubtful which of these two effects is likely to predominate in actual cases, though it would seem likely that the income effect would be more important to those with lower incomes and greater family responsibilities, and the substitution effect to those with higher incomes and fewer family responsibilities. It is often maintained, for instance, that high rates of surtax may be crucial in deterring men from accepting positions of greater responsibility such as those in top management, but at this level of income the disincentive effects of reduced additional net income may well be less important than the incentive effects of greater prestige, or the desire for power and authority, or the interest of the job itself.

Several studies have been made of the effects of income tax on incentives, but they are inconclusive, and there is little clear evidence of any appreciable disincentive effect. There is in fact considerable evidence that very few people are at all clear about what rate of tax they really pay on their marginal earnings, many for instance, ignoring the effect of the earned income allowance in reducing the rate.[9]

In the case of indirect taxes which are added to the price of commodities, the substitution effect tends to be reduced, since there is the additional choice of substituting untaxed goods, or lower taxed goods, as well as foregoing consumption. This is of course the less true the more inelastic the demand for the goods concerned is. In fact the big revenue-raisers are goods like tobacco, alcoholic drinks, and petrol for which demand is very inelastic. On the other hand, since taxes on goods in inelastic demand tend to be regressive in relation to incomes, the income effect incentive to work is likely to be stronger. Moreover the effect of the tax is disguised in the form of higher prices, so that influence is less obvious.

A flat rate National Insurance contribution, since it does not vary with income, can have no substitution effect, since its marginal rate is nil, and you cannot avoid it by taking more leisure, unless you are able to give up work altogether and live on social security, which is the only way in which you can avoid paying it and still have enough income to live on. On the other hand, the average rate of such a tax falls steeply as income rises, so that it is highly regressive, and thus its income effect should be favourable to work. In the case of an earnings-related contribution proportionate to earnings, marginal and average rates will be equal up to the earnings level where graduation ceases, above which the effects will be the same as those of a flat-rate contribution.

Thus there may be a conflict between the criteria of equity and economic effects. Equity considerations on the whole call for progressive forms of direct tax, with marginal rates exceeding average rates, whereas consideration of effects on incentives might lead to a favouring of indirect taxes and other forms of regressive tax, where the substitution effect is smaller and the income effect greater. This is one reason why we have a blend of direct and indirect taxes in our system, though political unpopularity also would probably prevent the balance being pushed further in the direction of progressive income taxes. In any case, the evidence on incentives is too uncertain to provide an authoritative basis for policy changes.

In cases such as those mentioned above where social security benefits are paid subject to a means test or an earnings rule, both the substitution and the income effects are likely to be disincentives to work, at least in their impact on benefit-receivers. If net income is reduced by the cutting of benefits as earnings rise, there is no incentive to earn an increased gross income, and there is every incentive to enjoy increased leisure, the net price of which is reduced, to nil in the case where the benefit reduction equals the earnings increase. On the other hand, as we have seen, such a system gives an incentive to forgo the social security benefit altogether, if it is possible to get full-time work which will give earnings higher than the rate of benefit.

In general one could conclude that on balance the Welfare State is perhaps more likely to have a disincentive than an incentive effect on work, but that this is likely to be so slight and so uncertain as not to be of much importance when set against the advantages which it brings from the point of view of equity.

Effects on the supply of savings

An increase of income tax on higher incomes is also criticized for having adverse effects on the supply of savings and, hence, of capital. Since the bulk of large scale personal saving tends to be done by those with higher incomes, a progressive tax is likely to reduce such savings more than a proportional or a regressive one. Those with lower incomes do not have much margin for saving anyhow and will have to reduce their consumption to pay a tax which falls on them, whereas those with higher incomes are more likely to cut their saving in order to maintain their accustomed level of consumption. The reduction of net income after tax thus has an adverse income effect. Moreover, the interest or dividend which is received on the savings when invested is also liable to tax, at the higher rates applicable to investment income because there is no earned income allowance deducted from it. If its amount exceeds £2,000 a year (less certain allowances) it is also subject to surtax. Thus not only is the original income out of which the savings are made reduced, but the net return on them is reduced also. This has the effect of increasing the price of a given value of future consumption to be obtained by saving and investment, in terms of the value of present consumption which must be foregone in order to achieve it. It thus encourages the substitution of present consumption for future. On the other hand, those who are saving in order to ensure a flow of future income of a given size will have to save more in order to make up for the reduction in the net rate of return after tax.

Thus the substitution effect of a tax increase on higher incomes is

THE ECONOMICS OF THE WELFARE STATE

likely to be adverse to saving, while the income effect will be adverse in its impact on the original income out of which the saving is made, but favourable in its impact on those who want to achieve a given future income stream. In general, a highly progressive system of income tax is likely to have adverse effects on the supply of personal saving. In practice, this is largely offset in Britain by the growing dependance on corporate saving, through the undistributed profits of companies. Recent tax changes have further encouraged this, with undistributed profits being subject since 1965 to corporation tax only, whereas distributed profits have also paid income tax at the standard rate. The present government has, however, announced its intention of changing this for a system of company taxes which discriminates in favour of distributed profits. Company saving is also supplemented by public saving, through surpluses on the current budgets of the central Government, the National Insurance funds, and the local authorities, as well as the trading surpluses of public corporations.

The supply of saving in Britain in 1970 was made up as follows[10]

	£ million	Per cent
Personal	2,890	26·4
Companies	3,038	27·7
Public corporations	752	6·9
Central Government[11]	3,738	34·1
Local authorities	533	4·9
	10,951	100·0

Personal saving was thus considerably outweighed in total by company saving and public saving. The extent of the latter was increased in 1970 by the pursuit of a deflationary policy designed to secure a surplus large enough to cover Government spending on capital account as well as on current account.

The emphasis on the supply of saving is likely to continue in view of the pressures on the economy. Investment, both private and public, must be kept up to increase the country's productive capacity and improve productivity. Public spending on social and environmental services is likely to grow, and to press against taxable capacity. Exports have to be increased to ensure an adequate continued surplus on the balance of payments. All these activities lead to an increase of spending power through the incomes they create, while at the same time absorbing resources which might have been used to meet the consumption demand to which increased incomes give rise. It is thus important to encourage saving in order to set resources free

131

for these other uses. This means encouraging personal saving as well as corporate and public.

This is one of the arguments in favour of meeting the public demand for income-related pensions by encouraging occupational pension schemes rather than through a State scheme of National Superannuation. Under an occupational scheme the contributions of employees and employers are funded and accumulated in order to provide a flow of income out of which to pay the pensions at a later date. Thus the contribution revenue becomes an addition to saving and is available for investment by the pension funds and insurance companies in industry and other productive enterprises. A National Superannuation scheme, on the other hand, would be financed on a pay-as-you-go basis, with current revenue from contributions being used to pay current benefits, and hence the only saving it would give rise to would be from the surplus, if any, of contribution over benefits. In so far as National Superannuation led to a reduction in the revenue of occupational schemes it would therefore tend to reduce the country's savings.

Effects of incentives to business enterprise

The argument on the effects of the present levels and forms of taxation and public spending on incentives to business enterprise is less clear cut. To deal first with taxation, so far as sole traders and partnerships subject to personal income tax and surtax are concerned, the argument is much the same as that concerning incentives to work. Taxation will reduce the net profit earned at the margin where the decision has to be made to undertake or not to undertake a certain enterprise. The substitution effect will tend to induce the trader to prefer leisure, or freedom from worry, by reducing the net income thus sacrificed, while the income effect will work the other way and lead to a tendency to undertake more ventures in order to maintain net income after tax. In addition, the fact that marginal income is taxed at progressive rates will lead to a tendency to prefer safer rather than more risky ventures, for the effect of the tax will be to disproportionately reduce the margin of higher return after tax on a remunerative, but risky, enterprise, if it comes off, relative to that on a safer enterprise giving a lower, but more certain, return.

The position of the smaller limited companies, controlled by a few large shareholders, may be similar to that of individual traders and partnerships. The fortunes of the firm will be reflected in the dividends received by these shareholders, and their actions will therefore be affected by their liabilities to income tax and surtax. But most of the country's more important businesses are now in the hands of large companies, where the controlling directors usually hold few shares themselves and where the equity holding is widely dispersed among an amorphous and constantly changing group of shareholders. There has been much discussion among economists about what the effective motivation towards enterprise really is in such companies. It is agreed that one aim must be to earn a satisfactory level of profits, to keep the shareholders happy and enable more capital to be raised by the issue of shares when required, as well as to stave off takeover bids from those who think they could get more profits out of the firm. Given a minimum level of profits, however, it is often argued that the growth of the firm itself, as measured by the volume of sales or turnover, may be a more important motive than the maximizing of profits in the textbook model.

A system of taxation such as Britain has had since 1965, under which distributed profits are taxed more highly than undistributed, might be held to be conducive to enterprise in such cases. It encourages the ploughing back of profits and thus should induce firms to grow more rapidly. The system of investment grants in cash, payable on new investments in manufacturing in replacement of the system of investment allowances against taxable profits, should have a similar effect in encouraging growth, since the grant is not dependent on profits being earned. On the other hand, it is often argued that the present system favours the large, well-established firm with secure profits out of which to finance its investment, but discourages the small, growing firm which needs to build up its investment by raising capital in the market and hence must pay good dividends. But further discussion of this would take us a long way from the Welfare State.

Government expenditure on the social services has little direct effect on incentives to business enterprise, since it benefits mainly those with lower incomes and large families, few of whom are in control of businesses. Indirectly, it has an effect as one of the factors making for full employment and a high level of consumption demand, and hence affecting the expectations of entrepreneurs in the direction of greater confidence.

SUMMARY OF ECONOMIC EFFECTS

The development of the Welfare State has thus brought about a considerable divergence in the ways in which resources are used, and incomes distributed, from what the market would have produced on its own. Services such as education, medical treatment and housing are produced to a much greater extent than would probably be the case in a free market, and with a different mix of types of product.

Other services, such as those for the welfare of children, old people and the handicapped, would probably not be produced through the market at all. A great deal of money income is diverted to those who cannot earn, especially old people, who would be unlikely to be able to provide for their needs to the same extent through their own savings or through commercial insurance.

The result is to redistribute income, in cash and in kind, towards those who would otherwise be worst off, those with little or no income from work or property and those with young families. This redistribution comes about mainly through public spending on the social services, which benefits mainly these groups. It is provided at the expense of the great bulk of moderate earners with fewer dependants, rather than at that of the wealthy. The net effect of the tax system taken by itself is probably distributionally neutral, since revenue from income taxes, which are mildly progressive, is matched by that from indirect taxes, which in total are mildly regressive. But out of total tax revenue must come not only the cost of these forms of expenditure like social services, the benefits of which can be allocated to individuals, but also the cost of unallocable expenditure such as that on defence and administration, and on economic and environmental services, such as aid to industry, up-keep of roads and urban redevelopment.

By means of this redistribution of income, the community provides itself with services from which social benefits are derived which are held to exceed the private benefits accruing to those who actually receive them. A better educated and healthier population and work force, care for the needs of groups in special difficulty, subsidized housing for those who cannot afford economic rents, a minimum income for those who cannot earn, these are held to benefit the whole community. As against the social benefits, there are some social costs to be set, notably the possible adverse effects on incentives to work, saving and business enterprise, or the inflationary effects of raising the propensity to consume. Some would add to this a reduction of freedom of choice among better-off families as to how to spend their incomes.

It is impossible to quantify the social benefits and social costs except on an arbitrary basis. Many of them are difficult to assess, and what is to be included and what value is to be put on them, involves value judgments on which opinions differ. Techniques such as those of cost–benefit analysis, which attempt to list the social benefits and costs of alternative courses of policy and to put prices on them as far as possible, are coming to have an accepted role in choosing between various methods of carrying out agreed aims, for example, the respective merits of underground railways and road improvements as means of dealing with urban traffic, or alternative sites for a third London airport. They are not adequate to deal with more fundamental choices, such as those concerning the amount to be spent on education as opposed to other social services such as the National Health Service, or other forms of public spending like defence or road building. Questions of general policy involving value judgments about the public welfare inevitably enter into such choices.

Controversy thus inevitably arises over the extent to which social service provisions should be made, and the forms which it should take, to maximize benefits and minimize costs, both private and social. This is the issue which lies behind the questions of policy which we have hinted at earlier; how far should the services be universal and how far selective, and how far they should be State provided and how far privately. We must return to them in more detail in the final chapter. But first, to gain perspective, it is useful to compare British experience with that of other countries with a similar economic, social and political background. In the next chapter, therefore, we look at some of the Western European countries, the United States and some of the developed Commonwealth countries, to see how they are tackling similar problems.

NOTES

1 A. T. Peacock and J. Wiseman, *The Growth of Public Expenditure in the United Kingdom* (Oxford University Press, 1961).
2 *Annual Abstract of Statistics, 1971*, based on Table 14.
3 *Public Expenditure, 1968–69 to 1973–74* (Cmnd 4234, HMSO, 1969), pp. 7–10.
4 *Public Expenditure, 1969–70 to 1974–75* (Cmnd 4578, HMSO, 1971), pp. 13–14.
5 These figures refer to non-retired households. Figures for retired households are similar.
6 Figures are not given for those groups of income range and family size where the number in the sample was less than ten.
7 Compare with the *National Plan* (Cmnd 2764, HMSO, 1965), Table 2–1, p. 24; and E. F. Denison, *Why Growth Rates Differ* (Brookings Institution, Washington, D.C., 1967), Table 21–17, p. 314.
8 Denison, loc. cit.
9 For a survey of the evidence, see C. V. Brown and D. A. Dawson, *Personal Taxation Incentives and Tax Reform* (P.E.P., London, 1969), Part Two, pp. 52–68.
10 The total includes net additions to dividend and interest reserves and tax reserves of businesses, but excludes stock appreciation. Source: *National Income and Expenditure, 1970*, Table 6.
11 Including National Insurance funds.

Chapter Eight

INTERNATIONAL COMPARISONS

The Welfare State is an international phenomenon. Similar factors to those which operated in Britain have led to a growth of Government expenditure on the social services, both in total and in relation to national product, at rates which in the developed industrial countries are remarkably alike. The less industrialized developing countries, with their much lower national incomes per head, are also much influenced by prevailing aspirations and are therefore constrained to spend on social services to a much greater relative extent than was the case in the West in the nineteenth century. Since conditions in these countries are, however, not comparable with those in Britain, we shall confine our comparisons to the countries of the developed West.

COMPARISONS OF SOCIAL SERVICE SPENDING

Table 8 gives some comparisons for recent years of the proportions of gross national product spent on the main branches of the social

TABLE 8 *Public expenditure on social services as a percentage of gross national product, in selected countries*

		Educa-tion	Health	Social security	Housing and com-munity amenities	Total
Austria	1966	3·9	4·1	14·1	2·2	24·3
France	1966	5·4	4·4	11·2	0·8	21·8
Japan	1965	4·0	1·7	4·2	0·4	10·3
Netherlands	1965	6·2	13·3		0·6	20·1
Norway	1966	6·0	2·0	12·1	0·1	20·2
Sweden	1965	6·0	4·3	9·2	2·7	22·2
Switzerland	1966	3·5	1·7	7·0	0·1	12·3
United Kingdom	1965	4·4	3·5	7·1	3·5	18·5
United States	1965	4·3	1·2	4·8	0·3	10·6

Source: *OECD Economic Outlook, Occasional Studies (July 1970)*; article on 'Public Expenditure Trends' by Mary Garin-Painter, Table 5.

services in a number of typical developed industrial countries in the mid-1960s.

The detailed figures for each class of expenditure cannot be compared too closely, for they reflect differences in the organization of services and the classification of expenditure by different governments. What stands out is the similarity in the general level of social service spending as a percentage of national product. In most cases it was around a fifth, a little more or less. The only exceptions were first Japan, where the lower level of income per head was reflected in a lower percentage, and where priority has been given to the industrial investment which has made possible the country's very fast rate of growth, rather than to social expenditure. Secondly, the United States and Switzerland also had lower percentages, reflecting in part a higher level of average income per head and in part a less developed concept of the Welfare State. Among the other more comparable countries the United Kingdom was in fact at the lower end of the scale, spending 18·5 per cent of national product, though this was for 1965, whereas figures for some of the other countries were for 1966. The main difference was that at that time we spent a smaller proportion of our product on social security than did our neighbours. This was before the introduction of earnings-related sickness and unemployment benefit and the replacement of National Assistance by Supplementary Benefits in 1966 but it is unlikely that the position has altered greatly. These figures also bring out the predominant part which social security spending has tended to play in most countries in total expenditure on the social services.

In the case of education, the proportion of national product absorbed by public spending does not vary very much, only between about 4 and 6 per cent. This is because the level of total educational provision in developed industrial countries is similar, and by far the greater proportion of the cost of providing it falls in the public sector. The differences which do appear, however, largely reflect variations in the proportion of private to public spending. Whereas in countries like Sweden, Norway and the Netherlands almost the whole cost of education, at least in the schools, is borne by the public purse, in Britain and the United States there is a sizable private sector. In Britain this is important at the secondary level, whereas in the United States it is found mainly at the tertiary level, which is in any case much more extensive there than it is in Europe.

In the case of health service expenditures, the differences in public provision between countries are much greater. The United States, Switzerland, Japan and Norway, for instance, spent only between 1 and 2 per cent of their national products on public personal health services, whereas the other countries spent from $3\frac{1}{2}$ to $4\frac{1}{2}$ per cent.

These figures reflect differences in the forms in which publicly provided health services are organized as well as differences in the extent
of provision. In the United States, for instance, government financial
responsibility on a national scale for personal spending on medical
treatment has begun only in the last few years, with the Medicare and
Medicaid schemes, mainly for the old. Other public provision is very
limited and mostly confined to treatment of the indigent under public
assistance. In Norway, on the other hand, the government in fact had
charge of a good deal more of current health expenditure than appears
in the above figure, since fees were charged for many services and
revenue from these is not included in public spending in the table. In
1965 fees covered almost 60 per cent of the cost of the services.

So far as Britain is concerned, the biggest difference between her
and the other European countries in the years in question lay in the
smaller proportion of her national product which was devoted to
social security, only 7 per cent as against 9 per cent in Sweden, 11 per
cent in France and 12 per cent in Norway and Austria. This figure
increased considerably in the next few years, with the introduction of
earnings-related sickness and unemployment benefits and supplementary benefits and the raising of family allowances, and by 1970 it
had reached 9 per cent. However, it was still relatively low compared
with those countries which had a more thorough-going earnings-
related system of benefits and contributions, instead of the basically
flat rate one which applied in Britain.

Table 9 shows some comparisons of average ratios of sickness

TABLE 9 *Average ratios of certain types of social security benefit
to average earnings, 1960 (Per cent of average weekly earnings)*

	Sickness benefit			Unemployment benefit	
	Single man	Married couple 2 children		Single man	Married couple 2 children
Netherlands	70	80	Netherlands	70	82
West Germany	65	75	West Germany	44	63
Austria	60	75	France*	59	76
Belgium	60	60	Italy	26	43
France	50	50	United Kingdom	27	59
Italy	50	50			
New Zealand	38	67			
Australia	23	45			
United Kingdom	23	48			

* In the case of unemployment benefit in France, both the statutory and the
non-statutory schemes are included.
Source: National Institute of Economic and Social Research, *Economic Review*
(August 1965).

benefit and unemployment benefit to average earnings rates in 1960, when the British system was entirely flat rate.

British rates of benefit relative to average earnings at that time compared very unfavourably with those in most of the other countries. This was more true in the case of single men than it was in that of married men with children, because Britain had fairly high dependants' allowances.

By the early 1960s the Western European countries had mostly also introduced more generous family allowances than those in Britain, at least before the big British increase of 1968. These were usually financed by earnings-related contributions paid wholly or mainly by the employer, though not in Scandinavia (nor in Germany after 1964) where family allowances were based, as in Britain, on the public service principle and financed wholly out of general taxation. Table 10 gives some comparisons for 1960 of the relationship in

TABLE 10 *Family allowances as a percentage of national income per head of the occupied population, 1960*

	Number of children				
	1	2	3	4	6
France	13·5	25·0	45·7	63·0	99·8
Italy	13·5	27·1	40·6	54·2	81·3
Belgium	7·7	16·2	30·5	45·5	81·0
Netherlands	5·3	11·1	16·9	24·8	41·6
West Germany	—	6·0	15·6	25·2	44·4
United Kingdom	—	3·8	8·6	13·4	22·9

Source: National Institute of Economic and Social Research, *Economic Review* (August 1965).

different countries between family allowances and average national income per head of the occupied population.

In France and Italy, for instance, and to a lesser extent in Belgium and the Netherlands, family allowances were big enough to make a very substantial difference to the average income of larger families. France, in particular, over and above its general system of allowances, has a system of additional allowances which are paid in cases of families with only one earner. In Britain at that time the addition to average incomes per head was comparatively slight.

Many countries in the 1960s had already introduced systems of graduated pensions intended to ensure that ultimately, when the scheme was fully in operation, those who retired would get pensions of up to two-thirds or three-quarters of their average earnings, over their whole working life or in the last few years, or some combination of the two. This was the case, for instance, in Germany, Belgium and Sweden. There is a distinction, however, between funded schemes such as that in Sweden where benefit entitlements are built up gradually, according to the number of years over which contributions have been paid, and the German approach where full pensions have been payable from the outset. Such schemes sometimes also include built-in adjustments to pension rates to take account of rises in the cost of living, and in the average level of earnings, after retirement. They are much more generous in their aims than the British system of flat-rate basic pensions, plus the very limited graduated additions introduced in 1961. The Labour Government's pension proposals of 1969–70, which were a casualty of the 1970 General Election, were based on similar principles.

TABLE 11 *Distribution of social security cash benefits between the main forms, 1960*

	Social insurance	Public assistance	Family allowances
West Germany	88	9	3
France	52	6	42
Belgium	73	1	26
Italy	64	3	32
Netherlands	72	7	21
United Kingdom	71	19	10

Source: National Institute of Economic and Social Research, *Economic Review* (August 1965).

As a result of these differences in the level of social insurance provision, social assistance under test of need and means has played a much larger part in British social security provision than it has in most parts of Western Europe, though it is more important in Scandinavia and also in North America than it is in the countries of the European Economic Community. The National Institute Economic Review article quoted above gives the figures above for 1960 which bring out clearly the difference between Britain and the EEC countries at that time. The greater role of social assistance in Britain, however, also reflects generally higher rates of assistance benefits than in many other countries, and hence a larger number of persons falling below the upper means limits of eligibility. This means that Britain comes out much more favourably in a comparison of minimum rates of social security benefit than it does in one of average rates. Those who are entitled to high earnings-related insurance benefits may do better in Europe, but those who depend on minimum rates of assistance do better in Britain.

Public assistance played a proportionately greater role in Britain than in any of the other countries covered and family allowances a smaller one than in any except West Germany. These figures, however, include in social assistance a number of social welfare expenditures on such items as school milk and child care. Since British expenditure on these items is relatively high, the figure for assistance for Britain is therefore inflated. The high level of social insurance benefits in West Germany shows up in a higher proportionate share of total expenditure than in any of the other countries, and the high level of family allowances in France shows up similarly.

VARIATIONS IN SOCIAL SERVICE PRINCIPLES AND POLICIES

The above comparisons make it clear that, within an overall picture of greatly increased spending on the social services, there are marked differences in the relative importance of various forms of expenditure. These in turn reflect differences in the principles on which the different services are organized and financed, and in the policies which underlie their provision. Comparisons between countries can be made clearer by bringing out some of these differences, which can be classified under the following headings.

Method of provision of services
scope of schemes
form of organization, single or multiple
direct provision of services as against cash grants or reimbursement of fees
methods of fixing benefit and contribution rates

These will be considered in turn and will be followed by a note on differences in housing policy, which do not fit easily into the above scheme.

METHOD OF PROVISION OF SERVICES

Three general principles can be distinguished on which services are provided, and most countries use all of them in varying combinations. These are social insurance, social assistance and public service principles.

Social insurance—that is the provision of benefits as of right to those who qualify by the payment of specified contributions, either by themselves, or their employers, or both.

This principle is used by most countries for their main systems of social security against old age, unemployment, sickness and dependence. There are certain exceptions, however, in Australia and New Zealand, the social assistance principle is the main one; in the countries of Eastern Europe, though there are contributions from employing enterprises, the system has many of the marks of the public service principle.

In many countries, including most of Western Europe apart from Britain, the provision of medical treatment is also carried out under social insurance, with insured contributors and their dependants having the right either to free treatment or to a refund of fees and charges wholly or in part. This method was used also in Britain before 1948, under the old National Health Insurance scheme, but was abandoned with the introduction of the National Health Service.

Social assistance—that is the provision of benefits financed out of general taxation, central or local, subject to test of the recipient's need and means.

In most countries this is the residual system, used to meet those cases of want or hardship not covered by other schemes. The extent of reliance on it therefore depends largely on how effective the social insurance and public service based schemes are in keeping the bulk of those whose means are inadequate above whatever minimum standards the country in question may have adopted. Thus Britain, with its tradition of flat-rate social insurance benefits, has made more use of National Assistance and Supplementary Benefits than most other European countries have done. In the United States, on the other hand, where social insurance schemes, though earnings-related, are limited both in scope of coverage and level of benefit, there is also great reliance on social assistance, though the provision for this is also limited in the types of need covered and varies considerably between states, both in level and coverage. A distinction can be made, however, between social assistance, strictly so called, providing means tested income maintenance based on a minimum standard of living, and other forms of social benefits on a means tested basis which usually have higher means limits and hence wider eligibility. The latter have both tended to grow in importance in recent years.

In Australia and New Zealand, for instance, social security has been generally based on a development of the social assistance principle and not on social insurance. In both countries there is a system of flat rates of benefit for all the main types of need, at comparatively high levels and usually subject to means test. In Australia they are financed out of general taxation, but in New Zealand out of a special proportional tax on incomes and on company profits.

In France also the statutory system of unemployment benefits is on an assistance and not an insurance basis, though there is also a voluntary scheme of social insurance against unemployment.

Supplementary use of means tests is also common in the case of many services in kind which are provided basically on the public service principle. Thus in Britain there are means tests for exemption from prescription charges and the charges for dental and ophthalmic treatment under the National Health Services, and also for eligibility for free school meals. Increasingly also, means tests are being used to relate eligibility for subsidized housing to income levels.

Public service—that is providing services as one of the rights of citizenship to all who are eligible, without test of means or contribution conditions, and financed out of general taxation.

This principle probably finds its most general application in the field of education, at least at the primary and secondary levels. Free schooling in publicly provided schools is here the rule, at least up to the minimum school leaving age, though access to education beyond this level may be more selective. An element of social assistance comes in, however, in the provisions for maintenance of senior pupils, which often involves parental means tests. The position in tertiary education is more complex. It is common for tuition to be provided on a public service basis in those cases where institutions are regarded as public bodies, though there is usually some form of selection of entrants on educational grounds. Thus in many European countries all those who qualify in the appropriate school-leaving examinations have the right to free university tuition and the same applies to the State universities in the United States (though not, of course, to the private ones). In British universities there are nominal fees, but the main part of running costs are borne by grants from the Exchequer, and the fees are covered by students grants. In general, the same principles apply to other forms of higher education also. Provision for students' maintenance, however, which is an important factor at this level of education, is more often subject to parental means test.

In the field of medical treatment, the British National Health Service is based on the public service principle for the most part, with the main forms of treatment being available to all free or at nominal charges, with no contribution conditions and with most of the cost borne directly either by the Exchequer or local rates. Health services are also provided on a public service basis in New Zealand and in the countries of Eastern Europe, and increasingly in Canada under various Dominion and provincial schemes. In most of Western Europe, as we have seen, health services are provided under social insurance, with entitlement to free treatment or refund of fees to those who are insured and their dependants.

The public service principle is less common in social security, though it is to be found in the British, Scandinavian and West German systems of family allowances. The social security systems of Eastern Europe also have public service elements in them, for although they are financed in part by percentage contributions on payroll by employing organizations, the State meets about half the cost directly and there are no contribution conditions nor contributions from employees.

Welfare services in many cases arose out of public assistance, services in kind for those in need being regarded as supplementary to cash relief. Hence they were often subject to means test, and this remains true in many countries. This is so in West Germany, where such services as residential accommodation, medical treatment for those not covered by social insurance, and care of handicapped where similarly not covered, are classed as 'social aid' and given under rather more generous means tests than social assistance in cash. In Britain, on the other hand, the trend has been to provide welfare services on a public service basis, without insurance contributions or test of means.

Housing policies are extremely complex and must be dealt with separately, but in general it is fair to say that these, too, whether they take the form of subsidized rents, loans for house purchase, rent controls or public building, contain a large measure of the public service principles, though also elements of social assistance in so far as rent subsidies are linked to incomes.

SCOPE OF SCHEMES

The extent to which social services cover the whole population or exclude certain groups is linked to the method of provision. The services which are based on the public service principle are usually available to all those in the categories covered, without any exclusions, as is the case with public education and the public service health services and family allowance systems. Social assistance services are normally available to all those in the categories of need covered who are not excluded by the means test, though there are variations in the categories of need which are in fact covered. Inadequate income alone is rarely accepted as a sufficient criterion of eligibility. Thus those in employment are usually excluded from public assistance, even though their income is below the accepted minimum.[1] In the United States, for instance, the coverage of public assistance schemes varies between states, and Federal grants-in-aid in supplementation of state resources are only paid for certain specific classes of need, such as the old, the blind, dependent children and the permanently disabled.

In the case of social insurance schemes, the scope of coverage is much more varied, and tends to reflect the history of the national system. In most countries, social insurance began with employed workers, but many groups of these were often originally excluded, notably white-collar employees above a certain income level (as in the British schemes), or agricultural workers, or domestic workers, or such categories as public employees or railway workers who had occupational pension schemes. In some cases, as in most of the Western European countries, there were separate schemes for different industries or different regions, or different religious and political groups, and these divisions may still remain.

The extent to which universality of coverage has been achieved depends in part on how far the service has been reorganized. In Britain, the replacement in 1948 of four separate schemes by a single system of National Insurance was accompanied by an extension of coverage to almost the whole population, including the self-employed and the non-employed (if they have a significant independent income) as well as the higher-paid non-manual employees who were formerly excluded. The fact that British benefits, especially pensions, were at fairly low flat rates, has meant that the national scheme was seen as complementary to professional pensions schemes and not alternative to them, so that there was no move for the exclusion of public employees and similar groups. The self-employed and the non-employed, however, are not eligible for the full range of benefits.

By and large this principle of wide general coverage also applies in the Scandinavian countries and in Eastern Europe. But in many Western European countries the self-employed are only partially covered and the non-employed are often excluded altogether. In some cases higher-paid earners, State employees and others in special schemes are also excluded. In Eastern Europe also coverage tends to be confined to employees, though there is often special provision for members of collective farms and agricultural co-operatives and sometimes also for self-employed craftsmen. In the United States domestic servants and casual agricultural workers are excluded from Old Age, Survivors and Dependants Insurance, as are the self-employed above a low income level, while public employees are separately covered; unemployment insurance has further exclusions which vary from state to state.

There are also variations in scope in terms of the range of risks covered. Most of the fully developed schemes of social security cover old age, sickness and invalidity, industrial injury, unemployment and family allowances, but there are a number of exceptions. In the United States, for instance, sickness benefit in cash is found only in one or two states, medical benefit is confined by and large to the old and the indigent and there are no family allowances. In Eastern Europe there is no unemployment benefit, except in Yugoslavia, Hungary and Bulgaria, it being an assumption that under Socialism there can be no unemployment. Japan has no family allowances. Medical benefits do not always provide free service or reimbursement of charges for all types of treatment. The extent to which free educational opportunities are available above the minimum school leaving age varies considerably, while the scope of public responsibility for the provision of housing varies even more.

FORM OF ORGANIZATION, SINGLE OR MULTIPLE

Closely associated with the scope of schemes, and reflecting the same historical factors, is the form of organization of the services, that is how far they are organized into single schemes covering the whole country and how far they are separate for different areas, industries, social groups or types of risk.

Education is perhaps the most generally unified of the services in its form of organization. In most countries the publicly provided schools form a single system under a national Minister of Education, though in federal countries like the United States, Canada, Australia, West Germany and Switzerland, education is primarily the responsibility of the states, provinces, cantons or *Länder*.[2] The degree of devolution also varies within nominally unified systems. In France education is centrally organized and tightly controlled from the national level and this tradition is common in those parts of Western Europe which share the same centralized tradition. In Britain, though the central Government decides the general lines of policy and the national Education Departments have general control over finance and great influence over how the system works, the local education authorities have a high degree of autonomy. This tradition is followed in the United States also and in the countries of overseas British settlement and also in Scandinavia. In the United States, in fact, the local school districts have a good deal more autonomy than British education authorities do.

In some countries the national school system includes large numbers of schools controlled in varying degrees by churches and other voluntary bodies, even though they are wholly or largely financed by the State. Thus in the Netherlands all schools are maintained by the State, but there are three separate systems organized by the local authorities and the Protestant and Roman Catholic churches. In Ireland also, both in the Republic and in the North, publicly supported Church schools form a large part of the system, especially at secondary level. In Scotland since 1918 the State has provided a separate system of Roman Catholic schools as part of the public school service, whereas in England and Wales the Church schools are still provided by the Church authorities, though the State pays 75 per cent of the capital cost and all the current operating cost.

These differences reflect historical factors and the varying roles of State and Church in the school provision of the past. In other countries, like France and the United States, where there is a much stronger tradition of the separation of Church and State, public support for private schools is often politically controversial, or even impossible.

In the case of health services, the form of organization tends to reflect the principle on which the system is based. In those countries where the public service principle prevails, such as Britain, New Zealand and the countries of Eastern Europe, organization tends to be on a unified basis, though, as we have seen to be the case in Britain, there may be a functional division. In fact, the more capital-intensive hospital service, in which salaried service prevails, is usually more highly centralized than the general practitioner services, with their jealously-preserved traditions of the freedom of the independent professional man.

Where the provision of medical benefits forms part of social security, the form of organization naturally reflects that of the social security system. In many of the Western European countries there is a tradition of separate sickness benefit funds, organized on the basis of industries and occupations or local areas, and sometimes also on a religious or political basis. Thus in the Netherlands in 1967 there were some 115 approved sickness funds and in West Germany some 2,000, and the pattern is similar in Belgium and France.

In the case of social security, as we saw above, the extent of centralization often reflects the extent to which an original system of separate funds has been reorganized on a unified basis. This was what happened in Britain in 1948 and was carried further in 1966, so that we now have two nation-wide National Insurance Funds and a nation-wide system of Supplementary Benefits and Family Allowances, all controlled and operated by one ministry. The same is true of the centralized systems of social security to be found in Eastern Europe, and of the centralized social assistance systems of Australia and New Zealand. In the United States, where social security is less extensive, there remain the original separate systems of Old Age,

Survivors and Dependants Insurance and of Unemployment Insurance, the former being purely Federal and the latter jointly Federal and State operated. A similar pattern of separate nationally-operated systems for health and pensions and for unemployment is to be found in Canada.

In much of Western Europe the tradition of separate local, industrial and sometimes political or religious funds, supervised by national authorities, remains predominant. This is especially true in the case of sickness cash benefits, which are closely associated with the funds administering medical benefits. It also applies to old age pensions in France, which are administered through local and regional funds, and in West Germany, where they are administered by the *Länder*. In most other cases old age pensions are centrally administered. In the Netherlands, however, invalidity pensions are administered separately for each industry. Unemployment benefit, on the other hand, is generally centrally administered, in connection with the national systems of employment exchanges, but it is operated through trade union funds in Sweden, Denmark and Finland.

Welfare services are normally decentralized, being operated through local authorities and local social security and health agencies. Housing services also tend to be decentralized in operation, though in most other countries the role of local authorities is less than in Britain and that of special Government housing agencies and of co-operatives and housing associations is greater.

DIRECT PROVISION OF SERVICES AS AGAINST CASH GRANTS OR REIMBURSEMENT OF FEES

In many cases governments have the alternative on the one hand of providing services in kind, free or at nominal prices, through their own agencies or, on the other, of providing cash benefits out of which goods and services can be bought, or reimbursing the charges incurred for the purchase of such goods and services.

In the case of social security, cash benefits are the normal rule, for the aim is to provide an income to those whose means are inadequate and leave them free to spend it as they wish. The giving of benefits in kind is limited to marginal cases, like free school meals or milk, where it is felt that there is an advantage in providing a particular good to those who otherwise might not get it adequately. Earlier practices, such as the provision of grocery tickets to families in need, are usually regarded as interfering with the family's freedom of choice in the way it spends its income. It is in fields like education and medical treatment, where the aim is to provide specific services believed to be socially desirable, to which those with low incomes do not have adequate access, that the choice arises.

In the case of education, direct provision of services normally applies at the school level. Schools are normally built and maintained, and teachers paid, by the State and its agencies, and education is provided free. This is true even where, as in the Netherlands, there are several parallel publicly provided school systems. Historically, this arises from a number of factors. Private, fee-paying school systems proved themselves manifestly incapable of providing mass education for all. In many countries, the public school system was seen as part of the process of nation-building, producing a population educated not only in reading, writing and arithmetic, but also in the country's history, traditions and aspirations. Thus in the United States the schools played a large part in the working out of the melting-pot concept, merging the children of immigrants into a common American culture. In Prussia, and later in Germany, they trained diligent, patriotic workpeople for the Reich. In France they spread the ideals of republican citizenship, as against the monarchist traditions of the past.

Moreover, education has long been organized on the basis of a salaried service, with often considerable numbers of teachers in one school, under a head teacher who is himself an employee, rather than on the basis of the self-employed professional, as in law and medicine. With the spread of public education from the primary to the secondary level, the sphere of the cash grant and the reimbursement of fees has tended to contract, till it is now only found in special cases, as where education authorities pay for children to go to independent schools. It is more common in the tertiary sector, where the payment of cash grants to students attending fee-charging institutions is often found, and where maintenance grants become more important. Thus in Britain part of the income of the universities comes from fees charged to students, who are reimbursed through their grants.

Although there has been considerable theoretical attention given to the possibilities of replacing direct public provision of free educational services by some system of cash grants or educational vouchers, there are few signs of such policies being put into practice. The whole historical trend of public education seems to be against such a change.

In the medical services, where private enterprise proved equally inadequate to meet mass needs, the tradition of the independent self-employed practitioner was predominant, apart from specific public services like the medical officers of health and the medical branches of the armed forces. This was especially true at the general practitioner level, though it is also applied to consultants in the voluntary

149

hospitals. It is reflected in the fact that in many countries those who receive medical treatment must pay doctors' fees and then claim reimbursement in whole or in part from their social security funds. This applies in France and Belgium, for instance, to all forms of treatment, and in Norway and Sweden to general practitioner and hospital out-patient treatment.

Other counties have chosen to go in for a system of public provision of services more analogous to that in education. In Britain, under the National Health Service, the hospital and local authority services are mostly on a full-time salaried basis, while general practitioners operate under a contract system, receiving capitation fees or treatment fees direct from the State and not receiving any remuneration from patients, even in those cases where they have to collect charges, as for prescriptions and dental and ophthalmic treatment. Similar systems exist in Germany, Denmark and Italy, in the countries of Eastern Europe and in Canada. In New Zealand the system is mainly on this basis, but there is some refund of fees to patients.

The welfare services, since they are intended to provide special help appropriate to particular disadvantaged groups, such as the old, children in need of care, families in difficulty, or the handicapped, by their nature involve mainly the provision of services in kind. Housing, on the other hand, being only in part a social service and involving the use of costly and long-lived capital assets, is not normally regarded as suitable for free provision and the usual method of giving benefit is by subsidy to rents for tenants or help with loans for owner-occupiers. There is a difference in approach, however, between the free market economies and the socialist economies. In the countries of the West, although subsidies to housing are often extensive and sometimes in practice indiscriminate, in principle the norm is regarded as being one of economic rents, with subsidies as an exception, intended to help those who are for various reasons cannot get access to adequate housing on fully economic terms. In the socialist countries housing tends to be regarded as in principle more of a social service and rents are consistently kept at a low level, well below the economic figure, with housing being allocated administratively.

METHODS OF FIXING BENEFIT AND CONTRIBUTION RATES

In the case of cash benefits, whether they are financed on the social insurance, the social assistance or the public service basis, the problem arises of how the rate of benefit should be fixed. Although there are differences of practice on such matters as the extent of provision of dependants allowances and the level of dependants allowances relative to benefits for single persons, the main difference of principle is between income-related and flat rate benefits.

In the case of social insurance, the predominant principle is that of income-related benefits. These are the general rule in the countries of the European Economic Community, though in the Netherlands the retirement pension is on a flat-rate basis, and the aim is usually to provide a level of income in the event of interruption of earnings which bears a reasonable relationship to average earnings, at least up to a certain maximum income level. In the case of sickness and unemployment benefits, this is usually at least 50 per cent and sometimes much more, e.g. 80 per cent in the Netherlands. In West Germany sickness benefit is 65 to 75 per cent of earnings, according to the length of time off work, plus dependants allowances, while unemployment benefit varies inversely with the average level of earnings. Sickness benefit for the first six weeks, however, in West Germany, is now provided completely by the employer and is at the rate of the full wage or salary. In the case of old age pensions, the maximum rate is usually similar, but the rates for those who have been insured for shorter periods is normally less. The two social insurance schemes in the United States are also earnings-related, though the fixing of fairly low maximum income figures above which the benefits become flat rate means that the actual percentage of earnings received by beneficiaries is not very high. In most cases where the income-related principle prevails, provision is however made for minimum and maximum benefit rates, below which and above which benefits become flat rate. This is to ensure that those with low earnings are guaranteed a basic minimum and those with high earnings do not exceed a maximum.

In a number of countries where the basic old age pension is on a flat rate, realization of the need for income maintenance in retirement has led to this being supplemented by an income-related pension, entitlement to which is built up as years of contribution continue. This is the position in Canada and Sweden, and something similar applies also in Norway and Denmark. The British graduated pension scheme of 1961 is a small step in the same direction and the earnings-related sickness and unemployment supplements of 1966 are a considerably larger one.

There is normally a maximum income level above which graduation of benefit is not carried, so that for those above this level benefits become flat rate. If this is fixed fairly low, therefore, the extent of income-related benefit is not very great. In the case of old age pensions, benefits tend to be related to average earnings over the working life, sometimes by some formula which gives greater weight

151

to later years of higher earnings than to earlier years when they were lower. The rate of benefit usually also depends on the number of years for which contributors have been assured. There may or may not be provisions for adjusting the pensions of those already retired, according to changes in the average earnings of the working population or in the cost of living.

Social assistance payments, which are usually regarded as supplementary to social insurance and intended to deal with needs not met by it, are generally at flat rates, subject of course to reduction according to the recipients' means.[3] In New Zealand and Australia, where social assistance at fairly high rates replaces social insurance, the benefits are nevertheless at flat rates; and this is also true of the social assistance based statutory system of unemployment benefit in France. Similarly, in those cases where cash benefits are paid on a public service basis, as in the British and West German family allowances, the payments are unrelated to income levels, though the rate per child increases with the number of children.

Income-related benefits are not normally found outside the field of social security. In the case of benefits in kind, like education, medical treatment and welfare services, the quality and quantity of the service to be supplied is related to the needs of the recipient, as assessed by expert judgment, and the whole aim is to get away from a situation in which those with higher incomes can get more or better schooling or doctoring than those with lower incomes. Where incomes are taken into account, there is more likely to be an inverse relationship, as when certain types of free services are made subject to a means test, or when a test of parents' means is applied to educational maintenance grants. A similar principle lies behind rebate schemes as applied to rents for subsidized housing.

In social insurance schemes where benefits are related to earnings, it is normal for contributions to be earnings-related also, while flat-rate benefits usually mean flat-rate contributions. In the case of social insurance, however, there is scope for further variation, in the extent to which contributions are shared between insured persons, employers and the State. The tripartite system, so well established in Britain, is not so firmly accepted in most other countries.

Government contributions out of general taxation are by no means universal. In France, the Government makes no direct contribution to the cost of social insurance benefits, though it bears the whole cost of unemployment assistance. In the United States also there is no Exchequer contribution, except that the Federal Government pays the administrative costs of the State unemployment insurance schemes. In most of the other countries of Western Europe the Government makes a contribution to some of the insurance funds but not to others, and the extent of its contribution varies considerably.

In general, most countries accept the principle of contribution by both insured persons and employers, but there are also important exceptions to this. Thus in France the whole cost of the very generous family allowances to employees is met by the employers,[4] and this is true of Italy also, though there there is a government subsidy towards allowances for agricultural employees. In Belgium and the Netherlands employees make no contribution to family allowances, but the Government shares the cost with the employers. In the United States, the costs of unemployment insurance fall entirely on the employers, except for the cost of administration, and there is a system of merit rating, by which employers' contributions vary inversely with their unemployment record. Employers also in most countries bear the whole or most of the cost of insurance against industrial injuries, for, unlike the position in Britain, the principle of employers' liability has usually been retained in the present-day statutory schemes.

In the countries of Eastern Europe the normal pattern is that the cost of social insurance benefit is met in part by percentage contributions on payroll paid by enterprises, with the Government meeting the rest of the cost; there are no contributions from insured persons. In Hungary and Russia, however, insured persons also make contributions towards pensions and sickness benefits.

VARIATIONS IN HOUSING POLICY

Since housing is in a kind of half-way position between the social services and the ordinary commercial market, it cannot easily be fitted into the above analysis of various aspects of social service policy. In fact, the differences between the housing policies of different countries largely reflect the extent to which the Government has found it appropriate to intervene in the commercial market. At the one extreme comes a country like the United States, where housing is mainly a matter of private ownership or renting and public intervention has been both limited and sporadic. At the other extreme are the countries of Eastern Europe, where urban housing at least is regarded as a public service, to be provided by enterprises and public authorities at very low rents.

Most of the countries of Western Europe come somewhere in between, with the majority of houses privately owned; public ownership in various forms is also on a large scale, and a well established system of rent control, rent subsidies and other forms of aids and regulations, arising out of wartime and post-war shortages, population movements and concern for slum clearance exists.

So far as the countries of Western Europe are concerned, Professor Donnison, in his book *The Government of Housing*, suggests that there are two types of attitude towards housing policy which in varying degrees are characteristic of the different governments. There is first of all what he calls a social housing policy, which he associates with countries like Britain, Switzerland, Ireland and Belgium, in which there is a large stock of existing houses, relatively slow growth of population and relatively little internal migration, as well as a well-developed market for housing. Hence housing policy is still thought of primarily as a matter of intervening in a basically free market to aid selected groups which cannot adequately help themselves. It may involve, as in Britain, large-scale government intervention in the provision of subsidies, large-scale local authority building of houses and extensive tax assistance to mortgage borrowers. Or, as in Switzerland, it may involve only limited subsidies to borrowers in a well organized and active private market for housing finance. In both cases, however, the underlying assumptions are similar.

With this he contrasts the more comprehensive housing policies developed in, for instance, France, the Netherlands, West Germany and Scandinavia, where for various reasons housing needs have come to be felt as something affecting the whole nation. This may be because of wartime destruction of houses, as in Germany and the Netherlands, or, as in France, because a long period of neglect and low rents has led to poor housing standards, or, as in Scandinavia, because of rapid urbanization and population movements. There is usually also an absence of an adequate private market for housing capital. Such conditions lead governments to an overall assessment of the country's housing needs, an overall planning of housing programmes, a mobilization of savings and the channelling of them into meeting those forms of need which are most urgent, and the use of taxation and subsidies for the same purposes. The Government may itself commission or build large numbers of new houses, or it may, as in West Germany, build none itself, but in all cases control and direct a comprehensive programme.

The distinction is not a clear-cut one and most countries have elements of both approaches. Britain, for instance, developed something like a comprehensive policy in the early post-war years, then veered away from it in the direction of encouraging the private market and confining public intervention mainly to slum clearance. In recent years she shows signs of groping towards a comprehensive policy again. The proposals to base local authority rent policies on the fair rent principle of the 1965 Rent Act, and to make subsidies available to private and local authority tenants alike on an income basis, are further examples of the same trend.

Because of different historical backgrounds and institutional structures, the actual methods of public housing provision vary greatly. Most countries have tried to avoid the kind of polarization between subsidized local authority houses to rent, subsidies through tax relief to owner-occupiers buying on mortgage, and rent controls but no subsidies for the tenants of private landlords. In Britain, this has tended to segregate the population into rigid groups according to housing category. It has been more common to work through a wide variety of institutions, such as housing associations and co-operatives, and to make use of a range of tax reliefs, loans and subsidies, to owner-occupiers and to private landlords and to tenants of both privately owned and publicly owned houses. Thus there tends to be greater flexibility. These differences arise in part because in most European countries there is less tradition of local authority independence than in Britain and hence more direct central control. Also there is, in many cases, a less well-developed system of financial institutions to provide loans for house purchase.

In the United States public housing policy has been more limited and more sporadic than in Europe. Housing provision is primarily a matter of the commercial market and increasingly of owner-occupancy. Public intervention is largely confined to regulating and facilitating access to house purchase loans and to the clearance of the worst slum areas. Public building of housing for renting by low income groups is very limited, and there is a tendency to rely on private enterprise for the redevelopment of cleared areas, with the result that the needs of the poorest are not met.

In the Communist countries of Eastern Europe the provision of housing is naturally treated as an integral part of Government investment policy, along with the building of factories and the provision of public utilities and social services. Since urbanization has proceeded very fast and since housing has had a low priority relative to industrial investment, the standard of housing that can be provided is often relatively low, especially in terms of the amount of space per family. In the towns, where flats are the rule, they are mainly built and owned by Government agencies, enterprises and co-operatives, but rents are generally very low, housing being treated as a social service and allocated according to need. In rural areas most houses are owner-occupied even where, as in Russia, the peasants are organized into collective farms; owner-occupancy of country villas by those who can afford them is also allowed.

HOW DOES BRITAIN COMPARE WITH OTHER COUNTRIES?

In the field of social security Britain has secured certain advantages from the thorough-going re-organization of her services which took place in 1948. The British system is more comprehensive than that of most other countries, in that it includes almost all types of levels of income-receivers within one scheme and aims to provide them all with the appropriate range of benefits on the same terms. It is also much simpler in organization, consisting of only two closely associated nation-wide funds; it thus avoids the proliferation of separate funds based on industries, areas and social groupings characteristic of many European countries. Protagonists of the European systems would, however, maintain that these reflect a different ideal, namely that of mutual self-help by groups associated on the basis of a common interest, as against the Beveridge conception of social security as one of rights of national citizenship.

On the other hand the British system has been less successful than those of Western Europe in ensuring to the bulk of its members a level of benefit, when they cannot earn, which does not represent a serious drop in their living standards. As a corollary of this, much more weight has been placed in Britain on the need to supplement social insurance benefits by means-tested social assistance payments. This is bound up with the fact that we have continued with a basically flat-rate system of benefits and contributions, whereas most other countries have used earnings-related systems, particularly for old age pensions.

High rates of benefit have, however, not been achieved without high rates of contribution. In particular, many European countries have put a much higher burden on employers. Table 12 gives some comparisons of revenue from social security contributions in relation to gross national product.

The large share of the national product that is absorbed by social security contributions in many West European countries is clearly borne out. In France, for instance, it is over three times as large in total, and over four times as large as it falls on employers, as it is in Britain or the United States; in West Germany it is more than twice as large in total and about two and a half times as large on employers. When making such comparisons, however, one must remember the relative scope of the services thus financed. In many countries where social security contributions are high, they include most of the cost of medical benefits, which in Britain are mostly financed directly by the Exchequer and in the United States are not provided at all. Family allowances also are paid out of employers' contributions in France,

TABLE 12 *Social security contributions as a percentage of gross national product, 1967*

	Total social security contributions	Contributions by employers
France	17·4	12·7
Netherlands	14·6	10·5
Italy	12·1	not available
West Germany	12·0	6·2
Norway	9·0	5·5
Belgium	9·8	6·8
Austria	9·4	7·5
Sweden	8·1	4·2
United States	5·7	2·9
United Kingdom	5·5	2·8
Switzerland	5·3	1·8
Japan	3·9	2·4
Canada	3·8	2·1
Denmark	2·2	0·8

Source: 'International Comparison of Taxes and Social Security Contributions', *Economic Trends* (May 1969), Table D, p. xix.

whereas in Britain and West Germany they are borne by the Exchequer and in the United States are not paid.

Britain is also distinctive in the comprehensiveness of the medical treatment provided to all under the National Health Service without contribution conditions, either free or at charges which are still nominal in spite of recent increases. This system has the advantage of placing fewer financial barriers in the way of obtaining treatment than in many countries, of requiring fees to be paid which must be reclaimed from the Social Security Funds. It also covers people who may not be included in a social insurance scheme.

Some have criticized the British system on the grounds that it also provides free benefits to many who could and would afford to pay the economic cost of medical treatment, or could provide for it by private insurance. Thus, at a time when the cost of medical treatment is rising fast, this reliance mainly on public funds may mean a slower growth in the nation's total spending on medical services than would be possible if part of the cost was privately met. Hence rationing by purse may be replaced by rationing by waiting time and queues.

Thus the Office of Health Economics, using statistics from the World Health Organization, has pointed out that in 1967–68 the

United States spent about 6·7 per cent of its gross national product on public and private provision of health services, Canada 7¼ per cent and Sweden 6¼ per cent, whereas France spent 4·9 per cent and the United Kingdom 4·7 per cent. Not only so, but whereas in the 'sixties annual expenditure on health services in money terms was growing at an average rate of 14·0 per cent in Sweden, 13·2 per cent in France, 11·8 per cent in Canada and 10·4 per cent in the United States, in Britain it was growing only at an average of 9·2 per cent. Thus not only did Britain devote a smaller proportion of her national product to health services than did countries like the United States, Canada and Sweden, where average income per head is considerably higher, but its spending was growing more slowly than in these countries. It was also growing more slowly than it was in France, where average income per head and the proportion of the product devoted to health were much the same as in Britain, but where the national product was growing faster.[5]

These figures include all forms of spending, private as well as public, and whether the public services are financed directly by the State as in Britain, or by reimbursement of fees as in France and Sweden. Hence to compare the relative effectiveness of health service provision one would need to know not only the relationship of health spending to national product, but also the distribution of the benefits of this spending between income levels and social classes and types of medical treatment. One would also need to know the relative movements of the costs of providing the services in different countries, as reflected in the fees and incomes of doctors and other practitioners. The fact that the United States, for instance, spends a greater proportion of its national product than Britain on medical services, and that this expenditure is growing faster, certainly does not necessarily mean that the bulk of the population, and in particular those less well off, are in fact getting better treatment. It may reflect in part a bidding up of the cost of medical service as a result of a rising demand from the better-off, who can afford to pay fees for doctors and for hospital treatment.

In fact, the slower rate of growth of health spending in Britain probably reflects above all the slower rate of growth of the national product, which makes it less easy to set aside the resources needed to provide for a service on which spending is everywhere growing faster than the national product. The evidence thus leaves open the question of how best to divert an increasing share of the country's spending to the needs of medical treatment and what the respective roles of public and private spending should be in this.

In the field of education Britain is facing much the same problems as the rest of Western Europe and is tackling them in much the same way. In all cases, the school system is overwhelmingly State-provided, though the private sector is bigger in Britain than in most other countries. All these countries face the problem of a rapid rise in the proportion of pupils staying on in full-time secondary education after the minimum school-leaving age. Hence the question arises of how far secondary education should continue on its traditional selective basis and how far it should become comprehensive, as it has always tended to be in North America. The evidence suggests that Britain has gone further in the direction of accepting comprehensiveness as a general principle than most other European countries. In all cases there is also the related problem of the growing demand for higher and further education and of the part to be played in meeting this by the universities and by other types of institution. Here Britain is perhaps more selective than certain other countries, such as France, where there is a stronger tradition that all those who pass the qualifying school-leaving examination have the right to enter the university. A higher percentage of university entrants is, however, counterbalanced by a much higher wastage rate of students during their course, and in the proportion of graduates completing their courses relative to the age group, Britain compares much more favourably.

In those countries where the organization of education is more centralized, changes in structure are often more dramatic. Thus France completely reorganized her secondary school system in 1959 and 1966, and her university system in 1968 (after the May disturbances had shown up its defects). In Britain, where local education authorities and universities have much more autonomy, changes in policy take place more slowly and experimentally.

Perhaps the biggest contrast is that between Western Europe and North America. In spite of the growing trend towards staying on longer at school, it is still the case that only a minority of the 15–18 age group are in full-time education in Europe, whereas in the United States and Canada it is the majority. Similarly the proportion of the over-18s in full time tertiary education in North America is much higher than in Europe, but here there is the added difference that a sizable proportion of American tertiary education is in the private sector.

In housing the main lesson from the experience of other countries is that a more comprehensive approach is required. It is not enough to confine public financial involvement to the provision of subsidies for local authority rents and tax reliefs for owner-occupiers buying on mortgage; this means that the poorest and those who find it most difficult to get adequate housing get least help. Nor is it enough to apply rent controls only to particular types of privately-owned rented houses. Although there is a good deal of uncertainty as to what the scope of the commercial market can effectively be in the housing field, and to what extent housing must be treated as a social service, Governments are being forced to take an overall view of the housing needs of all classes and areas in their communities, and of all forms of housing provision.

In the light of these comparisons between social policies and achievements in Britain and other comparable countries, we turn now to an appraisal of the position of thinking and policy on the Welfare State in Britain in the early 1970s. What are the problems which remain to be faced? How do recent organizational changes, following the change of government in 1970, suggest that they will be tackled? This will form the subject matter of the last chapter.

NOTES

1 The Family Income Supplement, introduced in Britain in 1971, is a deliberate departure from this practice, since it is intended to supplement the means of those who are at work.
2 Britain also, though a unitary State, has three separate education systems, in England and Wales, Scotland and Northern Ireland.
3 In West Germany, unemployment assistance benefits, however, are wage-related, though at lower rates than in the case of unemployment insurance.
4 The cost of family allowances for the self-employed in France is borne by contributions from the insured persons themselves.
5 Office of Health Economics, *Information Sheet 9* (September 1970).

Chapter Nine

THE FUTURE OF THE WELFARE STATE

THE UNSOLVED PROBLEMS

In our survey of the achievements and limitations of the Welfare State in Britain in Chapters Five, Six and Seven we found many deep-seated and complex problems yet to be tackled. Chapter Eight showed that many of these are common to all the countries of the developed world. It is useful to categorize them under the three main headings of rising aspirations, the continuance of poverty and inequality of opportunity, and growing strain on available resources.

RISING ASPIRATIONS

As incomes rise, even if not so far as was hoped, and as the social services develop, so the aspirations of those concerned in them and of the general public tend to rise. This is a self-reinforcing process, for the introduction of improved services, whether in education, medical treatment, welfare or social security, tends in itself to open up new forms of need and new prospects of further improvement and development. Once we extend secondary education in principle to all, we find that to make it a reality we must greatly improve the secondary schools attended by the bulk of the pupils and raise the school leaving age. Once access to higher education becomes less limited, the scope for extending it further and raising its quality comes to be realized and there are calls for more university places, more polytechnics, more colleges of all kinds. Once medical treatment becomes available without barrier of charge, the progress of medicine leads to calls for more costly forms of treatment to become more widely available, at the same time as the bottlenecks in the way of treating all those who need treatment become clear. Once welfare services begin to try to meet the needs of the old, the deprived children and the handicapped, more and more problems are uncovered, which could be tackled if money and manpower were available. As for housing, all our efforts so far seem only to be running to stay where we are in face of the creation of new slums, and new problems of overcrowding, sub-letting and the plight of the homeless.

At one time public opinion was all too ready to accept many of these evils as inevitable, or not the proper business of the State to interfere with. But our standards and our aspirations are higher now, and our knowledge of conditions is greater. We are less ready to accept such conditions as compatible with a reasonably prosperous Britain in the late twentieth century.

CONTINUANCE OF CONSIDERABLE POVERTY AND INEQUALITY OF OPPORTUNITY

Against the pattern of rising aspirations must be set the growing evidence of considerable continuing poverty and lack of opportunity. It seems clear that over the past twenty years the rise in average incomes and the official poverty line has been accompanied by an increase, rather than a fall, in the number of those falling below the supplementary benefit minimum level. This is not only due to failure of those entitled to supplementary benefits to claim them, which has been especially true in the case of retirement pensioners. Perhaps more disquietingly, it is also due to a low level of earnings for many of those at work, who are hence not eligible for social security benefits, except for family allowances and the new family income supplement. And this has applied not only where there is a large family with only one earner, but in an appreciable number of cases of families with only one or two children.

Nor has the extension of the services in kind guaranteed equality of opportunity. In the field of education, this has been the main burden of the criticism of selective secondary schools. It is also clear that children and young people from less favoured home backgrounds have deep-rooted disadvantages, which have been accentuated by the poor quality of the schools in many of the poorer areas of our cities. In the health services this is less acutely true, but quality standards still vary between areas, and the better-off can get access to private treatment. The welfare services are still in their infancy, but because resources are very limited, their extent and quality varies greatly and they are not adequate to offset the disadvantages under which many families labour. In housing, where public policy has often been uncertain in its aims and confused in its methods, inequality is even greater and the adverse effects of slums and overcrowding even more serious.

GROWING STRAIN ON AVAILABLE RESOURCES

There is thus a growing realization that more could be done and more should be done. Yet the developments already carried out and those clearly in prospect are already placing a great strain on our

162

resources. Expenditure on the social services has been growing about twice as fast as the national product, and the increase in the numbers of young people and old people in the population, together with the trend towards making fuller use of the services, will in themselves lead to a continued increase. The national product itself has been growing only slowly, and though it is to be hoped that the rate of growth can be raised from its average of $2\frac{1}{2}$ per cent or so, no one writing in 1972 would be very sanguine about this. Meanwhile there is pressure to keep down the growth of public spending, in order to set resources free for the exports we need to pay our way in the world, and to reduce the serious pressure of cost inflation in the economy. For the same reasons tax rates have been kept high, to produce a deflationary budget surplus; there is a desire to cut them, in order to give incentives to saving and business enterprise, rather than to keep them up to provide the means for more spending on social services.

There thus exists a serious problem of how to divert resources from private spending on consumption and investment, if the means are to be found to extend and improve the social services. This has led to considerable rethinking about what should be the relative roles of public and private spending in fields such as education, health and social security. Comparisons with other countries, which have had both a faster rate of growth of national product, and a more rapid rise in the share of it going to such services, have given further point to this discussion.

THE POLARIZATION OF APPROACHES TO THE WELFARE STATE

In the face of these problems, recent years have seen a tendency towards a polarization of attitudes into two contrasting approaches, which have come to be loosely associated with the policies of the two main political parties. These, which can be roughly labelled the 'liberal' and the 'collectivist' approach, are in some ways parallel to the selectivist-universalist dichotomy discussed in Chapter Six. In some ways, however, they cut across it, since they are concerned more with the proper role of the State than with the methods of provision of benefits. The labels are placed in inverted commas, since both words have multiple overtones, not all of which are reflected in this particular usage.

THE 'LIBERAL' VIEW

In describing the position of the holders of this view the word 'liberal' is used in the sense, more common in Continental Europe, of a belief in the overriding importance of the free market. Thus, while accepting that there is a public interest in ensuring that all have access to an adequate minimum of income and reasonable equality of opportunity, they would also place great weight on freedom of choice in the spending of incomes and on the virtues of the market in promoting the efficient allocation of resources. Hence, at a time of generally rising incomes, they would maintain that more and more people and families will want, and should be encouraged, to decide for themselves what type of provision they wish to make for their old age, what sort of medical treatment they prefer for themselves and their children, what kind of education they want their children to have. They would place great emphasis on the bureaucratic wastes and inefficiencies which are likely to arise when services are provided without charge and when the allocation of resources is left to administrative decision. They would maintain that more efficient allocation would be secured if greater scope were given to the price system and purchase through the market.

In terms of practical policy, those who hold this view would accept the necessity, for instance, of basic minimum State social benefits for those who cannot earn. They would want the State system to confine itself to basic flat-rate benefits, however, and would see the provision of above-the-minimum, earnings-related benefits as being more appropriately made by encouraging occupational pension schemes jointly financed by employees and employers. They would want to see suitable provision to make such pension cover fully transferable between employers, and might well advocate that it be made compulsory for all employers. For those not covered by social insurance or occupational schemes, they would advocate an improvement in the system of social assistance based on test of need and means, possibly working towards some form of negative income tax to get over the problems of means tests and failure to claim.

In the health services, they would want a greater emphasis on payment for services by recipients, whether by extension of National Health Service charges, or by giving encouragement through tax remissions to those who want to make use of private medical treatment. Some would envisage the replacement of the National Health Service, at least in part, by a compulsory system of private insurance against the costs of medical treatment, with free services confined to those below a certain income level or to certain special categories.

It is in the field of education that some of the most characteristic proposals have been made. Accepting that there is a public interest in securing adequate educational opportunities for all, and that this implies that education should be free, and compulsory up to a certain age, ingenious schemes have been proposed to combine this with freedom of choice. This could be done, it is maintained, through a system of vouchers, covering the cost of education, which could be issued to parents to spend at the school of their choice. They could be perhaps supplemented by payment of fees if they wanted some special kind of schooling, the charge for which was not fully covered by the value of the voucher. This would be combined with encouragement to voluntary bodies to provide different types of school, subject to inspection to see that they came up to minimum standards. Failing such a drastic change, they would favour the continuance of direct grant and independent schools, and tax reliefs and other help to parents making use of them.

In the higher education sphere, there would be support from those with these views for a system of loans instead of grants for students, to take account of the greater prospective earning power which graduates will enjoy. They would advocate also that a greater part of the costs of universities and colleges should be met out of fees paid by students (and reimbursed out of these loans), rather than by direct grants from the Government or the local authorities.

As far as housing is concerned, the differences are less marked, but they would tend to put greater stress on encouraging owner-occupiers and private landlords through improvement grants and mortgage assistance. They would also want to confine local authority house building largely to slum clearance; they would work towards the charging of economic rents and a fairly strict relation of rent subsidies to tenants' means.

The views of this school of thought are perhaps expressed most forcefully and characteristically in the publications of the Institute of Economic Affairs. These have the great virtue of helping both those who share their views and those who are unsympathetic towards them to see more clearly the issues of principle involved in the various proposals for the reform of the social services, and the costs and benefits involved in different types of provision. The names of Professors Peacock, Seldon, Wiseman and Lees are among the most prominent of those of the individual writers associated with the school.

THE 'COLLECTIVIST' VIEW

The use of this name for the contrasting view is perhaps even more in need of qualification. Those who hold it tend to be liberal social democrats in the pragmatic tradition of British radicalism, rather than in any sense advocates of collectivism in its totalitarian forms. That is to say that they are aware of the importance of freedom of choice by consumers and of the part which the market must play in making such choices economically, but they take a wider view of the limitations of the market and of the social benefits to be achieved by the communal provision of services. They maintain that, in cases such as education, medical treatment, welfare and social security, the overall benefit of the community is more likely to be achieved over most of the field if services are provided by the organs of the State and paid for out of taxation than if their provision is left to the price system and the market. Many individuals and families are unable, because of their limited income or their restrictive social background, to make the choices for themselves or their children which will result in the socially-optimum provision of such services. In other words, the more the better-off are left free to buy education, medical treatment or provision for old age for themselves, and the more these services are charged for at market prices, the more likely it is that the best teachers and doctors and the most money and material resources will go into providing these services for the rich, and the poorer the provision will be likely to be for those less well off.

Hence participation in the social services by everyone on more or less equal terms irrespective of income is seen as one of the rights and duties of citizenship. To ensure the improvement of the services, reliance is placed on securing the interest of the better-off and more articulate members of the community in support of better State schools, better State hospitals and clinics, better public welfare services, better State pensions.

In the field of social security, those who hold this view would tend to support the development of a full-scale State system of earnings-related social insurance. It is accepted that, in a community with rising real incomes, there is a demand for benefit rates related to earnings. However, it is believed that this can be achieved more effectively through a State system than through private occupational benefits. The terms of a State scheme can be adapted, by varying the Exchequer contribution, to provide more favourable terms for those less well off, who are unlikely to be adequately covered by a private scheme. A State scheme can also give those who are retired built-in guarantees of improvements in their pensions to keep pace with rises in the cost of living and in average earnings.

Support for State earnings-related social insurance is an example of how the liberal-collectivist distinction cuts across the selectivist-universalist division. What is being advocated is in fact a collectivist form of selection on the basis of earnings. By contrast, we can find examples of universalist positions being held by those who favour the 'liberal' approach; advocacy of basic flat-rate social security benefits would be one.

For those not adequately covered by earnings-related benefits, especially for those retiring in the near future (who can benefit little from them), the 'collectivists' would, however, prefer a raising of general flat-rate pensions to reliance on means-tested social assistance. They are very aware of the iniquities associated with the means test and the problems of failure to claim supplementary benefits.

In education, this group naturally favour comprehensivization, as being most likely to counteract the inequalities of opportunity arising from factors such as home background; they are opposed to State support for selective schools, such as the direct grant schools. The more extreme among them tend to favour the abolition of independent schools also, regarding them as perpetuators of social division. In the field of higher education, where limited resources mean that some selection is inevitable, they would want opportunities extended as widely as possible. They would favour a greater assimilation of the various types of institution in terms of quality, rather than a hierarchy of quality with the universities at the top reserved for a limited elite.

In the health services, they naturally support the maintenance and improvement of a free service and are opposed to the extension of charges or to any encouragement of greater use of private facilities by the well-to-do. In housing there is perhaps less difference of general principle, since the growing demand for owner-occupancy is recognized by all, but there would be a greater emphasis on the maintenance and extension of public building as a means of catering adequately for those most poorly housed. Controls over rents and security of tenancy to prevent exploitation, and less enthusiasm for moving towards economic rents and the revival of a free market, are also characteristic aims.

This school do not have such a well organized and active organ of publicity as their rivals, though the publications of the Fabian Society usually reflect their views. The best known names associated with them include those of Professors Titmuss, Abel-Smith and A. B. Atkinson. Many of those actively engaged in the social services tend to support their views, as also do organizations such as Shelter and the Child Poverty Action Group.

THE POLARIZATION OF THE POLICIES OF THE TWO MAIN PARTIES

Under the stress of the problems mentioned in the first section of the chapter and against a background of Britain's growing economic difficulties in the late 'sixties and early 'seventies, there has been a tendency towards a weakening of the consensus of policy on the social services which found expression in the Beveridge tradition. In fact,

167

the policies of the two main parties have tended to polarize along lines similar to the division of opinion just described, though in a more pragmatic manner, appropriate to parties which are themselves coalitions of different views.

Thus, under the Labour Government, in the years up to June, 1970, policy naturally tended to move in a 'collectivist' direction, since this reflected the traditions of the party. Hence when the problem of poverty among the families of low earners became prominent, the remedy adopted was a considerable increase in the rate of family allowances, which are administered on a public service basis without means test, though provision was also made for the benefit to be withdrawn from those with higher incomes by means of an adjustment of their income tax children's allowances. The most far-reaching example, however, was the National Superannuation and Social Insurance Bill, introduced in 1969, which provided for the introduction of a full-fledged system of earnings-related social insurance, which would eventually give retirement pensioners pensions related to their average earnings over their working lives, and adjusted after retirement to take account of changes in the cost of living and in national average earnings. It also proposed similar benefits for other types of interruption of earnings. The advent of the general election prevented its passage into law.

Similar policies were pursued in other fields, especially in education. The local education authorities were urged to submit schemes as fast as possible for complete comprehensivization of secondary schools, in terms of Circular 10/65 of the Department of Education and Science, issued in 1965. In the Education Bill of 1970 powers were being sought to enforce compliance by reluctant authorities. The system of fee-paying in certain local authority schools in Scotland was abolished. The Government was also considering the abolition of the direct grant system, on the ground that these highly selective schools militated against equality of opportunity and tended to rob the comprehensives of the brightest potential pupils. It was felt that there should not be a public subsidy for fee-paying schools.

It was clear that the change of government following the election of June, 1970, would involve a change of emphasis in the social services. The Conservatives favoured a policy of less, but more effective, government, with a reduction of direct public intervention in the economic field and a concentration on establishing conditions favourable to the working of the market. In the social services this would mean a concentration of public spending as far as practicable on to those whose needs were felt to be greatest, and encouragement of the better-off to rely more on spending for themselves.

In the first year of the Conservative Government's life, the lines of the new policy began to take shape. There was considerable concern to restrain the growth of public spending in order to make possible reductions of taxation, and in view of the built-in factors leading to a rise in social service spending, this led to some difficult choices. The expenditure restrictions announced in October, 1970, and spelt out more fully in the expenditure projections of January, 1971, give some hints for the future.[1]

In view of the steadily rising demand for more and better second-ary and higher education and the importance of maintaining and improving educational standards for the sake of the country's future prosperity, education escaped very lightly, with little more than higher charges for school meals. The future of the health ser-vices was still undecided, but the increases in the charges for pre-scriptions and for dental and ophthalmic treatment were signs of an attempt to put more of the rising costs directly on to the users. In particular, the replacement of flat-rate charges for dental and oph-thalmic treatment and eventually for prescriptions, by a charge of half the cost up to a maximum figure, represents a change of principle from a token charge towards a sharing of the costs between the State and the recipients.

An important innovation was the attempt to tackle the problem of poverty in the families of low earners directly, by means of a Family Income Supplement,[2] to be payable to those with low incomes subject to a means test related to the size of the family. The supplement is payable to those in full-time work and represents half the difference between their actual earnings and a prescribed amount varying with the number of children, subject to a maximum total payment. The prescribed amounts announced in March, 1971, were £18 per week (increased in April 1972 to £20) plus £2 for each child, with a maxi-mum payment of £4 (since increased to £5).

This scheme has, however, been much criticized. Only half the deficiency of income below the poverty line level is made good, not the full amount. Moreover, the fact that Family Income Supple-ment entitlements are reduced as income rises means that there is a considerable effective rate of tax on marginal earnings. This is the more so when account is also taken of other possible loss of benefits, such as reduction of rate or rent rebates, or loss of entitlement to free school meals or free medical services.[3]

There were a number of other cases of special help being given to particular groups felt to be in need. A special retirement pension was introduced for the small group of people, now in their eighties or more, who were too old to become eligible for National Insurance pensions when they were first started in 1948. This was followed in March, 1971, by the announcement of special supplements to be paid as of right to pensioners over eighty years old (the age addition) and also to the chronic sick (the invalidity allowance), the amount in the latter case to vary inversely with the age at which their disability began. There is also from December, 1971, an attendance allowance for the very severely disabled who need constant attention, on the lines of that available under Industrial Injuries Insurance.

In the educational field there have also been some reversals of policy. Immediately after the election, the new Secretary for Education and Science issued a new Circular (10/70), replacing the obligation on local education authorities to prepare schemes of comprehensivization by a new obligation to prepare schemes for secondary school reorganization taking account of local needs and wishes. In practice the effect of the change has been less than expected. The logic of events is inducing authorities to accept comprehensivization as an aim, and the withdrawal of the threat of compulsion has been followed by a willingness of several recalcitrant authorities to prepare schemes envisaging a flexible approach to this aim. The Education Bill of 1970, giving powers of coercion to the Department, was in any case one of the casualties of the election, but in Scotland a new Act was passed giving authorities the right once more to charge fees if they wished.

Similarly, the lines of a new housing policy emerged in a government statement of November, 1970. The Government has decided to extend the system of regulation on the basis of fair rents, as defined in the Rent Act of 1965. It is intended that the rents of local authority houses shall be fixed on the same basis, that of a market rent in the absence of excess demand. However, it is accepted that in Scotland, with its tradition of low rents, local authority rents cannot be raised to this level at once, and the target must rather be a rent level that will enable the authorities to balance their housing accounts. Subsidies will eventually be related to tenants rather than to houses. They will take the form of rent rebates below the fair rent and will be related to tenants' means. They will be made available to the tenants of private landlords as well as to those of local authorities. These policies have now been embodied in the Housing Finance and Housing Finance (Scotland) Bills, which came before Parliament in 1972.

THE MAIN TASK AHEAD

Whichever of these two main attitudes, or, more probably, whatever varying compromises between them, are applied to particular cases, there remain certain important problems which must be tackled.

In the field of social security, the main unsolved issues are how to provide the bulk of the population with earnings-related cover against inability to earn, and how to tackle the problem of poverty adequately. In the health services there is the fundamental problem of how to meet the ever-rising costs of providing adequate medical treatment, and the subsidiary problem of the organizational structure of the services. In education the main issues are how far comprehensivization should be carried and what the pattern of higher education should be. The welfare services face the need to weld the various separate and often partial services into a comprehensive and effective organization. In housing there is a need for a more all-embracing and socially based policy in place of the piece-meal and often inconsistent approaches of the past. All this is in a situation where the social services are now big business in their claims on trained manpower and other material resources, but, unlike commercial big business, do not produce an easily measurable product which can be sold on the market for a price. Rather, the community must raise the resources by various forms of taxation, and choose how best to use them by means of administrative decisions.

SOCIAL SECURITY

Now that rising real earnings have brought the bulk of the working population to a position well above the subsistence level, it is clear that there is a general demand for some system of income maintenance that will ensure that income when unable to work is not too far out of line with what is earned while working. The question then arises how far this should be provided through the State system of social insurance and how far it should be left to private or occupational provision. So far as short-term interruptions of earning through sickness and unemployment are concerned, this is not a serious financial problem. The earnings-related supplements of 1966 have gone a long way to meet it, together with the obligation of the employer to make redundancy payments, and the growing practice among employers of making up earnings during short periods of sickness. Chronic long-term sickness or unemployment raise much more serious difficulties, as does widowhood, but the biggest problem arises with retirement. Here permanent cessation of earnings creates the need for a sustained level of benefit that will not involve a severe drop in living standards, while the large numbers involved and the long continuance of payments impose a severe financial burden on any insurance scheme.

The present Conservative Government is known to favour reliance on occupational pension schemes to meet most of this need, and so in spite of what has happened in Germany, Sweden and other countries, we are unlikely to see a fully-fledged national super-annuation plan without a change of government. The White Paper *Strategy for Pensions* of September, 1971[4] outlines the Government's plans.

The State basic social insurance scheme will be retained at flat rates of benefit, to provide a minimum guarantee against poverty, subject to review of rates every two years to guard against inflation. Contributions, however, will be earnings-related over a range between about one-quarter of average earnings (below which they become voluntary) and one and a half times average earnings, above which they become flat rate. This extends further the principle of earnings-related contributions, already reflected in the differential contribution increases according to income introduced in September, 1971.

Provision for earnings-related income maintenance above the minimum level is to take the form mainly of occupational pensions. These will be subject to the supervision of an Occupational Pensions Board. Schemes will have to provide for the full preservation of accumulated pension rights accrued in each period of employment, when changes of employment take place.[5] There will be a stipulated minimum rate of pension, with half rates for widows. The pension must be protected against increases in the cost of living, either by linking to the cost of living index, by providing for a prescribed rate of increase of benefits, or by some other method approved by the Occupational Pensions Board.

In addition, there will be a State reserve scheme for the benefit of those who are not eligible for recognized occupational schemes, such as those in irregular employment and those who have just started employment. This will be fully-funded and run on commercial lines without Government contribution. The terms proposed will tend to discourage reliance on the reserve scheme as an alternative to being contracted out into an occupational scheme. For instance, there will be no income tax relief on employees' contributions[6] and no provision for the 'blanketing in' of those who retire after only a short period of contribution, at more favourable benefit rates. Indeed, rates of pension will depend strictly on contribution record, though the fund will be able to pay bonuses if it is successful with its investments. Membership will be compulsory for all employees between 21 and retiring age who are not covered by a recognized occupational scheme.

The self-employed will not be included in the proposals for occupational pensions and the reserve scheme. They will continue to pay flat rate contributions because of the difficulty of assessing them on earnings, but will be subjected to an additional contribution of 5 per cent on Schedule D earnings between £1,000 a year and the upper limit of income on which employees' graduated contributions are assessed.

These proposals represent a conception of the role of the Government in social security which sees it as being primarily to provide a minimum basic income for all, financing it by a measure of income redistribution through graduated contributions and flat rate benefits. Cases where this minimum is not adequate for need should be met by means-tested supplementary benefits. Income maintenance for the retired is seen as primarily the concern of employers and employees jointly through occupational pensions, with the Government's role confined to encouraging extended coverage by such schemes and controlling their terms to make them fairer as between those with different conditions of employment. In addition, the Government will provide a reserve scheme for those who cannot be expected to be covered by private occupational schemes.

At first sight the proposed developments seem akin to the system of provision for old age in the Netherlands, where there is also a flat-rate basic pension financed by graduated contributions based on earnings, and where this is supplemented by a wide range of occupational pension schemes, based both on industries and individual firms. In fact, however, the balance is the other way round, for the basic pension rate in the Netherlands is regularly adjusted to keep pace with rises in the cost of living and in the statutory minimum wage. It already averages 90 per cent of the latter, and the aim is to raise it to the level of the statutory minimum. On the other hand, occupational pensions in the Netherlands are at much lower rates and are definitely regarded as supplements to the basic pension, the accepted aim being to ensure ultimately that between the two forms of pension all old people will receive some 70 per cent of their average earnings when working.

A serious limitation of any system of universal income-related pensions, whether based mainly on social insurance or on occupational pensions, is that the full rate of earnings-related benefits can only be enjoyed by those who have contributed over the whole, or at least a major part, of their working life. The financial burden of transferring pension payments of, say, two-thirds or three-quarters of their earnings in the last few years of employment, to those for whom income-related contributions had only been paid for a few years, would involve a level of contributions either from taxpayers or from employers too high to be borne without adverse effects on incentives or on business costs.

Hence there will be a period of some twenty years or so in the early days of any scheme of universal graduated pensions, during

173

which those who retire will only be entitled to pensions at a much lower level, probably little more than a supplement to their basic flat-rate pension. It is only as their graduated contribution record is built up over the years, on whatever formula is adopted, that they will gradually become entitled to a level of pension that eventually will reach the target proportion of their average earnings. This will not unduly affect those who are members in good standing of long established occupational schemes, such as those in the professions and the public service, who are mostly in relatively high income groups anyhow. It will, however, seriously affect those with lower incomes, who in the past have not been covered by such schemes, or have been in schemes where the pension rates have always been very low, and in any case are related to the much lower earnings which they received in the early days of their working lives.

There is likely to remain, therefore, a considerable problem of poverty among those who are already retired or likely soon to become so, as well as among those who cannot earn because of chronic sickness or disability, or long-term unemployment, and also among widows and other unsupported women with young children. As well as this, there is the considerable problem of poverty among those in work with low earnings.

There are essentially three ways in which this problem of residual poverty can be tackled by means of social security benefits.

First, by a raising of the level and availability of means-tested benefits, for example, a raising of the rates of supplementary benefits and a further extension of the newly introduced family supplement. This method has the advantage of concentrating benefit on those whose need is greatest and avoiding the giving of extra benefits to those who already have higher means. Thus for a given total expenditure it is possible to provide higher rates of benefit to the needy than could be done through raising the flat-rate basic social insurance benefits. It is also more flexible, and if properly administered allows special help to be given to those who have special needs, by the discretionary benefits, or through the system of rent allowances covering actual rents. Help can also be given quickly in cases of emergency.

Against this, it has the disadvantage of being dependent on the beneficiaries knowing about and claiming their entitlements, which is never certain among the poor and ignorant. It also involves the costs and the element of arbitrary decision inherent in the operation of means tests, as well as a substantial rate of effective taxation on additional earnings, where these result in reduction or loss of benefit entitlements. Hence there may be considerable disincentive effects on willingness to seek better paid employment.

Second, by raising the basic level of social insurance benefits and family allowances payable to all as of right. This has the advantage of ensuring that all those who are in need and are already covered by these schemes get their extra benefits automatically, without having to claim them and without the costs and arbitrariness associated with means tests. Whether or not it involves effective taxation of extra earnings and disincentives to work depends upon whether an earnings rule is applied, as in the case of retirement pensions, limiting the amount which can be earned without reduction of pension.

This is, however, a much costlier method, since it involves giving higher benefits to all, whatever their means, except when an earnings rule applies. Thus retired people who had occupational pensions, or income from dividends, would benefit from a rise in the basic pension on the same terms as those who had no income except from social security. This would be modified to the extent that such extra benefits increased their taxable incomes, and perhaps, as in the case of the family allowance increases of 1968, it might be possible to claim back the extra benefit from those above a certain income level through adjustments in income tax allowances. If this method were adopted, the scope for means-tested relief would be much reduced, though there would still be a place for it in the social security system, to deal with exceptional cases of need arising from such causes as high rents, heavy expenses or sudden emergencies.

Professor Atkinson, for instance, has put forward a scheme for a 'New Beveridge Plan', outlined in *Lloyds Bank Review* for April, 1971. It involves an increase in standard national insurance benefits of 44 per cent for a single man and 33 per cent for a married couple, to bring them up to a level equivalent to that proposed by Beveridge. For those at work there would be a minimum wage of £13 a week, which is roughly the same level for a one child family. The needs of families with children would be taken account of by increased family allowances. There would be an income tax 'clawback' through reduced allowances to reduce the benefit gained from these increased by those with higher incomes. The cost of such a scheme would be high; it is estimated at £525 million a year; but it is claimed that such a scheme provides benefits as of right and avoids the high rates of effective tax on additional earnings involved in negative income tax schemes, as well as the sharp cut-off of extra benefits as soon as the minimum poverty line is reached.

Third, by integrating the social security system more closely with the income taxation system through some form of negative income tax. As mentioned in Chapter Six, this can take two main forms. First, there is the Social Dividend type of scheme, where every family is paid a weekly sum varying with family size, which replaces both social security benefits and income tax allowances, and all income other than this is then subjected to a proportional income tax. Such a system, if it is to replace existing benefits adequately, involves a very large transfer of income via the State, both to those who need it because they cannot earn enough to live on, and to those who do not, because they have adequate means. Hence it involves high rates of tax, and the combined effect of dividends and tax payments is likely to be seriously disincentive. Nor are the social dividend payments likely to be high enough, or flexible enough, to make it possible to dispense altogether with other forms of social security.

It has been estimated, for instance, that to pay rates of social dividend adequate to replace the present national insurance benefits, family allowances and supplementary benefits, and also provide the revenue at present drawn from income tax, surtax and employees' insurance contributions, would involve a proportional rate of tax on all income other than social dividend of something like 50 per cent.[7]

The second type of scheme is that more properly called negative income tax. This essentially involves an extension downwards of entitlements to negative income tax, in the form of cash allowances, below the income level at which income tax liability begins. That is to say that, just as those whose income exceeds the total of their tax-free allowances at present pay tax on the difference, so those whose income falls short of their entitlement to tax-free allowances would receive payments based on the difference. The break-even point would depend on the size of family, since the total of tax-free allowances would include the personal, married and children's allowances. If the rate of negative income tax was the same as that of positive tax, the shortfall of income would not be made good completely, but only in part. For instance, if the break-even income for a family of a certain size was £700 per year and the family's actual income was £600, then with a tax rate of 30 per cent, which is near the present rate on earned income, the family would receive an allowance of only £30. If they had no assessable income at all, i.e. no income except perhaps social security benefit which might well be exempted from assessment, they would still only receive £210. This is not very much, but it might be enough to make all the difference as a supplement to minimum flat-rate social insurance benefit. The system can, however, be adapted to ensure that every family gets, from its earnings plus its entitlement to negative tax, an amount equivalent to a guaranteed minimum income varying according to family size. The level at which this guaranteed minimum was fixed would affect the rate of tax necessary to finance the scheme and meet the needs of general tax revenue, as under the first type of scheme. The amount of money to be transferred via the State from taxpayers to recipients would, however, be considerably less.

A scheme of this sort has been proposed by the Institute of Economic Affairs (*Policy for Poverty*, IEA Research Monograph 20 1970). This would involve the payment to each family whose income was below the Supplementary Benefit scale appropriate to it, including average rent, of an allowance sufficient to bring it up to this level. Thus there would be 100 per cent making good of the income deficiency, as against only 50 per cent under the Family Income Supplement scheme. On the other hand, this Reserve Income Supplement, as it is called, would be reduced pound for pound with any increase of income, from earnings or social security or other source, until it fell to nothing once the guaranteed income level was reached. The scheme thus involves 100 per cent effective rates of tax on marginal income rises, and hence a greater substitution effect disincentive to work than increases in standard insurance benefits would have. On the other hand, the net cost is much lower, estimated at only some £150 million, according to Professor Atkinson (*Lloyds Bank Review* (April 1971), p. 24).

Such a scheme has a number of advantages. It enables those whose incomes are too low for them to gain any advantage from the present income tax allowances to share in the benefit from them, since they receive supplements to their income. In so far as such payments replace supplementary benefits and other forms of social assistance, they cut out the need for those entitled to claim benefits and hence the danger of their failing to do so. The unpopular personal means test is replaced by an impersonal assessment of means through a tax return. Such a system is also less disincentive to earnings than means-tested social assistance, since there is a constant marginal rate of effective tax as income increases, the negative tax allowances being reduced by a constant percentage as income rises to the break-even point, and marginal income continuing to be taxed at a constant rate as it rises above this level. There is no sudden cut-off involving effective tax rates of 100 per cent or more. It is likely to be more disincentive, however, than a flat-rate basic social insurance benefit without an earnings rule, since it does involve a marginal rate of tax as income rises. On the other hand it is much less costly than the latter.

The main disadvantage is that of administrative cost and difficulty, since it would be necessary to assess millions of small incomes

177

which at present do not need to be assessed for income tax purposes. Also, as with extended basic insurance rates, it is unlikely that a negative income tax system could replace means-tested assistance altogether, because some provision must be made for exceptional or sudden cases of need. (See Appendix, p. 191.)

One obvious way of dealing with the problem of poverty due to low earnings would be to introduce a statutory minimum wage, on the lines of that in the United States. This has never existed in Britain, though there is a system of wages councils with powers to fix minimum wage rates in industries where employers and workers are poorly organized. The main problem about fixing a statutory minimum is that unless it were fixed at a fairly high level, say £15 to £20 a week, the main benefit would go to subsidiary workers such as wives and young people, rather than to adult male heads of families. If it were fixed at a high level, and especially if the same rates were fixed for both men and women, the addition to the wage bill would be great, and there might be serious effects both on industrial costs and also on the employment prospects of marginal workers who would not be thought to be worth employing at the higher rates. A Department of Employment and Productivity enquiry in 1969, for instance, concluded that if the minimum were fixed at 7s 6d (37½p) an hour for both men and women, which would give a weekly rate of £15·75 for a 42 hour week, the likely addition to the wage and salary bill would be up to £3,800 million a year, or one-sixth of the total. Inflation since then would mean that higher rates would have to be fixed to have the same effect on poverty. Moreover the benefit would take no account of the number of earners in a household. Consequently there has been little emphasis on this solution.

What are the most likely trends? The cost of providing flat-rate social insurance or public service benefits available to all at rates adequate to meet all needs is likely to be so great as to rule it out as a practicable solution. Further development of the social insurance principle is more likely to take the form of a development of income-related contributions and benefits, as has happened in a number of other countries such as Germany and Sweden. A future Labour Government would probably return to its proposals for National Superannuation. Under the Conservatives, policy will probably move more in the direction of some form of means-related social assistance. In either case the need remains for some method of ensuring that help is effectively given to those for whom it is most essential, and this may lead to experiments with some type of negative income tax, though probably in a partial and modified form.

The most serious problem facing the future of the health services is the steeply rising cost of providing adequate medical attention. This arises out of technical developments in medicine, the need to compete for scarce supplies of highly skilled man-power, and the population trends which increase the proportion of old people and young people in the community. Medical progress itself has added to this by making it possible for people to live much longer and to be kept alive often at high cost when otherwise infirm. Conditions which formerly could not be treated can now be dealt with by means such as intensive care units, kidney machines and transplant operations, but only at very great cost. There are also growing needs for more spending in areas which so far have had less priority, such as the care of the chronic sick and the long-term mentally ill and mentally subnormal. There is still a heavy backlog of unmet capital expenditure on new hospitals, particularly those to accommodate these latter types of case, who occupy accommodation often for years and decades on end and have been too often consigned in the past to obsolete Victorian buildings, with a low standard of medical and nursing care.

Many critics of the present system have doubted whether a health service based on public service principles can ever provide adequate revenue to meet these needs, and have quoted in evidence the figures suggesting that Britain is lagging behind in the proportion of its national income it spends on health services, to which we referred in Chapter Eight. In face of competition from other social services, such as education, and the needs of other forms of public spending, such as defence, roads and urban redevelopment, the means available are likely always to be limited, whereas potential demand is virtually unlimited.

What other sources of finance are available? One possibility is to raise more revenue from those able to pay by increases in charges, which until recently have covered only about 5 per cent of the total cost of the National Health Service. The Government has gone some way in this direction in the increases announced in October, 1970, in prescription, dental and ophthalmic charges which came into operation in April, 1971. There are, however, obvious limitations in this method. Means tests must be operated to exempt those who cannot afford the charges and there is a grave danger of deterring from receiving treatment those who are not eligible for exemption, or fail to apply for it. At the time when the 1971 increases were introduced, there was grave concern about the small extent to which the right of exemption from charges was being taken advantage of, and fear of considerable hardship if these rights did not become better known when charges were raised.

Is it practicable to go any further in the direction of introducing

179

prices in order to raise more money from those able and willing to pay? Few would seriously advocate going so far as to abandon the principle of a public service National Health Service and return to fee-paying private practice, with a free service only for the poorest section of the community. It is generally accepted that the State will have to maintain financial responsibility for providing a basic service, access to which is not barred to anyone for lack of means. In particular they must retain the heavy burden of maintaining and extending the general hospital service, the costs of which are far too high for them to be equitably passed on to users by means of fees. It has been suggested, however, that the present national health contribution, which is collected as part of national insurance, might be supplemented by a system of compulsory insurance contributions paid by those above a certain income level, which would cover the cost of providing them with personal medical care by general practitioners and possibly part of the cost of hospital care as well. Others would go further, and would urge encouragement for the better-off to opt out into private medical cover, through voluntary health insurance or direct private fee payment. They would propose giving those who do so exemptions from compulsory contributions or other appropriate tax relief.

The danger remains that the more successful we are in persuading the better-off to opt out of the State system into private provision, the more we deprive the State system both of tax revenue and of the services of the best human and other resources. There is a real danger of the best doctors and nurses, the latest equipment and the most modern buildings becoming concentrated into the private sector, where working conditions are better, and the public service becoming merely an inferior residual provision for the less wealthy. The dilemma therefore remains of finding some means of channelling more resources into the service without incurring the twin dangers of encouraging first and second class services and of imposing serious hardship on those caught by the operation of a means test.

In spite of the limitations of the National Health Service as we have known it, the ideal of the public service giving free treatment to all without barrier of means and financed entirely out of taxation remains the most attractive one and should not be lightly sacrificed. Should it prove impracticable to provide enough revenue for such an ideal to be carried out completely due to limitations of taxation, a system of compulsory supplementary health insurance contributions from the better-off to what would still be basically a public service, in which the quality of treatment would not depend upon the level of payment, is one which deserves consideration. On grounds of equity and of social benefit, it has advantages over a system of encouraging voluntary private provision, where the quality of service received varies with ability to pay. Many would maintain that this would be an inequity that would outweigh any gain in freedom of choice for the better-off to decide how much they want to spend on medical treatment, though this is of course a value judgment reflecting fundamental views on the nature of social welfare. What future course the Government will in fact take remains uncertain at the time of writing.

A second unsolved problem facing the health service concerns its future form of organization. The tripartite structure of 1948 has been much criticized though, as we saw, it was probably inevitable given the structure of local government and of the previous medical services. Proposals to bring the three branches together under Area Health Boards in areas larger than those of the present local health authorities, but smaller than the hospital regions, were put forward in the Government's Green Paper on the Future of the National Health Service, published in 1968. These gain an added appropriateness with the proposed reorganization of local government, for the upper-tier authorities of the new system look like being about the same size.[8] It is not proposed to make the health services part of the functions of the new local government units; objections by the medical profession are probably too strong for that. Rather, the local authorities would lose their health service functions to the new boards, which would remain agents of the central Government. But if the health service area boards covered the same areas as the upper-tier local authorities, this would make the hand-over easier and would also mean easier co-ordination between health services and the local authority welfare services.

EDUCATION

Whereas over the health services there has been relatively little controversy up to the present (although serious causes of dispute lie ahead), the position in education is in many ways a contrast. The last few years have seen bitter controversy over the respective roles of selective and comprehensive secondary education, made fiercer because it has directly involved the two main political parties. So far as secondary education is concerned, however, it now looks as if the future may be more peaceful, for the principle of comprehensivization has been generally accepted. Dispute only remains over the pace at which it should be implemented, and what role should remain in the fringes for selective institutions such as the direct grant and independent schools.

Nor is the general principle of State provision of education on a public service basis likely to be seriously questioned, in spite of the arguments of those who believe in vouchers and the like. The importance of adequate educational opportunities as a source of social mobility and as an investment in the country's future productivity are too well accepted. The public have also got too used to a system of publicly provided free education for it to be politically practicable for this to be seriously challenged. It is significant that in the Conservative Government's cut-backs in growing expenditure announced in October, 1970, education escaped almost entirely, apart from the rise in the price of school meals. Indeed, the trends of future education spending reflect largely the projected trends in the numbers of pupils and students, including those towards longer full-time education. Any attempt to cut back on them would mean that in future generations those with equal qualifications would get poorer opportunities.

The most controversial field is likely to be that of higher education, which remains highly selective in spite of widening opportunities. Whether a time will be reached when selection at eighteen plus will seem as unsatisfactory as selection at eleven plus, and when the community will want, and be able to afford, to give everyone a full-time education up to the age of twenty-one or twenty-two remains doubtful. It is far from certain that all would want this or could profit from it, even if we could afford to dispense with the product of their labours in employment. But in spite of the rapid growth of numbers in all higher education institutions, there remains a hierarchy, with universities very much at the top, the polytechnics and the colleges of education just below them and the other types of technical college lower still. The growing numbers who will stay on at school until eighteen and achieve minimum standards such as two A levels will force serious problems of choice on us. Do we deny a university education to many who would have attained it if they had reached the same level a few years earlier, when numbers were smaller? Do we go to the enormous expense of expanding the universities to take all who qualify at a minimum level? If we do this, can they remain the type of institutions they now are, orientated primarily towards an elite whose interest is expected to be in scholarship? Can they become much larger and offer much more diverse courses without losing their concern for the advancement of fundamental learning and knowledge? Or do we accept that there must continue to be a hierarchy of different types of institutions meeting different needs and catering for different types of abilities from that which we now have? We have hardly begun to look for answers to such questions as yet.

Moreover, all our planning of the future development of higher education has been done against the background of a sellers' market for graduates, in which it could be assumed that demand for highly educated skill was so high that there would be no difficulty in absorbing into employment as many as could be trained. The recession of 1971–72 meant that for the first time graduates were experiencing difficulty in finding employment in industry and commerce. It is to be hoped that this recession is only temporary, but as the greatly expanded output of the universities, polytechnics and other higher education institutions comes on to the market, it is being forecast that the automatic sellers' market is coming to an end as supply catches up with demand, so that graduates can no longer expect to walk straight into their choice of occupations. Higher education planning will therefore have to take more account of forecasts of demand for various kinds of skill, a notoriously difficult exercise in which past attempts have not been conspicuously successful. It will no longer be enough merely to plan to give higher education to all those who obtain the minimum school leaving qualifications to entitle them to it.

In the welfare services the main problems are likely to be administrative, as the unified Social Work and Social Service Departments get under way. The problem of welding staffs with very different backgrounds and extent of training into a unified service which can meet the needs of families in a comprehensive way will offer many difficulties. The problem of the relationship of these services to the related fields of education, health, social security and the administration of justice remains acute. The reorganization of the health services will bring new difficulties, with the transfer of the local authority health services, so closely bound up with welfare, to the separate and much more clinically dominated area health boards. There is also the problem of getting the means to extend the welfare services and enable them to break out of their Cinderella position, so that they can play their part in the total Welfare State pattern in the most effective way. Domiciliary care by trained social workers is often much more effective as well as much cheaper than residential care in meeting the needs of the handicapped. If there must be residential care, it can often be cheaper and more effective in a 'welfare' home than in a hospital. Yet we often spend pounds on hospital care for the want of the pence to develop the welfare services.

HOUSING

In housing the trend is likely to be towards the more explicit acceptance of a social housing policy of the type discussed in Chapter Eight.

This is not so much a question of the extent of the direct role of public housing provision as against private. On this there is likely to continue to be a difference of approach between the two main parties, with Labour putting more weight on local authority building and the Conservatives more weight on private building and home ownership. Rather, it reflects a growing recognition of the fact that no concept of the Welfare State is valid which does not include a concern to ensure that all citizens have access to adequate housing at a price that is reasonable in relation to their means. Experience has made it abundantly clear that this cannot be achieved by the unfettered working of the free market. Hence, since the Government must inevitably be involved in housing, it is desirable that it should have a coherent and well thought-out policy covering all types of houses and all types of housing needs.

A number of aspects of the housing problem have emerged over the years for which clear-cut policies have to be evolved. They include:

i *The provision of housing for the deprived*, that is, those groups such as large families with young children and very low incomes, fatherless families or immigrant families which often find it difficult to get reasonable accommodation at all and are forced to take nominally furnished rooms with little security or protection from the Rent Acts.

ii *Slum clearance and redevelopment*, especially of the hard core of long-neglected areas in the largest towns, but also of the twilight areas of older housing on the fringes of the 'hard core', which tend to degenerate into slums through multi-occupancy and general decay. This includes the question of what form of redevelopment should take place in the cleared areas, and in particular how far the displaced inhabitants can be rehoused there and how far they must be moved to distant housing estates or to tower blocks.

iii *Migration and industrial location* Housing policy cannot be considered apart from trends in industrial location and consequent movements of population. Many populous areas have been based on industries like coal mining, shipbuilding or cotton, which have since declined. In the past local authorities have planned the rehousing of their populations with little consideration of whether the industrial base of their areas would continue. Similarly, national policy on industrial location has tended to waver between the concept of inducing new industries into all areas of heavy unemployment and the more hopeful concept of building up growth points in the relatively declining regions, which can become viable centres of new industrial expansion. In either case, housing policy must be related to location policy, so that there are houses for the workers where their work is going to be.

Moreover, Britain can expect an increase of up to fifteen million in its total population by the end of the century, and policy decisions must be taken about where these growing numbers are going to live and work. Should population be left to build up in the areas where economic expansion, left to itself, is most likely, such as south-east England and the Midlands? Or should there be a deliberate attempt to develop new large centres of industry and population in areas at present relatively undeveloped, such as Humberside or the Solway Firth, or Tayside or Inverness and Easter Ross?

iv *What form of tenure?* Recent years have seen a continuance of the marked trend towards owner-occupancy. This has been spurred on by the progress of inflation, for rising house prices have meant that houses have been among the few assets to keep their value in real terms, and it has seemed sensible to most of those who could afford it to buy houses rather than pay rent. For long, the new owner-occupiers came mainly from those who in earlier periods would have rented privately owned houses, the supply of which for new tenants has virtually dried up. More recently, however, steep rises in local authority rents have led many potential council house tenants also to become owner-occupiers, except in Scotland with its tradition of low council house rents.

How far should these trends be further encouraged, for instance by making it easier for those with moderate means to borrow money for house purchase, along the lines of the option mortgage scheme, or by more generous local authority mortgages? What should be the future role of the local authorities? Should they encourage the trend to home ownership, by selling off some of their houses to their tenants, by encouraging building for sale in redevelopment areas, and confining their own letting activities as far as possible to those who have to be rehoused because of slum clearance and those who cannot afford to pay economic rents or mortgage charges? Or should they accept that they have a role in meeting the general housing needs of their areas, by building houses to let at different rents, including economic rents in the case of those able to afford them, and in particular by themselves owning most of the houses built in redevelopment areas?

And can anything be done to revive the private ownership of houses for letting? Is it possible to make private landlordship once more an attractive business proposition, through more generous improvement grants, more flexible rent regulation combined with subsidies to needy tenants, and provision for depreciation allowances on house property? And what are the prospects of encouraging other forms of tenure, such as housing co-operatives and housing associations which have played a minor part in Britain?

vi *Adjusting subsidies to needs* The answers to these questions are bound up with the final question of how subsidies can be better adjusted to needs. It must be accepted that those with low incomes are unlikely to be able to afford the full economic price of housing of the minimum quality held to be socially acceptable. On the other hand, the desire of the better-off to choose and own their own houses is too strong in Britain for the market to be likely to be superseded by a situation in which housing is accepted as a social service, to be provided free or at a nominal rent and allocated administratively. Subsidies will be necessary, therefore, and the problem is to ensure that they go to those whose needs are greatest, as they have manifestly failed to do in the past. There is also the question of where the subsidies should come from, how far out of general taxation and how far out of higher rents paid by those who can afford them.

Prospective housing policy trends

What specific lines of policy are likely to be developed to meet these problems? The present Conservative Government has now embodied its general approach to housing in the Housing Finance Bill and the Housing Finance (Scotland) Bill of 1972. There will be a move towards a more comprehensive policy in which all types of housing provision will play their part, and an attempt will be made to consider all types of housing need. However, the emphasis will be on a greater role for the private sector and an assimilation of conditions between private and public sectors. Thus the principle of rent regulation as established under the 1965 Rent Act, with fair rents fixed by Rent Officers, is being extended to cover the lower valued privately rented houses at present subject to controlled rents under the 1957 Rent Act.[9] It is also being extended to furnished properties except that, following the recommendations of the Francis Committee,[10] the Government has decided not to extend to tenants of furnished premises the security of tenure enjoyed by tenants of unfurnished premises, on the grounds that to do so would dry up the supply of furnished lets. Eventually there will be a uniform system of rent rebates for all tenants, both of local authority and of privately owned houses, which will be related to incomes. In England and Wales the aim is that local authorities should charge full regulated rents, i.e. those which would reflect market value in the absence of scarcity. In Scotland this is not yet a practicable aim, and rents will be fixed so as to enable local authorities to balance their accounts without deficit.

At the same time, further encouragement is being given to owner-occupancy. In March, 1971, the local authorities were given extended powers to grant mortgages of up to 100 per cent, with the aim of helping those with smaller means and those who want to buy older properties, both of whom have difficulty in getting mortgages from building societies.

Thus the trend seems likely to be towards the regulation of rents rather than their control at fixed levels, and towards assimilating as far as possible the conditions under which rent levels are decided and subsidies given in the public and the private sectors. Taken together with a growing concern to see that plans for urban renewal fit in with those for regional development of industry and regional distribution of population, these are all signs of a more positive and comprehensive approach to housing policy, seen no longer in isolation, but as an integral part of the Welfare State.

CONCLUDING THOUGHTS

It is clear that in Britain, as in all the Western world, the Welfare State is here to stay. There may be differences in the way it develops, according to which party is in power: the Conservatives favour more use of the market and more relating of benefits to recipients' means, and the Labour Party favour more use of State services provided communally as of right to all citizens. But it is not for nothing that the social services absorb nearly a quarter of the national product and that, even under the Conservative plans for slowing the rate of growth of public expenditure over the next five years, social service spending is expected to grow much faster than other forms of government spending. In particular, the two main services in kind, education and the health services, are estimated to be likely to grow at a rate of 5·2 per cent a year, in real terms, whereas transfers such as social security grow more slowly, at 2·7 per cent a year.

The fact is that public education, the National Health Service, comprehensive social security and the developing welfare services have become part of our way of life. The growing numbers of children and young people, the growing numbers of old people, and the rise in the real cost of services like education and medical treatment relative to other goods, will ensure that even at present levels of provision, their share in the national product will grow. And the pressures to improve standards are strong. Too many people in fact have too much of a stake in the Welfare State to make it likely that fundamental changes in its nature will take place.

Since this is so, and since resources are limited, especially in our relatively slow growing economy, it is the more important that we should be clear about our priorities. If we cannot do everything, what should come first? More education, or more medical treatment, or more welfare services, more social security or subsidized housing? How should these be rated against other needs, such as improvement of the environment, roads, aid to industry, regional development or defence? Within each field, how do we choose between spending relatively more on higher education or on nursery schools, on treatment of acute diseases like cancer or kidney disorders as against care of the mentally handicapped, on welfare for children or old people, or slum clearance as against houses for those moving to new centres of industry? Given our priorities as between the main policy aims in each sphere, how can they best be carried out, for instance by larger or smaller schools, by students living cheaply at home, or more expensively away from home, by care in hospitals or community care of the less acutely sick, by residential institutions as against the care of children or old people in their own homes?

In all these, and similar, cases, different decisions mean a choice between policies which vary both in the costs involved in carrying them out and in the type and quality of the services which they provide. Reliance on public services for the satisfaction of wants means that the sphere is constantly growing in which the decisions about what goods or services are to be supplied and how they are to be supplied can no longer be made through the market and the price system. Increasingly, such choices must be made by deliberate political and administrative decision, not by the reaction of consumers and producers to price changes.

Thus the problem of securing economic efficiency in the social services is part of the wider problem of the economics of the public sector, to which increasing attention is now being given. Certain techniques have been developed, such as cost-benefit analysis, to help those who have to make the choices to assess more clearly the variables between which they must choose. For instance, if a choice must be made between major road developments and the building of an underground railway to meet prospective transport demand, or between alternative sites for an airport, or between alternative methods of carrying out schemes of flood control, irrigation, water and electric power supply in a river basin, cost-benefit analysis can throw considerable light on the issues involved. The prospective benefits to be obtained from the alternative schemes can be listed, both direct ones, such as extra passenger journeys or vehicle trips, and indirect ones such as reduction of congestion or travelling time, and an attempt can be made to put a value on them. The corresponding costs can also be assessed; these include both direct costs of borrowing capital and carrying out construction, and indirect, or social, costs such as pollution or noise or loss of agricultural land. Again an attempt can be made to value them. But, as the experience of the Roskill Commission on the Third London Airport has shown, many of these valuations must necessarily be based on somewhat arbitrary assumptions and there remain intangibles, such as damage to the environment, or loss of wild life or historical monuments, which are difficult to put figures on. The ultimate decision must be a political one, as when the Government rejected the Roskill recommendation and chose Foulness instead of Cublington as the site for the prospective airport.

In any case, cost-benefit analysis gives little help in choices between programmes giving incommensurate benefits, such as between more spending on education or more spending on health services, or between either of these and defence or industrial research. Nor can it easily be used in those cases where the product cannot be quantified; this is true of most of the social services. Measurement of cost-effectiveness in education or the health services is always handicapped by the difficulty in assessing how much 'more' of the service one is getting for a given increase of expenditure, in the sense of the changes that are taking place in the quality of the product.

The decision, therefore, as to what extent and what kind of social services shall be provided must necessarily be a political one, reflecting the values and priorities prevailing in the community at the time. We have seen plenty of examples of this and have tried to classify them under such headings as universalism versus selectivism, or the 'liberal' against the 'collectivist' ideal. We have also discussed many of their implications for practical policy, such as the extent of comprehensivization in education, how far there should be charges for health services, whether the State should provide for income maintenance as well as minimum subsistence, and so on.

But once the general lines of policy have been chosen, the role of economics is important in choosing the most effective way of attaining the desired ends, in terms of economical use of resources and of alternative ends which may have to be sacrificed because resources are scarce. For instance, if the policy aim is to be advanced secondary education for all, can this be most effectively attained by having a large number of sixth forms in all the existing secondary schools, or by transferring advanced pupils to centralized sixth form colleges? If provision for the welfare of the handicapped is to be improved, how far can this be effectively and economically done by improving the domiciliary services, or how far are specialized residential institutions needed? Techniques of cost-effectiveness can be devised to measure the costs of the different methods, both financial and social, and the effects each is likely to have on the quality of the product.

The economics of the Welfare State are thus part of the wider theme of the economics of the public sector. In the choice of policies to be pursued by politicians and administrators, a vital part is played by the evolution of public opinion. This greatly influences the programmes put before the electorate by the political parties and the way in which these programmes are carried out or modified by governments once they gain power. We have tried in this book to trace the course of this evolution of prevailing opinion. We have seen how *laissez-faire* slowly gave way in late Victorian times to a belief in positive intervention to help different groups of people felt to be in need; how the piece-meal development of social services in the first half of this century led to the acceptance of a comprehensive reorganization on universalist lines after the Second World War; and how experience of the limitations of Beveridge system and the imperfect fulfilment of the Beveridge aims led to renewed differences in the fundamental understanding of what the Welfare State should be and how it should be organized.

This is the point at which we must leave the story, in the hope that this account will be of help to those who seek to understand the Welfare State, and who as citizens will have their part in influencing how it will develop in the future.

NOTES

1 *New Policies for Public Spending* (Cmnd 4515, HMSO, October 1970), and *On Public Expenditure, 1969–70 to 1974–75* (Cmnd 4578, HMSO, January 1971).

2 Under the powers of the Family Income Supplements Act, 1970.

3 A survey of the effects of increased Income Tax and National Insurance contributions, and of the loss of benefits from Family Income Supplement, rent rebate and rate rebate, appeared in *New Society* (8 May 1971) (T. Lynes, *Family Income Supertax*). It related to families in Birmingham over the income range £13 to £23 per week. It appeared that a two-children family was liable to experience an effective net tax rate on additional income of over 100 per cent as its income rose from £17 to £22, while a four-children family would have a similar experience over the income range £15 to £18.

4 White Paper, *Strategy for Pensions* (Cmnd 4755).

5 The alternative of refund of employees' contributions will no longer be permitted.

6 Though this is offset by the charging of employee's contributions at a lower percentage rate on earnings than employers' contributions.
7 Atkinson, *Poverty in Britain and the Reform of Social Security*, pp. 171–3.
8 In England and Wales it is now proposed to have two tiers of health authorities; an upper one based on the present 14 planning regions concerned with overall planning of the services, and a lower one with some 35 authorities concerned with the actual operation of the services. In Scotland there will be only one tier of authorities, corresponding to the new regional local government authorities.
9 Controlled houses which comply with the standards prescribed by the Housing Act of 1969 became subject to rent regulation from 1 July 1971.
10 Cmnd 4609, March 1971.

Appendix

The Government's proposals on Tax Credits

In a Green Paper *Proposals for a Tax Credit System* (Cmnd 5116, October, 1972) the Government proposes a form of negative income tax as discussed on pages 176–8 above.   The present income tax personal and family allowances would be replaced by tax credits—i.e. an amount of credit to be set against income tax liability. Tax would be levied on the whole income at the proposed rate of 30 per cent, but the amount of credit would be deducted from the amount of tax liability. If the liability exceeded the credit, the balance would be deducted by the employer as income tax; if the credit exceeded the tax liability, the difference would be paid out to the taxpayer. For example, if the credits were set at £4 for a single man, £6 for a married man and £2 for each child, a single man earning £20 a week would have a tax liability of £6 approximately and a credit of £4, and would thus pay £2 in tax. A married man with two children earning £20 a week would have a tax liability of £6 and a credit of £10, and would receive a payment of £4. It is hoped that this system could eventually replace supplementary benefit and family income supplement for all but the very lowest income-receivers.

Bibliography

1. Historical development of the Welfare State
M. Bruce, *The Coming of the Welfare State*, Batsford, 1961
T. Ferguson, *The Dawn of Scottish Social Welfare*, Nelson, 1947
—— *Scottish Social Welfare, 1864–1914*, Livingstone, 1958
Fried and Elman (editors), *Charles Booth's London*, Penguin, 1971
B. B. Gilbert, *The Evolution of National Insurance in Great Britain*, Michael Joseph, 1966
—— *British Social Policy, 1914–1939*, Batsford, 1970
P. Gregg, *The Welfare State*, Harrap, 1967
T. H. Marshall, *Social Policy*, 2nd edition, Hutchinson, 1967
M. E. Rose, *The Relief of Poverty, 1834–1914*, Macmillan, 1972
—— *The English Poor Law, 1780–1930*, David and Charles, 1971
Social Insurance and Allied Services (Beveridge Report), Cmd. 6404, HMSO, 1942

2. Description of individual services
M. Brown, *Introduction to Social Administration in Britain*, Hutchinson, 1969
J. B. Cullingworth, *Housing and Local Government*, Allen and Unwin, 1966
H. C. Dent, *The Educational System of England and Wales*, 4th edition, University of London Press, 1969
—— *Education in Great Britain*, 4th edition, Oxford University Press, 1964
D. Donnison, *The Government of Housing*, Penguin, 1967
H. Eckstein, *The English Health Service*, Harvard and Oxford University Presses, 1959
J. Farndale, *Trends in the National Health Service*, Pergamon, 1964
A. Forder (editor), *Penelope Hall's Social Services of England and Wales*, 2nd edition, Routledge, 1971
V. George, *Social Security*, Routledge and Kegan Paul, 1968
S. L. Hunter, *The Scottish Educational System*, 2nd edition, Pergamon, 1972
B. Jackson and D. Marsden, *Education and the Working Classes*, Penguin, 1966
B. Lawrence, *The Administration of Education in Britain*, Batsford, 1972
A. Lindsay, *Socialised Medicine in England and Wales*, University of North Carolina Press, 1962
I. Morrish, *Education since 1800*, Allen and Unwin, 1970
Nuffield Provincial Hospital Trust, *Challenge for Change*. Essays on the Next Decade of the National Health Service, Oxford University Press, 1971
J. Parker, *Local Authority Health and Welfare Services*, Allen and Unwin, 1965
H. Rose, *The Housing Problem*, Heinemann, 1968
N. J. Smith, *A Brief Guide to Social Legislation*, Methuen, 1972

W. O. L. Smith, *Education in Great Britain*, 4th edition, Oxford University Press, 1964

J. Vaizey, *The Costs of Education*, Allen and Unwin, 1958

3. *Current issues of social policy*

A. B. Atkinson, *Poverty in Britain and the Reform of Social Security*, Cambridge University Press, 1969

—— *Unequal Shares: wealth in Britain*, Allen Lane the Penguin Press, 1972

D. Bull (editor), *Family Poverty*, Duckworth for the Child Poverty Action Group, 1971

Institute of Economic Affairs, *A Policy for Poverty*, 1970

T. H. Marshall, *Social Policy*, Hutchinson, 2nd edition, 1967

W. A. Robson and B. Crick (editors), *The Future of the Social Services*, Penguin, 1970

R. Titmuss, *Commitment to Welfare*, Allen and Unwin, 1968

—— *Income Distribution and Social Change*, Allen and Unwin, 1962

P. Townsend and N. Bosanquet, *Labour and Inequality*, Fabian Society, 1972

Index

Note: n. after a page number indicates that the reference is to a note.

Abel-Smith, B. and Townsend, P. 89, 104*n.*, 167
Abercrombie Plan 41, 47*n.*
Approved Societies 28, 34
Artisans' Dwellings Act, 1875 18
Aspirations, rising 162
Assessment principle 53
Assistance Board (1940) 27, 42, 55
Atkinson, A. B. 89–91, 104*n.*, 167, 175, 177
Austria 136–41
Australia 138, 142–3, 146–7, 152

Barlow Report 41, 47*n.*
Belgium 138–40, 147, 152, 154, 157
Bevan, A. 60
Beveridge Report 7, 37, 41–7, 49, 56–7, 65, 89, 97, 100–1, 156, 167, 175, 190
Beveridge, Sir W. (Lord) 20, 27, 41–7
'Full Employment in a Free Society' 43, 47*n.*
(*see also* Beveridge Report)
Birmingham 18
Booth, C., 'Life and Labour of the People of London' 20, 22*n.*
Brown, C. V. and Dawson, D. A. 135*n.*
Bulgaria 146
(*see also* Eastern Europe)
Butler Act (*see* Education Act, 1944)

Canada 143, 146–8, 150–1, 158–9
'Cathy come home' (television feature) 96
Chadwick, E. 15
Charity Organizations Society 13
Child Poverty Action Group 112, 167
Children Act, 1948 45, 70
Children's Act, 1908 31
Children and Young Persons' Act, 1933 31
'Children in Trouble' (1968) 71
Cockerton Judgment, 1899 17
'Collectivist' view 165–8, 189
Colleges of Education (*see* Higher Education)
Commission on the Health of Towns, 1844–5 15

Comprehensive schools 68–9, 159, 167–8, 170, 181, 189
Conservative Government (1970–), policy of 168–70, 178, 182, 186–7
Cost-benefit analysis 189
Curtis Committee, 1945 45, 70
Customs and Excise, Board of 35

Denison, E. F. 123, 135*n.*
Denmark 148, 150–1, 157
(*see also* Scandinavia)
Direct grant schools 69, 165, 168, 181
Disraeli, B. 11
Distribution of Industry Act, 1945 45
Donnison, D. 154

Eastern Europe, countries of 142, 145–6, 147, 150, 153, 155
Edinburgh 32
Education 6, 16–17, 21–2, 29–30, 33–4, 46–7, 49, 116–17, 119–22
As a social investment 122–5, 182
Conclusions on 187–90
Effects on economic efficiency 126–135
Increased demand for 111–13
International comparisons:
Expenditure 136–41
How does Britain compare? 158–159
Principles and policy 141–53
Polarization of approaches to 163–170
Post-1945 reorganization 65–72
limitations of 92–4, 97, 102–3
Tasks ahead 170, 181–3
Unsolved problems 161–2
Education Act, 1870 16
1872 (Scotland) 16
1902 17, 22, 29
1918 29
1918 (Scotland) 30
1944 41, 44, 47, 65, 92
1946 (Scotland) 65
Education Bill, 1970 168, 170
Education and Science, Department of 168

194

Efficiency of the economy, effects on 126–35
Employment and Productivity, Department of 178
Executive Councils (National Health Service) 61

Fabian Society 167
Factory Acts 14
Family Allowances 1, 43, 49, 57–8, 91, 97, 100, 124, 139, 147, 168, 175–6
Family Allowances Act, 1945 44, 57
Family Expenditure Survey 119–22
Family Income Supplement 160n., 169, 174, 190n., 191 (Appendix)
Family Income Supplements Act, 1970 190n.
Family Welfare Association 13
Finland 148
(see also Scandinavia)
First World War 18, 23, 31, 37, 39, 108–9
Forms of organization, international comparisons 146–8
France 57–8, 136–41, 143, 146–8, 149, 152–3, 154, 156–7, 158–9, 160n.
Francis Committee 186
Full funding principle 52–3

Garin-Painter, M. 136
Geddes Axe 29
General practitioner services 61–4, 92, 149–50, 180–1
Germany 138–41, 144, 146, 147–8, 149, 150–2, 154, 156–7, 160n., 171, 178
Glasgow 18, 33
Gregg, P. 8n.
Guillebaud Committee 63

Hadow Committee 30, 44
Hall, M. P. 82n.
Health, Ministry of 35, 60
Health and Social Security, Department of 60
Health Services 6, 18–19, 28–9, 33–8, 46–7, 60–4, 92, 97, 102–3, 111–112, 119–22
As a social investment 122–5
Conclusions on 187–90
Effects on economic efficiency 126–135

International comparisons:
Expenditure 137–41
How does Britain compare? 156–180
Principles and policies 141–53
Polarization of approaches to 163–170
Tasks ahead 170, 178–81
Unsolved problems 161–3
(see also National Health Service)
Hicks, U. K. (Lady) 39, 47n.
Higher education 30, 92, 116, 161, 165, 167, 170, 182–3
Hill, Octavia 18, 21
Hospitals:
National Health Service 60–4, 92, 102–3, 112–13, 166, 179–81
infectious diseases 19, 28
in western Europe 150
mental 19, 28
public 19, 28
voluntary 18, 28, 92
Wartime Emergency Service 40
Housing 18, 21, 31–2, 34, 45, 49
Conclusions on 187–90
Economic effects of expenditure on 126–35
International comparisons:
Expenditure 136–41
How does Britain compare? 159–160
Principles and policies 149–50, 153–5
Polarization of approaches to 163–170
Post-war period 73–81, 95–7, 103, 111, 116–17, 122–5
Subsidies 31–2, 74–6, 103, 119–22, 123, 154–5, 165, 170
Tasks ahead 170, 183–7
Unsolved problems 161–3
Housing Act, 1890 18
1919 31
1923 32, 78
1924 32
1961 76
1969 77–8
Housing Finance Bill, 1972. 79, 170, 186
(Scotland), 1972 79, 170, 186
Housing Subsidies Act, 1967 78
Human capital, investment in 122–4
Hungary 146, 153
(see also Eastern Europe)

Incentives, to work, effects on 127–30
  to save, effects on 130–2
  to business enterprise, effects on 132–3
Income, distribution of 2, 119–22
  national, relatively slow growth of 113–4
Independent schools 69, 165, 181
Institute of Economic Affairs 114, 165, 177
Interdepartmental Committee on Physical Deterioration 20
Ireland 147, 154
  Northern 160n.
Italy 150, 153, 157

Japan 136–41, 146, 157

Keynes, J. M. (Lord) 36, 43
Kirk sessions 10, 13
Kuznets, S. 2, 8n.

Labour Government, 1964–70, policies of 51, 76, 168
Labour, Ministry of 35, 89
Laissez-faire 4, 10–12, 190
Level of demand, effects of social services on 126–7
'Liberal' view 163–5, 189
Lipton, M. 81n.
Liverpool 15, 18
Local authority health services 61–4, 181, 183
Local Authority Social Services Act, 1971 72
Local Government Board 12, 15, 21–2
  for Scotland 13
London:
  City of 16
  Dock Strike, 1889 19
  Housing in 18, 75–6, 95

Malthus, T. R. 11
Mansion House Fund, 1885–6 19
Maternity and Child Welfare Act, 1918 28
Means test 23, 26–7, 29, 55, 57–8, 90–1, 98–100, 130, 140, 142–4, 164, 167, 174–5, 179
Medical Relief Disqualification Removal Act, 1885 19
Medical treatment (see Health services)
Merchant Taylors School 9

Methods of fixing benefit and contribution rates, international comparisons 150–3
Method of provision of services, international comparisons 141–4, 148–50
Merit wants 6
Minimum wage 178
Musgrave, R. A. 6, 8n.

National Assistance 1, 42, 44, 49, 55–6, 89–90, 137, 142
National Assistance Act, 1948 44, 70
National Assistance Amendment Act, 1962 70
National Assistance Board 55–6, 88
National health insurance 24, 28, 33–8, 42, 61, 142
National Health Insurance Act, 1911 24
National Health Service 36, 42, 44, 49, 60–64, 71, 116, 187
  Conclusions on 187–90
  Economic effects of 122–35
  Green Paper on the Future of 181
  Growing demand for services 111–113
  International comparisons 142–3, 150, 157
  Limitations of, in post-war period 92, 97–8, 102–3
  Polarization of approaches 163–70
  Tasks ahead 179–81, 183
  Unsolved problems 161–3
  (see also Health services)
National Health Service Act, 1948 46
National Institute of Economic and Social Research 138–40
National insurance 1, 41–7, 49–53, 57, 83–5, 89–91, 98–102, 111–12, 114, 119–22, 129, 145, 156, 169, 175–6, 180, 190n.
National Insurance Act, 1946 44, 50
National Insurance Fund(s) 52–3, 101, 116, 135n., 147
National insurance (industrial injuries) 27, 49, 54–5, 84–5, 170
National Insurance, Ministry of 55
National superannuation 101, 132, 166, 168, 172, 178
National Superannuation and Social Insurance Bill, 1969 101, 168
  White Paper on 101

Negative income tax 99–100, 164, 175, 176–8, 191 (Appendix)
Netherlands 136–41, 146–8, 149, 151, 153–4, 157, 173
Newsom Committee 92–3
New towns 45
New Zealand 142–3, 147, 150, 152
Norway 136–41, 151, 157
    (*see also* Scandinavia)
Notification of Births Act, 1915 28

Office of Health Economics 157–8, 160*n*.
Oundle School 9

Peabody Trust 18
Peacock, A. T. and Wiseman, J. 38*n*., 39, 47*n*., 106–8, 135*n*.
Pensions:
    Graduated scheme, 1961 51–2, 101, 140, 151
    Growing demand for 111–12
    International comparisons 139–40
    Occupational 101–2, 132, 145, 164, 166, 171–4, 175
    Old age 22
    Old age non-contributory 26, 44, 56
    Reserve scheme 172
    Supplementary (1940) 27, 35, 40
    Widows, orphans and old age contributory 25, 33–8
    (*see also* national insurance, social insurance, social security, war pensions)
Plowden Committee 92
Poor Law 9–10, 12–13, 26, 36, 55, 90
    Board 12
    Commission 12, 15
    doctors 19
    guardians 12
    infirmaries 18–19, 28
    New Poor Law of 1834 12–13
    Royal Commission on 12, 21
    unions 10, 12
Poor Law Amendment Act, 1834 12
Population trends 50, 70, 82*n*., 111
Poverty, extent and causes 20
    continuance of 87–91, 162
Public assistance 26, 35–6, 42, 55
Public health 14–16, 21
Public expenditure:
    distribution of 3–4, 37–8, 39–40, 105–10
    factors counteracting rise of 114–15

factors making for continued rise of 110–14
    rise of 3, 37–8, 39–40, 105–10, 163, 169
Public Health Acts 15
Public service principle 143–4, 150, 152, 168, 178

Quality of life, improvement of 124–5

Rachmanism 76
Regional Hospital Boards 61
Rent Act, 1957 75–6, 96, 186
    1965 76–7, 96, 170, 186
Rent control 31, 74, 96, 155, 159, 167, 186
Report on the Sanitary Conditions of the Labouring Population, 1842 15
Ricardo, D. 11
Robbins Committee 92
Roskill Commission 189
Rowntree, B. S. 20, 22*n*., 34, 88
Royal Commission on the Housing of the Working Class, 1884–5 18
Royal Commission on the Poor Law, 1905–9 21
Rugby School 17
Russia 153, 155
    (*see also* Eastern Europe)

Sadler 14
Savings, supply of, effects on 130–2
Scandinavia 140, 144–5, 154
    (*see also* Denmark, Finland, Norway, Sweden)
School meals 20, 73, 80, 99, 148, 168, 182
School medical service 20, 22, 28
Scope of schemes, international comparisons 144–6
Scotland:
    Education in 10, 16, 22*n*., 65–72, 147, 160*n*., 168, 170
    Health services in 60–64
    Housing in 32, 73–81, 95, 185, 187
    Poor Law in 10, 13
    Public health in 16
    Welfare services in 71–2
Scott Report 41, 47*n*.
Second World War 7, 33, 37, 40, 70, 108–9, 127, 190
Seebohm Committee 72
Selectivism 46, 96–105, 163, 189

Shaftesbury, Lord 14
Shelter 112, 167
Shrewsbury School 17
Smith, Adam 11
Social assistance 23, 26–7, 49, 140–1, 142–3, 144, 150, 152, 156, 164, 167, 178
Social dividend (see Negative income tax)
Social insurance 23, 33, 41–7, 49–54, 140, 141–2, 150–2, 156, 164, 168, 172, 175, 178
Social security 6
    Beveridge Report and 41–7
    conclusions on 187–90
    in period 1900–48 23–27
    in post-1945 period 49–60, 87–91, 96–104, 111–12, 116–17, 119–22, 122–4, 130
    international comparisons:
        expenditure 136–41
        how does Britain compare ? 156–160
        principles and policy 141–53
    Ministry of 89–90, 104n.
    polarization of approaches 163–70
    tasks ahead 170–81
    unsolved problems 161–3
Social services:
    conclusions 187–90
    effects on economic efficiency 125–135
    international comparisons:
        expenditure 136–41
        How does Britain compare? 156–160
        policies and principles 141–55
    limitations of, in inter-war period 33–8
    polarization of approaches 163–70
    public expenditure on 3–4, 6–7, 37–38, 105–10, 110–15, 116–19, 136–41, 163
    Tasks ahead 170–87
    unsolved problems 161–2
Social Work (Scotland) Act, 1968 71–2
Speenhamland System 10, 12, 22n.
Spens Committee (1938) 45
Statute of Apprentices 11
Strategy for Pensions (White Paper) 190n.
Supplementary benefit 49, 55–6, 84–5, 89–90, 98–9, 117, 126, 127, 137–138, 142, 147, 162, 174, 176–7

Supplementary Benefits Commission 88
Sweden 136–41, 148, 151, 157–8, 171, 178
    (see also Scandinavia)
Switzerland 136–41, 146, 154, 157

Tax credits 191 (Appendix)
Taylor, G. 104n.
Technical colleges (see higher education)
Temple, Archbishop W. 1
Town and Country Planning Act, 1948 45
Toynbee Hall 20

Unemployment 19, 42, 52, 127
    assistance 26, 33–8
    Assistance Board 26–7
    insurance 24–5, 33–8
    insurance (agricultural) 25
    (see also national insurance, social insurance, social security)
United States 103, 135, 136–41, 142–3, 144, 146–7, 149, 151, 152–3, 155, 156–7, 158–9, 178
Universalism 46, 96–105, 163, 189, 190
Universities (see higher education)
University Grants Committee 30
Uppingham School 17
Uthwatt Report 41, 47n.
Utilitarianism 14

Wage stop 91, 127–8
Wareing, J. 104n.
War pensions 49, 58–9
Webb, Mrs Sidney 21
Welfare services 31–2, 45–6, 49, 116, 122–5
    development after 1945 70–2, 94–5, 97, 111–12
    conclusions 187–90
    international comparisons 141, 144, 148, 150, 152
    polarization of approaches 163–70
    tasks ahead 170, 182
    unsolved problems 161–2
Welfare State:
    concept of 1, 4, 7, 46, 114
    concluding thoughts on 187–90
    economic effects of 122–35
    international comparisons 136–60
    limitations of 87–103, 125

polarization of approaches to 163–170
redistributive effects of 121, 124
tasks ahead 170–87
unsolved problems 161–3
White Paper on Employment Policy (1944) 41, 44, 47*n.*

Workmens compensation 22, 27, 42, 54
World Health Organization 157–8

Yugoslavia 146
(*see also* Eastern Europe)

Date Due

JUN 14 '78			